W9-BQY-129

BLOCKS
AND BEYOND

Strengthening Early Math and Science Skills Through Spatial Learning

by

Mary Jo Pollman, Ph.D.

Early Childhood Education
Metropolitan State College of Denver

Baltimore • London • Sydney

Paul H. Brookes Publishing Co.
Post Office Box 10624
Baltimore, Maryland 21285-0624
USA

www.brookespublishing.com

Typeset by Integrated Publishing Solutions, Grand Rapids, Michigan.
Manufactured in the United States of America by
Sheridan Books, Inc., Chelsea, Michigan.

Library of Congress Cataloging-in-Publication Data

Pollman, Mary Jo.
Blocks and beyond : strengthening early math and science skills through spatial learning / by Mary Jo Pollman.
p. cm.
Includes bibliographical references and index.
ISBN-13: 978-1-59857-101-1 (pbk.)
ISBN-10: 1-59857-101-X
1. Mathematics—Study and teaching. 2. Science—Study and teaching. 3. Problem-based learning. I. Title.
QA11.2.P596 2010
372.7–dc22 2010015190

British Library Cataloguing in Publication data are available from the British Library.

2014 2013 2012 2011 2010

10 9 8 7 6 5 4 3 2 1

Contents

About the Author

Mary Jo Pollman, Ph.D., Professor, Early Childhood Education, Metropolitan State College of Denver, Campus Box 21, Post Office Box 173362, Denver, Colorado 80217-3362

Dr. Pollman is Professor of Early Childhood Education at Metropolitan State College of Denver. She received her doctoral degree in early childhood education from Florida State University. A former lab school teacher at Florida State University as well as a kindergarten, first-, and third-grade teacher, Dr. Pollman has continued her study of early childhood education in Australia, Italy (Reggio Emilia), Japan (fellowship), Germany, and Canada. Her fascination with the work of Friedrich Froebel, a trained mathematician and architect and the father of kindergarten, led her to walk in the footsteps of Froebel in Oberweissbach, Bad Blankenburg, Rudolstadt, and Berlin, Germany, in 2007.

At the national level, Dr. Pollman is presently Vice President in charge of membership of the National Association of Early Childhood Teacher Educators (NAECTE) and a member of the Professional Development Panel of the National Association for the Education of Young Children (NAEYC); she has reviewed early childhood programs for the National Council for Accreditation of Teacher Education. Dr. Pollman is a past president of the Presidents' Council of the Association for Childhood Education International (ACEI). At the state level, she has served as a past state president of the Alabama Association of Early Childhood Teacher Educators and the Colorado ACEI. She is currently an active board member of Colorado Association of the Education of Young Children and the Colorado ACEI and holds other current memberships in organizations such as the National Council of Teachers of Mathematics and National Council for the Social Studies. A frequent presenter at NAEYC, NAECTE, and ACEI, Dr. Pollman has written many articles and position statements dealing with issues in the field of early childhood.

About the Contributor

Sandra Phifer, Ph.D., Associate Professor, Metropolitan State College of Denver, Campus Box 21, Post Office Box 173362, Denver, Colorado 80217-3362

Dr. Phifer taught in elementary grades and was science coordinator for an elementary school. She has taught in elementary education at the college and university level for the last 16 years. Her favorite class is teaching inquiry mathematics and science methods for licensure students. She is presently President of the Colorado Association for Childhood Education International and a past president of the Colorado Association of Teacher Educators. She received her doctorate in educational psychology and cultural studies from the University of Nebraska–Lincoln.

Preface

Just as there are landmarks and paths to follow in map reading and spatial understandings, there are landmarks and paths to follow in writing a book such as this. Like Alice in *Alice in Wonderland*, who had to make many twists and turns because the path was not always straight, I had to struggle on the pathway in order to get to the final destination of writing this book.

The path of writing this book took me from my original love of block playing, to the exploration of early childhood teaching in three countries, and finally back to the original roots of early childhood.

I began my college teaching career doing block-play workshops in the early 1980s, and since then I have taught every subject on both the graduate and undergraduate levels in the field of early childhood. I was and continue to be interested in how blocks can be integrated into all the areas of the curriculum and in standards. Block playing became a focal point of my teaching in math, science, art, literature, and social studies. As I continued on my quest for excellent visual-spatial representation of children's work, I traveled in 1996 to Reggio Emilia, a small town in Italy known the world over for its high-quality early childhood programs. There I saw the intensity of how children looked at objects and recreated them from different perspectives and different media, and I knew this was helpful in promoting spatial understandings. Two years later I picked up a book, *Inventing Kindergarten* (1997), by Norman Brosterman, in an art book store in Denver and was so intrigued with it that I read the entire book very quickly. *Inventing Kindergarten* expanded upon the significance of how Friedrich Froebel, a trained architect and mathematician, may have influenced famous architects, mathematicians, and artists such as Frank Lloyd Wright, Buckminster Fuller, Mondrian, and Paul Klee. It also cited how Froebel's kindergarten movement may have influenced the Bauhaus movement of art and architecture. Even though this is not definitive research, it does say a great deal to the public when an architect like Frank Lloyd Wright reflects back on his life and says that the Froebelian blocks influenced his interest in architecture.

In the late 1990s I pondered how children in the United States scored lower in the spatial and geometric sections of the Trends in International Mathematics and Science Study (TIMSS) than they did in number sense and problem solving, and I continued to see this trend on these tests in 2003 and 2007. The divergence in the spatial and geometric scores led me to start conducting workshops on Froebel's work because I was making connections to spatial and geometric understandings that are not typically imparted in the schools. As I delved further into Froebel's creative endeavors, I realized that they were much more profound than I had at first thought. I wanted to share how his work touched on nature, design, and mathematics in ways we could benefit from today.

The experience of studying in Japan in 2002 led me to observe how the children used tangrams and origami at a spatially precocious level at early ages. They used many of the materials that Froebel mentioned in his writings and, more astonishingly, had some Froebelian kindergartens, unlike the United States at the time.

In 2007, I visited Germany and actually walked in the footsteps of Froebel in the cities of Oberweissbach, Bad Blankenburg, Rudolstadt, and Keilhau. At each museum and in each school, I saw dedicated people keeping alive the work of Friedrich Froebel by carefully preserving and sharing it. I also visited Bauhaus museums in Weimar and Berlin and saw the work of artists and architects who would have gone to Froebelian based schools.

The next stop on my sojourn was in 2008 at the only Froebelian kindergarten in North America, in Mississauga, Canada. I met Mrs. Barbara Corbett, director of the the Froebelian Education Centre, who has worked to preserve and promote the work of Froebel in North America through a school based on Froebelian philosophy.

As time went on, I knew the United States needed to promote interest in the science, technology, engineering, and mathematics (STEM) courses because we did not have a significant number of people who were going into these fields. Research has demonstrated that spatial development is an important component of these STEM courses. So what was I to make of my interest in blocks, my Froebelian interest, my foreign travels, and my profound preoccupation with helping children develop spatial skills? I needed to write a book about ways to help teachers develop strategies in math and science—as well as in the arts, literature, social studies, and technology—that use spatial skills. This book is useful in the following ways:

- For teacher educators in early childhood, this book promotes a balance between current research and practice in curriculum areas, particularly math and science, related to spatial development. It can be used as a supplement to undergraduate and graduate texts in math and science and other curriculum areas such as arts, literature, social studies, and technology.
- For daycare directors and school supervisors, it can be used for workshops and book studies in order to learn how to raise our awareness of spatial and geometric issues in the curriculum.
- For teachers of preschool through third grade, it can be used to enrich understanding of how cognitive and spatial development needs to be encouraged—not only in math but in all areas of the curriculum.
- For distributors of toys and teacher materials, this book provides opportunities to show teachers and parents how to use their materials.
- For parents of young children, the activities and materials in this book can be used to promote their child's interest in the STEM courses.

- For all early childhood teachers who have lost the connection with their foundational roots, this book can help reconnect them to the roots of kindergarten and to the essential tools in them, and their importance for mathematical, scientific, and artistic development. It can help early childhood teachers see the STEM courses in a different light and show them how to promote the STEM courses through spatial development and the materials in this book.

REFERENCE

Brosterman, N. (1997). *Inventing kindergarten.* New York: Harry N. Abrams.

Acknowledgments

In the *Wizard of Oz,* Dorothy had a path to follow on the Yellow Brick Road and needed assistance from her friends the Scarecrow, the Tin Man, and the Cowardly Lion. In writing this book, I had a path to follow and received the intelligence (brain), the heartfelt support and feeling (heart), and the strength (courage) to follow the manuscript through to completion by having a cadre of scholars and supporters of this project, both in the United States and abroad. They provided the impetus for me to develop the traits that were deep in me. Without their help I could not have completed this book.

I thank family, friends, and students who have contributed: Jan Pollman, Judy Knapp, Jessica Knapp, Jaclyn Knapp, Jillian Rhodes, and Michel Vallee. My special thanks to Jennifer Pollman, who created many of the illustrations in the book. Thanks to all my students, who through the years knew of my passion for block playing and implemented in their lessons some spectacular ideas; Sarah Wilson and Fukuko Yoshida especially stimulated my ideas for the book.

This book could not have been possible without Karine Drechsel, former director of the Metropolitan State College of Denver Child Development Center. She paved the way for the trip to Germany and accompanied me with her fluent German and gracious way, helping me communicate with the kind and generous people of Germany who were my excellent hosts in the cities of Oberweissbach, Bad Blankenburg, Rudolstadt, and Keilhau. I would also like to thank the director of the Froebel Education Centre, Dr. Barbara Corbett, in Mississauga, Canada, for her generous time during a busy school day.

I express my sincere thanks to the Early Childhood Teacher Educators throughout the country who supported this work by letters and comments: Dr. Mary Ruth Moore, Dr. Janet Taylor, Dr. Amanda Branscombe, and Dr. Rosalind Charlesworth.

I thank my Metropolitan State College of Denver colleague in teacher education, Sandra Phifer, who contributed Chapter 6 (Spatial Development and Science), as well as Malinda Jones, who took on a heavier load in early childhood during my sabbatical. In addition, thanks to math professors Dr. Shahar Boneh and Lew Romanango for their scholarly level of mathematical support. I also thank Mary McCain, director of the Auraria Early Learning Center, Denver, Colorado; and Cheryl Caldwell, Supervisor of Early Childhood, Denver Public Schools.

Portions of *Curriculum Focal Points for Prekindergarten through Grade 8 Mathematics: A Quest for Coherence* (2006) were reprinted in Appendix E with permission from the National Council of Teachers of Mathematics.

I would like to express gratitude to the Metropolitan State College of Denver; to Dean Sandra Haynes, Dean of Professional Studies; and to the Sabbatical Leave Committee who saw the merit in this work. Last but not least, special recognition goes to Astrid Zuckerman, who first took interest in this project; Jan Krejci; and Julie Chávez; as well as the Paul H. Brookes Publishing Co. Editorial Committee and the anonymous reviewers who took time to read this. You took a rough manuscript and helped develop it into a scholarly book.

In memory of my late husband, Daniel Alfaro,
who always encouraged me to pursue my dreams.

BLOCKS
AND BEYOND

Theoretical Background

An Overview of Research on Spatial Development

Daniel Alfredo, a recent immigrant from Costa Rica, recently moved to his new classroom in a new school. Daniel is 4 years old and attends a prekindergarten class taught by Mrs. Rhodes. Daniel enjoys playing in the classroom's block-play center. This is the only area Daniel has chosen to play in during the first 3 weeks at the new school. The following events occurred during this time period.

On September 1, Daniel moved to the block-play area and began to make an enclosed shape. He used six blocks to make a design. He did not answer when Mrs. Rhodes said, "Will you tell me what you made?" He only stared into space. He did not say a word after Mrs. Rhodes asked, "Did you make a house?" He just stared. Mrs. Rhodes then took a photograph of his structure, showed it to him, dated it, and placed it in his portfolio. She also picked up some books about houses and placed them at the block-play center a few days later.

On September 8, Daniel created designs in the block-play center. He used triangle blocks and placed them above the unit blocks. He did not say a word. The teacher showed him books on different types of houses, and he glanced at a few pages. Later Mrs. Rhodes took a picture of his building, showed it to him, dated it, and placed it in his portfolio. The books on houses were again placed at the block-play center.

On September 14, Daniel looked intently at the books of houses before he began to play. He built a much larger structure with an arch block entrance. He used a narrow wedge block for a door and different unit sizes to make his structure fit together. He placed blocks on top of one another. He used repetition in the four rooms he completed. After he was finished, he came to Mrs. Rhodes, touched her skirt, and said, "My house." She wrote "Daniel's house" on his structure. This was the first time Daniel talked to Mrs. Rhodes. Mrs. Rhodes took a photograph of his structure, showed it to him, dated it, and placed it in his portfolio.

There can be an underlying reason for Daniel's behavior. Daniel may not have talked to the teacher initially because he did not feel secure enough to express himself in a new classroom in which he did not understand or speak the language. Instead, he expressed himself through spatial understanding. The teacher was sensitive enough to express her acceptance of Daniel's use of his spatial and geometric abilities, enhanced by literature to improve both his structures and language development.

As illustrated in the vignette above, spatial thinking is a critical element of education, and today's teachers have the opportunity to equip children with the skills they need to succeed in the 21st century (National Research Council, 2006). Teaching spatial thinking to young children lays the foundation for learning science and mathematics throughout their academic careers and beyond. Spatial thinking is also essential to daily living skills, such as in the concepts of locations, maps, distances, directions, shapes, and patterns.

It is the intent of this book to provide readers with background on spatial literacy, including current research and theory as well as new approaches to teaching spatial development in the early childhood classroom. *Learning to Think Spatially,* a report by the National Research Council (2006), stated that spatial literacy is critical and that, although spatial thinking underpins many sets of national K–12 standards, it is generally not emphasized at any educational level. According to the report, spatial development is addressed explicitly in the math standards but only implicitly in the science standards. Attention to spatial thinking is especially significant in the field of early childhood education, where spatial development begins. Two reports, *Mathematics Learning in Early Childhood: Paths Toward Excellence and Equity* from the National Research Council (2009) and the National Mathematics Advisory Panel report from the U.S. Department of Education (2008), pointed out that attention to spatial development is especially significant in the field of early childhood education and that formal instruction is necessary to ensure that children build on this knowledge.

Historically, in the United States, it has been thought that reading, writing, and arithmetic were the most important subjects. However, spatial thinking is critically important for the disciplines of science, technology, engineering, and mathematics. Moreover, there is a strong need to enhance spatial thinking and identify individuals who are spatial thinkers. Spatial thinking is integral to daily living. People, nature, human-made objects, and structures exist in space, and the interactions of people and things must be understood in terms of locations, distances, directions, shapes, and patterns. Currently, spatial thinking is not systematically taught in grades K–12 despite its significance and its role in science, mathematics, and social studies standards.

Some studies have specifically found spatial thinking to be related to proficiency in overall mathematics (Ansari et al., 2003; Stewart, Leeson, & Wright, 1997). "Mathematics" in this sense, and as used in this book, is *mathematics literacy* and is not strictly concerned with "numeracy," as has been the instructional emphasis in the past. Mathematics literacy includes not only knowledge of numbers and operations but geometry, measurement, data analysis, and algebra. Spatial visualization takes place in the right part of the brain. The right brain is known to derive thinking and perception as a whole. Spatial visualization is different from verbal reasoning. Verbal reasoning takes place in the left part of the brain. The left brain is known for sequential and logical thinking and for the ability to combine parts into a whole and to put things in order (Newcombe & Huttenlocher, 2000). Because of location in distinct and separate parts of the brain, the processes of spatial visualization and verbal reasoning are related but nonetheless distinct. It has been found that mental rotation and spatial abilities are better predictors of performance on the mathematics section of the Scholastic Aptitude Test (SAT) than math anxiety or self-confidence in math (Casey, Nuttall, & Pezaris, 1997).

What Is Spatial Literacy?

Spatial literacy is often referred to in other literature as *spatial reasoning, spatial cognition, spatial concepts, spatial intelligence, cognitive mapping,* and *mental mapping* (Elliot, 1987; Gardner, 1983; Kitchin & Freundschuh, 2000; Newcombe & Huttenlocher, 2000). For the purpose of this book, the best way of defining *spatial literacy* is to describe it as the ability to problem-solve operations, such as mental rotation (a spatial skill that involves thinking about objects in different spatially oriented ways), perspective change (visualizing things from different perspectives), coordinated use of space (coordinating how different space is used in relation to other space), representation (representing one object to mean another object or place, as in a map), and reasoning (ability to understand how items are arranged in space and in relation to one another). These definitions have been modified and assessed in various studies in a number of ways in order to promote a better understanding of spatial and cognitive development.

What Are Some Gender Differences Regarding Spatial Literacy?

It is speculated that some physical and biological processes could account for the differences between boys and girls in spatial literacy and mathematical opportunities. Some research has demonstrated that spatial tasks are easier for young boys than young girls, indicating that boys have an advantage over girls from as young as 4½ years on tasks of mental rotation (Voyer, Voyer, & Bryden, 1995). *Mental rotation* is a spatial skill that involves thinking about objects in different spatially oriented ways. For instance, mental rotation can be seen within a class setting whereby children see different constructions of each other using the same five blocks (see Chapter 2 for more information on mental rotation in the use of Froebelian materials in forms of nature, in forms of beauty, and in forms of knowledge). Spatial skills like mental rotation are difficult to verbalize; it has been hypothesized that this may explain why boys perform better on mental rotation tasks, as girls generally prefer verbalizing whereas boys are more comfortable explaining their reasoning by arranging objects and movement. Studies also indicate that preschool boys perform better than girls on solving mazes (Fairweather & Butterworth, 1977; Wilson, 1975) and copying models of LEGOs (McGuinness & Morley, 1991).

The ages at which these spatial skill differences are said to occur vary according to different research studies. Some researchers have found consistent gender differences on a battery of spatial skills by age 10 (Johnson & Meade, 1987); some have found that these spatial skill differences by gender appeared by age 4 in the speed with which the children build three-dimensional forms (McGuiness & Morley, 1991); and others have found that sex differences exist by age 5 on two-dimensional spatial tasks and mental transformations (Ehrlich, Levine, & Goldin-Meadow, 2006; Levine, Huttenlocher, Taylor, & Langrock, 1999; Levine, Vasilyeva, Lourenco, Newcombe, & Huttenlocher, 2005).

Why Do Boys Seem to Have Stronger Spatial Skills than Girls?

The question has been raised whether experience playing with certain toys could account for boys scoring higher than girls on tests of spatial skills. Many studies have determined that boys play more frequently with blocks, manipulatives, puzzles, balls, and transportation toys than girls do (Servin, Bohlin, & Berlin, 1999). Studies have also shown that girls are attracted to toys in the home living area (Servin et al., 1999). The amount of puzzle play for both boys and girls is related to the degree of mental transformation ability (McGuiness & Morley, 1991). Additionally, studies have determined that boys play more video games than girls do; such games rely on and nurture spatial skills (Quaiser-Pohl, Geiser, & Lehmann, 2006).

Findings indicate that boys have an advantage on certain spatial tasks, but the advantage may be influenced and affected by the use of spatially oriented toys, activities, and video games. It also could be true, or at least is speculated, that males are more encouraged to play with blocks, manipulatives, puzzles, balls, and transportation types of toys than girls are. This could possibly further enhance boys' advantages in spatial activities. Traditional preschool activities, such as block play, have been used successfully to develop spatial knowledge in girls (Casey, Erkut, Ceder, & Young, 2008). Perhaps the underrepresentation of women in math, science, technology, and engineering fields could be related to the types of toys which girls are encouraged to play with in early childhood. This makes it essential to encourage play with toys such as blocks, manipulatives, puzzles, and balls to enhance spatial skills in all children.

An intervention study of preschoolers using a research-based mathematics curriculum indicated that girls can learn as much as boys about spatial and geometric development in a classroom that emphasizes spatial skills. These findings demonstrate the need for more emphasis on spatial and geometric development for girls as well as boys (Clements & Sarama, 2008a).

Why Is It Important to Identify Spatially Talented Students?

Spatially talented students are often not identified unless they happen to also be mathematically or verbally gifted (Shea, Lubinski, & Benbow, 2001). It is important to identify spatially talented students early on so that they can be adequately supported in developing and furthering their spatial abilities. The Woodcock-Johnson III Tests of Cognitive Abilities, Diagnostic Supplement Block Rotation subtest (Woodcock, McGrew, & Mather, 2000) is a test that can be used to identify students with spatial abilities (Schrank, Mather, McGrew, & Woodcock, 2003); most generic IQ tests also have sections devoted to spatial intelligence. Students who exhibit spatial talent in the early years continue to exhibit these types of reasoning skills throughout their academic careers, thus making identification of such students important.

Evidence has suggested that high school students with spatial skills are typically drawn to environments that involve technology and manipulation of forms (Humphreys, Lubinski, & Yao, 1993). Studies have shown that such students are attracted to the technical fields, such as software engineering, airplane design, architecture, or trade fields such as car mechanics, drafting, plumbing, or construction. However, research also indicates that such students should not be limited to trade fields; spatially talented persons have the potential to be highly proficient in many engineering and scientific fields including, for example, mechanical engineering, industrial design, surgery, advanced mathematics, physics, biology, astronomy, and chemistry (Xie & Shauman, 2003). Because of the strong emphasis on literacy and math in K–12 schools, highly spatially oriented students who rely on reasoning with shapes rather than reasoning in words or numbers may feel left out of the mainstream.

In order to overcome the lack of emphasis shown toward spatially focused individuals, a variety of changes in early childhood education can be made with relative ease. Students who have spatial learning abilities can be motivated by incorporating more block-building activities, promoting puzzle activities in the classroom, using books that promote both spatial and geometric concepts, and using correct spatial terminology and language in the classroom. For specific ideas on how to incorporate spatial reasoning throughout the early childhood classrooms, see Chapters 3–8.

What Research Has Been Done to Improve Spatial Development?

Developing geometric and spatial knowledge in children can develop growth in math and science skills as well as in other cognitive abilities (Clements & Sarama, 2009). This section explores research regarding topics such as gestures, visualization, block play, mapping, computer skills, puzzle play, and children's stories. Case studies illustrating practical use in the classroom are also included in each subsection.

Gestures

Five-year-old Mark came to school one day and said to the teacher, "Mrs. Adams, I know how to get home from school on my bicycle." He gestured with his entire hand (fingers pointed) to the right and left, and left again. Then Mark stated, "I go to the second house on this side (to his right side)." Mrs. Adams asked what the gestures meant and he said, "to the right, left, and left again." In this case, Mark used gestures to underline his understanding of spatial relations of two locations (home and school) and illustrate knowledge for the teacher that he might not be able to demonstrate with words alone.

Gestures are very important to spatial development. Gestures can capture information (McNeill, 1992; Kita & Ozyurek, 2003) and are quite often utilized when describing spatial words and concepts (Krauss, 1998). Gestures are frequently used when navigating through space and directions (Emmorey, Tversky, & Taylor, 2000; Schaal, Uttall, Levine, & Goldin-Meadow, 2005). In a study by Ehrlich, Levine, and Goldin-Meadow (2006), it was found that children ages 4 and 5 who performed better on a spatial transformation task often used movement through gestures. It was also found that boys scored better on the spatial development tasks and gestured more about movement than girls did (Ehrlich et al., 2006).

Visualization

The children in Mrs. Carley's second-grade class had become designers of containers for their blocks. They were instructed to design containers for their cubes. They were each given one piece of 1-inch grid paper and eight 1-inch square cubes.

The children were told to work with partners and design with the help of the grid paper. This task required the children to develop different ways they could construct a box. They then recorded their information on paper. They had to think about length, width, and height. One student made a tall box, a rectangular one to hold the eight cubes. Another student made two rows of four. Others designed their blocks in the shape of the letter L. With this exercise the children were introduced to the concepts of length, width, and depth.

Visualization provides learners with strategies to promote spatial ability. Research has found that visualization promotes problem-solving skills (Ben-Chaim, Lappan, & Houang, 1989). Visualization helps children interpret, use, and reflect upon pictorial images and then represent images in various ways. Because visualization is an important aspect of spatial learning, it is imperative that teachers help young children visualize and think of many different ways to represent their visualizations. Graphics and diagrams can be used to promote spatial visualization and perspective taking (Szechter & Liben, 2003). Representation of visualization can take place in structured diagrams or grids, as well as in different media and technology.

Block Playing

Before an architect designs a skyscraper, he or she spends time in the city where the building will be constructed. Similar to the architect's approach, the children in Mrs. Jones's kindergarten class in an inner-city school visited downtown Denver. When the children came back to school, they were divided into groups of three or four. Each group decided what they were going to build. The children drew a street plan with the main street and several side streets on large 3-inch grid paper. They decided where the streets would be, where the parking lots would be, and where the stop signs would be.

They decided what buildings should be constructed. They decided to build a skyscraper, post office, school, store, gas station, and hospital. The children had previously studied layouts of cities and had seen many pictures of these structures in books. The children decided how tall their buildings would be, how wide, and where the buildings would be placed in relationship to one another. To accomplish their design, the children determined how many grid squares their buildings took up and which building had the largest area. The teacher guided them in using words such as on top of, above, below, next to, beside, *and* inside. *One 5-year-old boy decided to connect the city to the interstate highway with special curves, bridges, and ramps. His ability to produce these elements showed an understanding of the inclined plane and mental rotation. When the teacher later had him draw the design on paper, he was able to repeat his design.*

This example of city building illustrates how block play with unit blocks enhances spatial thinking as well as number sense and measurement. Drafting a design helps the children with graphic skills and the design in turn helps with the construction of the actual buildings. With teacher guidance in the use of spatial concepts, blocks can augment spatial understanding.

Block play in the early years has an important effect on spatial thinking and mathematical thinking later in middle and high school. Wolfgang, Stannard, and Jones (2001) found that children's block play performance in preschool is a predictor of mathematics achievement in middle school and high school. Golbeck (2005) has studied block play skill scores and related these to performance on spatial knowledge and graphic skill in writing and drawing. It has also been discovered that preschool children, at least intuitively, use many high-level geometric concepts in block play that are usually taught in elementary school. If used effectively with teacher guidance, blocks can be used to enhance spatial knowledge (Seo & Ginsburg, 2004). See Chapter 8 for more information on and a discussion of block play.

Mapping

At circle time in kindergarten, Mrs. Knapp read Rosie's Walk *by Pat Hutchins (1968). This classic book is about a hen that went for a walk in the barnyard and a fox that cannot follow the path to catch her. It uses concepts such as* over, under, around, *and* through *in the trail that the hen makes in the barnyard. This book sparked the children's interest in exploring their school on a walk, just as the hen had explored the barnyard. Mrs. Knapp had previously taken pictures of various places in the school. After she read the book, she showed the pictures of the school to the children. Mrs. Knapp told the children that they were going to take a walk through the school. She said, "As we walk, we will look for the bathroom, the cafeteria, and the principal's office and think of ways to remember where we are and where we are going." She showed the pictures and the labels for each picture and told the children they would be labeling the places.*

Then the children went for a walk. They walked down the hall past two rooms, past the water fountain, and labeled the bathroom that was on the right, immediately after the water fountain. They then walked past two more classrooms and located the principal's office on the left. The children labeled the principal's office. Then they turned right and went down a short hall and passed the ticket station for the cafeteria where the tickets for lunch were collected. They labeled the cafeteria with a sign near the ticket station.

The group came back to the classroom and discussed what they saw in each of these spots. Using chart paper, Mrs. Knapp drew a red dashed line to mark a path leading from the front door of the classroom to the bathroom, a blue dashed line to mark the path to the principal's office, and a green dashed line to mark the path to the cafeteria. As Mrs. Knapp created each path, she talked about the distances between the bathroom and the classroom. She also discussed the distance between the cafeteria and the classroom as well as the distance between the principal's office and the cafeteria.

She made a legend at the bottom of her chart using red, blue, and green colors for the paths. Mrs. Knapp also included miniature pictures of the places in the school and labels. Two boys used string as well as a tape measure to measure each path according to the colored legend, then determined if they measured the same length going forward from the classroom and backward to the classroom. Mrs. Knapp labeled the rooms and the classrooms they had passed. One girl explained, "I can remember where the bathroom is because we pass my sister's room."

This example demonstrates how measurement can be used to promote an understanding of space and how mapping skills contribute to spatial literacy. Such an activity enhances boys' interest in distance and direction and can be used as well to enhance girls' interest in landmarks.

Mapping skills or learning of routes are important to spatial literacy because these skills help guide children to orient themselves in space. Studies of mapping skills reveal that males do better with distance and direction, whereas females do better with landmarks (Beilstein & Wilson, 2000). Therefore, boys should be given more verbal directions and girls should be given more landmarks, such as the water fountain or a sister's classroom as in the example above, that can assist them in remembering. The example demonstrates how distance, directions, and presentation of landmarks and pictures can be successfully shown to children, thereby increasing understanding through methods that both males and females use to learn routes. (See Chapter 5 for more information on mapping.)

Computers

In Mrs. Bender's first-grade class, children used attribute blocks, or blocks that can be classified by color, size, shape, and thickness. The children then classified these blocks by shape and size. They later were exposed to the same attribute blocks on the National Library of Virtual Manipulatives web site (see www.nlvm.usu.edu/en/nav/vLibrary.html) and classified them by shape and size again in a different medium. This web site offers manipulatives in virtual form that children can use in the classroom. Geometric web sites such as this one make motions on the computer more accessible to further viewing and reflection. Throughout the year, they used geoboards, pattern blocks, three-dimensional blocks, and other types of materials in class and later used them on the web site. This allowed the children to practice using the manipulatives in two meaningful contexts.

This example shows that children who have been exposed to concrete manipulatives can later successfully transfer these skills to web-based virtual manipulatives.

Computer usage aids the metacognitive aspects of spatial activity. Using computers can foster a deeper conceptual thinking and visualization of what the child has experienced concretely. In early childhood settings, children can explore shapes in a playful way and use shapes similar to their play objects by using computer programs and web sites (Johnson-Gentile, Clements, & Battista, 1994; Moyer-Packenham, Salkind, & Bolyard, 2005). There are now many web sites and software programs that aid the teacher in guiding the child in geometrical and spatial contexts to enhance understanding of what they have experienced in real life and on paper (see Chapter 7) for more information about computers and technology in the classroom).

Puzzles

Children in Mrs. Gagnon's first-grade class were matched with a partner to make designs using a tangram. The tangram is a set of seven geometric shapes consisting of five triangles (two small, one medium, and two large), a square, and a parallelogram. These seven basic shapes can be used to make an amazing number of other shapes, and together all seven pieces can form a square. One child was instructed to make a design with the tangram while the partner looked on. The partner was then asked to copy the shape. The child who originally made the design described orally to the other child how the design was completed.

This activity shows how a child can see the puzzle as a whole and then have instructions to make the tangram puzzle. One student said, "I made a tower. First, I made a square out of the two large triangles and placed the square shape at the bottom. Then I worked really hard and made two triangles and a parallelogram into a rectangle. I placed the rectangle I made on top of the large square. Next, I placed a small square on the rectangle and the medium-sized triangle on the top for the roof."

The amount of puzzle play for both boys and girls is related to development of the concept of mental transformation (McGuiness & Morley, 1991). Puzzles and tangrams require that the child think about the object as a whole. The child must also think about which way to place individual pieces and transform them in a way such that they fit together to form a whole. Puzzle play is a powerful tool for encouraging the development of mental transformation, matching shapes, and problem solving. Chapter 3 provides further discussion on puzzles and mental transformations with shapes.

Children's Stories

The children in Mrs. Crawford's preschool class had been interested in bridges. One day they walked over a bridge near a stream. Mrs. Crawford pointed out how the bridge connected two pieces of land and that there was water underneath. When she got back to class, she read The Three Billy Goats Gruff *and the children acted it out. She read* London Bridge Is Falling Down *and they played the game that follows the same story line. She also brought in books about bridges and images of some of Monet's paintings of bridges. A few days later, she went over to the block-play area and decided that the students could make a bridge for the Three Billy Goats Gruff and the Troll who lived underneath the bridge in the story. She placed two blocks vertically and asked the children what else they would need for the bridge. Sam placed another block on top. Mrs. Crawford then asked if the bridge was long enough. The children decided that they wanted to build a longer bridge and added more vertical blocks. Subsequently, they constructed a ramp to go to the top so the Three Billy Goats could go up. Then they added another ramp so the Billy Goats could go down. The children then tested the bridge to see if the Billy Goats could get over it without the bridge falling down. They also tested the height of it to see if the Troll could fit under it.*

This activity served to expand the children's knowledge, because it introduced a new structure to the children who had previously only been stacking blocks, and the activity promoted the concepts of the inclined plane, length, width, and strength of the bridge to hold material. It also demonstrated how a bridge is used to connect two pieces of land.

As explained earlier in this section, practical activities such as block play and children's stories (Kersh, Casey, &Young, 2008) regarding spatial topics have also been used to develop spatial knowledge (Casey, Erkut, Ceder, & Young, 2008). Children's literature has always been a source for creative drama, and the block area lends itself naturally to prop construction and sequencing of the literature story. See Chapter 4 and Chapter 8 for more detailed discussions.

What Does the Research Say About Spatial Development and Math?

Contemporary research has shown that young thinkers are both mathematical thinkers and spatial thinkers, yet young children receive a limited emphasis or introduction to mathematics before they enter elementary school (Geary, 1994). In international studies, the United States ranked 13th in math scores out of 38 countries tested (Mullis et al., 2000), a trend that was also evident in the most recent Trends in International Mathematics and Science Study (TIMSS) results in 2003 and 2007. The TIMSS results did show that improvements have been made in the overall scores of children in the area of mathematics in 2007.

According to evaluations of the results of these international studies, elementary students in the United States are failing to learn basic geometric concepts and geometric problem solving. American students are not ready for the study of more difficult concepts, especially compared with students from other countries (Carpenter, Corbitt, Kepner, Lindquist, & Reys, 1980; Fey et al., 1984). Students from Japan and Taiwan scored more than twice as high as U.S. students on a test of geometry in both first and fifth grades.

Why Are Students from Asia Outperforming Students from the United States?

As early as preschool, children in the United States score lower on spatial imagery than children in Japan and China (Starkey et al., 1999; Stigler, Lee, & Stevenson, 1990). This could be because, unlike their Asian counterparts, some children in the United States are not given enough support for visual representation through drawing, paper folding, and puzzles. However, research has shown that certain settings with geometric and block play emphasis (see Chapter 8 for further information on block play) in the United States do help children develop spatial abilities (Clements, Battista, Sarama, & Swaminathan, 1997). One of the few research-based early childhood math programs, the *Building Blocks Curriculum* (Clements & Sarama, 2007a), was designed to enable young children to build mathematical concepts through learning trajectories. It has a strong spatial component and has produced positive outcomes (Clements & Sarama, 2007a, 2009). There is a dearth of recent research on the Froebelian curriculum, a highly developed spatial program, because of a historical lack of written curriculum and paucity of programs that use it; however, there has been a renewed interest in the curriculum (see Chapter 2 for more information about Froebel's curriculum).

As the outcome of the spatial research indicates, it is important to break from the narrow vision of early childhood geometric and mathematics study and build on the legacy of research and curricula that have supported spatial development. Thinking about spatial development from an international perspective as well as through curricula in the United States that promote spatial development will help facilitate a better understanding of the conditions that support spatial development.

How Do Japanese Classrooms Promote Spatial Development?

In observing and examining classrooms and homes in Japan in 2002, the author noticed the prevalence of exercises in paper folding in both settings. In one of the Japanese schools she visited, she saw a tree decorated with origami designs, made by children for the celebration of the Tanabata Festival holiday. The tree traditionally is decorated with origami figures made by the children at home.

Japan has more people per square foot than any other place on Earth, so space is very valued. Even in the home, the tatami mat—the traditional straw mat made in uniform sizes used as a floor covering in Japanese homes—is representative of space being used geometrically and efficiently. Asian countries are well known for making use of the tangram, which is a set of seven wooden or plastic pieces containing five triangles of proportional sizes, a parallelogram, and a square (see Figure 1.1). This tangram puzzle alone can teach many of the geometric concepts recommended in National Council of Teachers of Mathematics Focal Points (2006).

How Do Italian Classrooms Promote Spatial Development?

In a 1996 study in Italy at the Reggio Emilia preschools, the author observed a whole room filled with blocks. Children used the blocks as a medium to represent different things. Along with the blocks, the children's representation of their long-term study of a chair was prepared in different media such as pâpier mâché, drawing paper, and blocks. The perspective offered by the

Figure 1.1. A tangram.

chair from different views (from the front, back, left side, and right side) helped the children see the object from different angles and in greater detail, which is not often the case in schools in the United States. In classrooms in the United States, children have a variety of different blocks in early childhood classrooms, but many teachers do not utilize them in ways conducive to spatial development. Even though there are concrete objects being used in classrooms, often these concrete objects consist of such items as teddy bears for counting or other manipulatives that may not lend themselves to the development of spatial orientation. Some objects are used as assessments of whether children can distinguish the differences between a triangle, circle, or square, but usually the lessons do not extend to in-depth use of transformations and examining different forms of the same shape in two- and three-dimensional forms.

Teaching spatial development does not require new, expensive materials or even disregarding existing curricula. Upcoming chapters in this book will provide readers with new perspectives on how to approach teaching of spatial literacy based on research and theory and tied to curriculum areas commonly found in the early childhood classroom.

SUMMARY

Spatial thinking is very important for the disciplines of science, technology, engineering, and mathematics (the group of disciplines known as STEM). Therefore, it is critical to understand how spatially talented persons are identified and how spatial development takes place in the youngest children in the school system. The intent of this book is to provide the reader with new perspectives on how to approach spatial literacy in early childhood education using planned, research-based activities.

2

A Curriculum that Promoted Spatial Development

Friedrich Froebel, a Trained Architect and Mathematician

According to the National Research Council's report titled *Mathematics Learning in Early Childhood: Paths Toward Excellence and Equity* (2009), there has been a coordinated national effort to provide high-quality instruction for America's children. This may be because children have not always had the opportunity to use a challenging mathematics curriculum (Geary, 1994). However, there was a curriculum that did provide a challenge for children, especially in the area of spatial development. This was the curriculum of Friedrich Froebel, who is known as "the father of kindergarten." Froebel was a German mathematician, architect, mineralogist, and educator who, over time, became a familiar name in Europe, America, and Asia at the end of the 19th century. In the 1850s, he created a rather complex pedagogy for young children up to age 7 that was based on many geometric forms. He coined the word *kindergarten,* which means *children's garden,* and the term became familiar in early childhood settings. Froebel chose the name "kindergarten" because he was interested in encouraging the development of children in a way analogous to that of the gardener who promoted growth in plants. His emphasis was on using songs, nature, storytelling, "gifts" (or objects that represent symbolic ideas and can be used for construction, design, and mathematical concepts), and educational toys such as blocks and origami.

Friedrich Froebel.

Friedrich Froebel: A Brief Biography

Friedrich Froebel was born in 1782 in eastern Germany. His mother died when he was 9 months old. In his early schooling, he had difficulty reading and he was not a good student. The only subject that came easily for him in school was arithmetic. One day in 1792, his maternal uncle, Herr Hoffman, came to see him. Hoffman had lost his wife and child and was very interested in young Froebel, who had a difficult relationship with his stepmother and a strained and distant relationship with his father. Hoffman took him in. After Hoffman became Froebel's guardian for several years, Froebel went to a school for boys and received excellent training. He loved both the freedom he experienced with his uncle and the garden his uncle had developed.

When Froebel returned to his parental home at the age of 15, he served a 2-year apprenticeship as a forester, surveyor, and assessor. He discovered his love of work in agriculture. During this time he studied botany, natural history, and geometry. He also became very fascinated with nature, taking nature walks throughout the glens in Germany. While observing nature, Froebel classified specimens with great personal delight. He remarked that his religious study as a child was transformed into religious study with nature. His interests in geometry and botany were made known to his father, and with his father's help he enrolled at the University of Jena in Germany in 1799.

At the university, botany was Froebel's favorite subject, but he also liked map drawing and geometry. Froebel also attended lectures on applied math, arithmetic, physics, chemistry, accounting, cultivation and management of forest trees, architecture, house building, and land surveying.

After his uncle died, Froebel received a small inheritance and went to Frankfurt to study architecture in 1805. He soon started to contemplate how he could use architecture to enlighten humanity. At the same time, he was introduced to the headmaster of the Frankfurt Model School, which was developed on the principles of Johann Heinrich Pestalozzi, a Swiss elementary school teacher. Pestalozzi rejected memorization and advocated sensory exploration and observation as the basis for learning. Froebel was offered a job at the Frankfurt Model School and later studied with Pestalozzi at Yverdon in Switzerland. He soon found himself in opposition to the existing teaching methods because he felt that Pestalozzi lacked organization and did not feel that Pestalozzi made known the specific underlying reasons for what he did (Downs, 1978). Froebel wanted to combine subjects into a connecting whole, as opposed to learning about each subject separately, yet Froebel also found he wanted to learn much more about other subjects. In 1811 he studied at the University of Göttingen, continuing his scientific studies in physics, chemistry, mineralogy, and natural science. He received a post at the University of Berlin as the assistant to the Mineralogical Museum. There he attended lectures on mineralogy, crystallography, and geology. The developing branch of crystallography was becoming a science based on geometry and not just a philosophy. His intensive work with crystals made Froebel realize that the shapes of crystals were combinations of triangles, squares, and cubes, eventually influencing his ideas for his curriculum.

Froebel's Environment and Curriculum

Froebel's interest in the field of education developed into a belief that children should be nurtured and taught from a very early age, and not at age 7 or even later, which was the practice at the time. Froebel's conviction that very young children were rapidly acquiring knowledge and could be taught and stimulated in learning became the basis for his concept of kindergarten (Bultman, 2000).

When Froebel decided to begin developing a kindergarten curriculum, he focused on the importance of surrounding environments, both in nature and in the room. He made sure there was a garden and he symbolically used the circle for "circle time," a time when children sang songs. His geometric interest was evident in many of the tables in the kindergarten classroom developed by Froebel because they had squares cut into the wood. These squares provided visual scaffolding in geometric forms. Froebel's materials show an understanding of the importance of hand–eye coordination, small-motor coordination, and form. The materials were also used to promote play, creativity, geometry, physics, and storytelling.

Froebel's Gifts

Froebel designed toys for use with his curriculum. Froebel referred to these toys as "gifts," because the word *gift* conveys both pleasure and responsibility (Corbett, 1989). Froebel designed each gift to be given to a child in a self-directed activity. Gifts represent symbolic ideas in concrete form, and they were designed to show the child's knowledge of the world. The number of gifts vary depending on what source is consulted. Some of Froebel's followers modified the gifts later on.

In Froebel's curriculum, handwork activities were used in conjunction with the gifts. Occupations, the name Froebel gave to the handwork activities, included things like drawing, perforating, sewing, twining, braiding, paper cutting, paper folding, and clay modeling. Sticks, rings, twining, and paper cutting helped make the child familiar with lines. Points and lines were used in sewing. Weaving gave the child ways of putting lines together to form a surface. Paper folding showed the child ways in which surfaces can be changed. The solid objects, such as clay, could be manipulated creatively.

In general, all of Froebel's gifts represented forms of nature, forms of beauty, and forms of knowledge. Froebel thought it was important for children to create something using gifts with these three concepts.

1. **Forms of nature** include life, the physical world, and familiar objects. For example, children might create something they saw on the way to school or on the playground, or a building in the city.
2. **Forms of beauty** include art, pattern, and symmetry. For example, children might create something using an element of art that is aesthetically pleasing.
3. **Forms of knowledge** include science and math. For example, children might learn about the physics of the materials by showing how solids such as the sphere or cylinder will roll and some such as the cube or cylinder will stand still, or they might learn math concepts such as addition and subtraction.

The Froebelian gifts help children learn how nature (the physical world), beauty (design), and knowledge (math and science) are interrelated. Belief in this interrelationship has been held by many scientists and philosophers (e.g., Leonardo Da Vinci, Albert Einstein). The gifts represent these three forms: nature, beauty, and knowledge.

Gift Descriptions

Each of Froebel's gifts will be described in the following sections, along with an explanation of how it relates to the forms of nature, beauty, and knowledge. It should be noted that in practice, a child would create a form of nature, beauty, or knowledge and then describe it. The teacher would enhance the conversation with ideas relevant to the structure, and then one child would summarize the work of all the children. To give the contemporary teacher more ideas on using Froebel's gifts (forms of which can be ordered from FroebelUSA, www.froebelgifts.com; see p. 152), a section in Appendix A of this volume extends the forms of knowledge into mathematical concepts commonly taught in preschool and elementary school classrooms. The activities in Appendix A are in line with the National Council of Teachers of Mathematics (NCTM) Standards (2000). Although some of these activities seem rather complex for the kindergarten of today, the National Research Council's report on mathematics learning in early childhood (2009) indicates that children are capable of learning much more in the area of math than once thought, especially in the area of geometry. There is also some evidence that Froebel's Kindergarten could have had older children (up to age 7) than our present-day kindergartens.

Gift 1: Six Woolen Colored Balls Gift 1 consists of six woolen balls colored in the spectrum of the rainbow—red, orange, yellow, green, blue, and violet. The balls are divided into primary colors (red, yellow, and blue) and secondary colors (orange, violet, and green). There are many round objects that can be compared with the six balls of the first gift, such as sports balls (e.g., baseballs, basketballs), fruits (e.g., oranges, apples), and playthings (e.g., marbles, balloons). The balls, according to Froebel, needed strings, because the strings helped the child manipulate the ball for positional and directional concepts that could be taught with the balls. The strings helped the child demonstrate certain concepts with the balls. This was chosen as the first gift because a ball was considered a perfect form. Many other objects and shapes can be created from a ball. For instance, a cube can be cut from a ball, as can a triangular prism.

There are also ways the gift of the six woolen balls can be used to teach language. Froebel wrote songs to sing with the child along with each gift that he presented. In the case of the six woolen balls, Froebel sang a song explaining primary and complementary colors.

According to Froebel, the ball first appears to be part of the child. The child can play with the ball, and the parent or teacher can pull out the string so that the child can gain strength. Froebel believed it was important not to speak to the child directly and let the child figure out what to do with the balls. There should be a comparison of opposites, and at first, the child should discover them by letting the ball roll up and over and letting the ball roll down and under. Later, the teacher can help develop vocabulary with the balls by using more direct instruction. A picture from the Froebel Memorial Museum in Bad Blankenburg, Germany, showed 30 phrases being used with the ball, such as "swing over," "swing under," "place beside," "roll over," and "roll under." A box was used with the ball; the teacher placed the ball in it, beside it, over it, and under it. Then, the child moves from using the ball to using other objects (e.g., oranges, nuts, and flowers) with the same words.

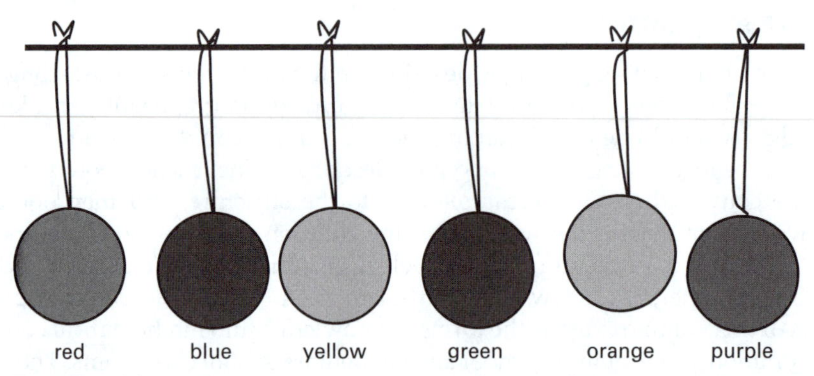

Figure 2.1. Gift 1.

Froebel emphasized the unity of each child's developmental domains and the inner connection between individual children, the spiritual worlds, nature, and the human race. In addition, the circle represented circle time used in the kindergarten when all the children gather around for a lesson and songs and use the balls to represent something.

See Figure 2.1 for a pictorial example of Gift 1. This gift was mainly used for positional vocabulary and directional vocabulary. It should be noted that there are differing opinions as to where Gift 1 should be introduced with forms of nature, forms of beauty, and forms of knowledge. Some Froebel authors suggest that this should start with Gift 2 or Gift 3 (Liebschner, 2001). For the sake of consistency, this text will use the same format for all gifts, because there is variation among authors and the Froebel Museums in Germany in the interpretation of how they should be used.

Gift 1

Forms of Nature: The child uses the figure to represent things from the child's life. A sphere is a solid round shape. Some examples of spherical forms of nature include oranges or balls.

Forms of Beauty: In the forms of design, the unity of what makes the shapes complete can be discussed with the children. The sphere can be represented as perfectly round. Primary and secondary colors can be discussed.

Forms of Knowledge: In physics, the sphere will roll and the child can practice rolling the ball. In math, one can count, add, subtract, multiply, and divide. The child can use the balls and develop vocabulary of position and direction words.

Gift 2: Wooden Sphere, Cube, and Cylinder Gift 2 (see Figure 2.2) consists of the wooden sphere, cube, and cylinder, all of which are 2 inches in diameter. The cylinder was added because it is a mediator between the sphere and the cube. This gift forms the basis for all other gifts. Froebel placed much symbolic importance on the wooden sphere, cube, and cylinder. To Froebel, this gift represented variety, contrast, and synthesis. This was similar to the German philosopher Georg Hegel's concept of thesis, antithe-

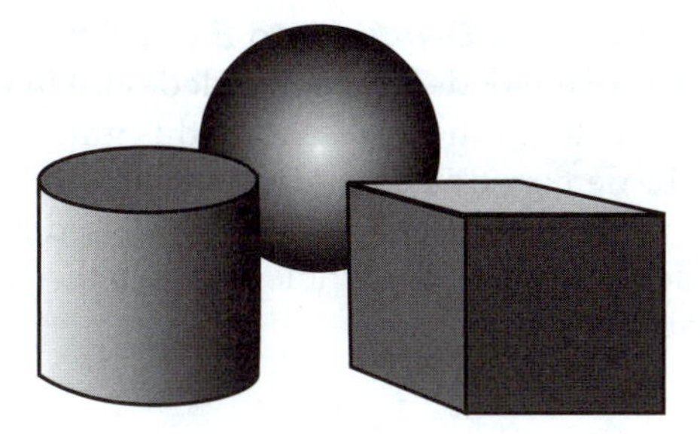

Figure 2.2. Gift 2.

sis, and synthesis in which a thesis is a proposition that a person advances and offers to maintain an argument, an antithesis is opposition to the ideas, and synthesis is a combination of parts or elements in a whole. When used in contrast with the first gift, the child would be able to learn the difference between soft and hard, rough and smooth, and light and heavy. According to Froebel, it is important for the child to see these contrasts. The sphere represented continuity, a figure with no flat planes, while the cube represented a figure with diversity (i.e., a figure with surfaces, angles, and lines). This was important to know because it promoted keen observation on the part of the child if a deeper meaning was understood. Meanwhile the cylinder represented something simultaneously static and dynamic or coherent, with curves and flat surfaces. The sphere and the cube are opposites. The sphere has no flat planes, whereas the cube has no curves. The sphere is an object of motion, whereas the cube is at rest. The sphere can be spun around on its axis. The sphere can be found in a cube.

Gift 2

Forms of Nature: The child uses the figure to represent things from the child's life. A sphere is a solid round shape. Some examples of spherical forms of nature include oranges, balls, marbles, or bubbles. A cylinder is a solid tube-like shape with the end faces shaped as circles. Some examples of cylinders include tennis ball cans, most batteries, and marshmallows. Corn on the cob, sugar cane, and centipedes are also cylindrical in nature. A cube is a solid shape, and it is not a flat surface. It has six faces. Each face is a square. Some examples of cubes are houses or dice.

Forms of Beauty: In the forms of design, the unity of what makes the shapes complete can be discussed with the children. The sphere can be represented as perfectly round. For instance, children can examine what the cylinder looks like from the top view, the front view, the side view, and the bottom view, and decide which two are just alike. Children also can be asked to draw the top, front, and side views and to examine the cube for its 6 faces, 12 edges, and 8 vertices.

Forms of Knowledge: A cube on a string, being hung over a stick, will move up when the string is pulled down and down when the string is moved up. In physics, the sphere and cylinder will roll whereas the cube and cylinder will stand still. In math, there are surfaces, edges, and corners.

Gift 3: Wooden Cube Divided into Eight Smaller Cubes Gift 3 (see Figure 2.3) consists of a wooden cube, divided once in each direction to produce eight smaller cubes. When presenting this gift, the initial wholeness of the cube should be demonstrated first by turning the box upside down so the children can see that the large cube is also composed of eight smaller cubes. This process of demonstrating the whole and then the parts should also occur during the opening of Gifts 4–6.

Gift 3

Forms of Nature: Because wholeness is respected, children can produce something with the entire gift of eight cubes. For instance, they may produce something that they saw on the way to school. They might reproduce a flower, a car, a tree, a house, a box, or the sun. Children then share their creations. In one observation of material at the Froebel Museum in Oberweissbach, Germany, the children had designed many different kinds of chairs for people with Gift 3 and its eight cubes. Designs that were made using transformations of the eight cubes include a three-seat bench, a garden bench, a three-seat garden bench, a reclining bench, a chair, an arm chair, a throne, two chairs, and bleachers. In teaching how to reproduce an object, children in a small group can be encouraged to share their creations. It is useful to have one child try to summarize what took place and describe the creations of each child in the group.

Forms of Beauty: Designs can be patterns that are symmetrical, asymmetrical, or radial. In a symmetrical pattern, both sides are designed to appear equal. An asymmetrical pattern has one side that is not equivalent to the other side. A radial pattern is produced when everything is emanating from the center. For instance, the petals on a flower come out from the center, and designs with the cubes can follow this pattern and come out from the center. A pattern is defined or identified as a shape or design that is repeated. Patterns can be repetitive, alternating, progressive, or flowing. For example, the teacher could say, "Let's make a short, tall, tall, short pattern" or "Let's make a small, small, big, big pattern" or "Let's make a narrow, wide, narrow pattern." Progressive patterns could be demonstrated by adding a little bit more on to the design. *Emphasis,* a principle of design that stresses a particular part to keep the attention of the viewer, can be discussed. *Scale,* another principle of design, can be discussed by explaining that the design is actually smaller than the real thing. If a child has made the design of a man, it could be pointed out that the head is smaller than the leg. Designs can be rotated one at a time to show different designs.

Forms of Knowledge: Counting, addition, subtraction, multiplication, division, and fractions can be used with the blocks. Blocks can be composed and decomposed in preparation for fractions.

Gift 4: Wooden Cube Divided into Smaller Oblong Blocks Gift 4 (see Figure 2.4) is a 2-inch cube divided into eight oblong blocks 2 inches ×

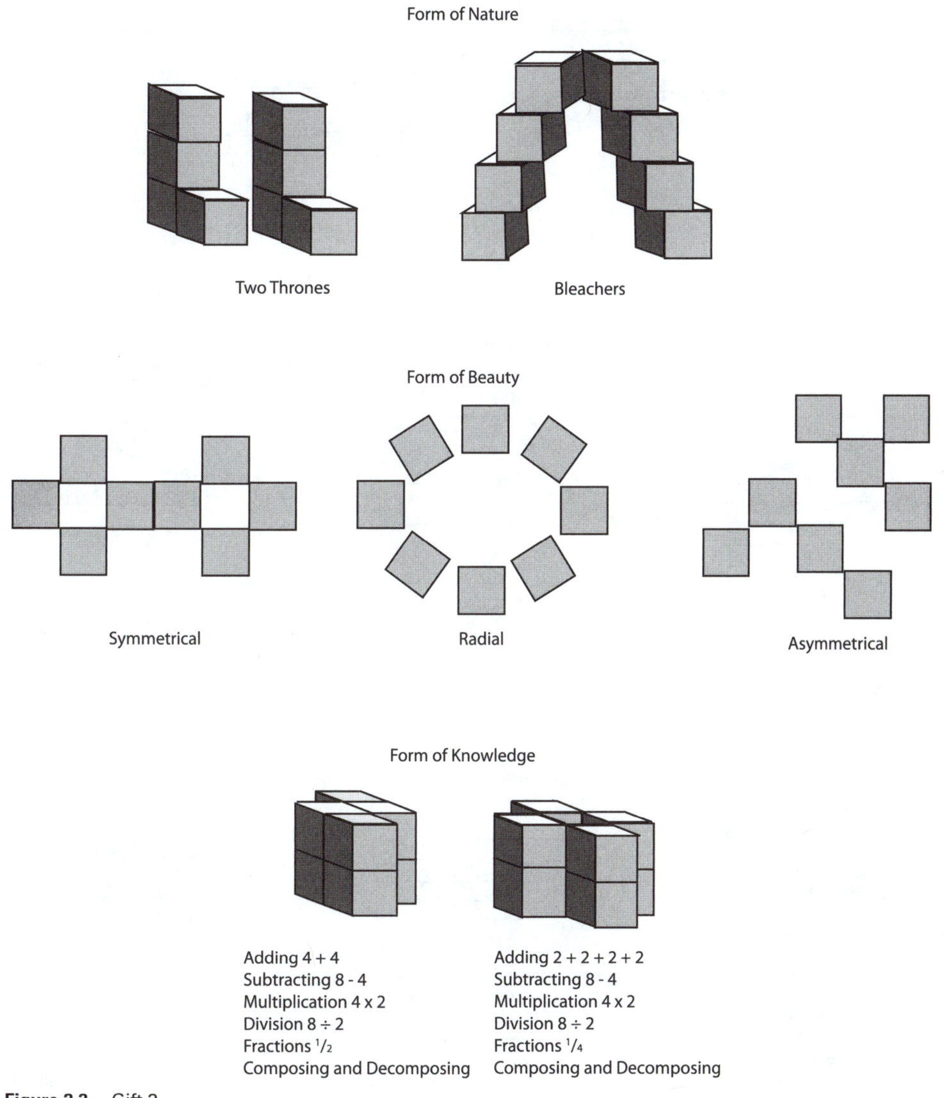

Figure 2.3. Gift 3.

½ inch. Gift 4 is only slightly different from Gift 3. The gift should be presented by demonstrating the initial wholeness of the cube first, before showing students that the cube is divided into smaller oblong blocks. The oblong block pieces can produce modular construction, a form of construction used in the housing industry that is easy to produce because of its geometric proportions. In addition, proportion can be discussed in the classroom. This gift prefigured some of the floor plans of Frank Lloyd Wright, Mies van der Rohe, and the windmill paintings of Piet Mondrian, Theo van Doesburg, and Lyonel Feininger (Brosterman, 1997).

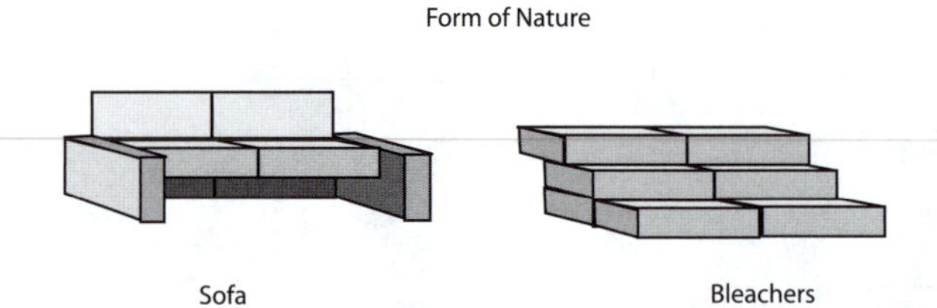

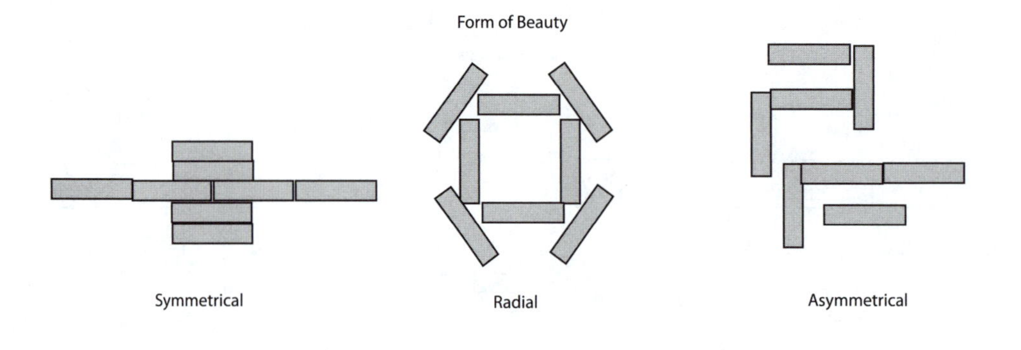

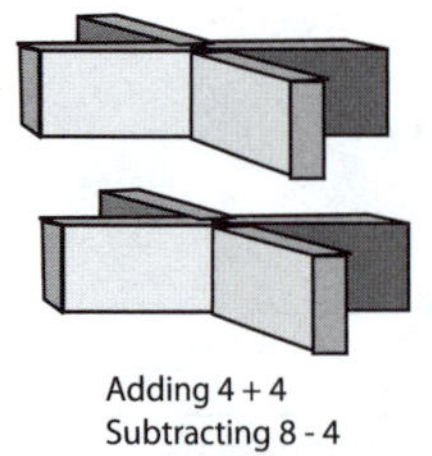

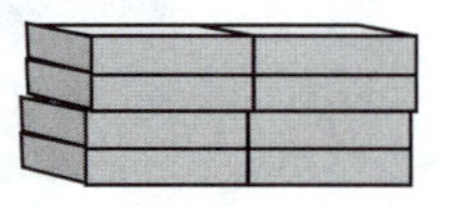

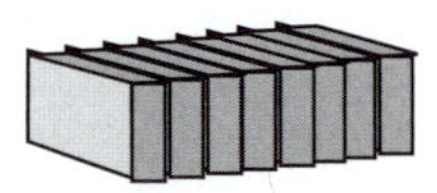

Figure 2.4. Gift 4.

Gift 4

Forms of Nature: Bricks, tiles, and steps can be designed, along with other forms of nature. Again, as in the example of forms of nature in Gift 3, children can make different designs of the same object, such as a chair. They can compare their creations with cubes and rectangular prisms and discuss why the cube designs are different from the rectangular prisms used in Gift 4.

Forms of Beauty: As mentioned above, the forms of design, such as balance (symmetrical, asymmetrical, and radial) can be discussed. In addition, scale, emphasis, and unity can also be discussed.

Forms of Knowledge: A rectangle is a four-sided figure with opposite sides equal and parallel, with each interior angle being a right angle. The face of the rectangular prism is a rectangle. Counting, addition, subtraction, multiplication, division, and fractions can be used with the blocks in Gift 4. Composing and decomposing of the blocks in preparation for fractions can also take place, and concepts such as half, quarter, vertical, horizontal, rectangle, height, width, and length can be introduced.

Gift 5: Large Wooden Cube Divided into Smaller Cubes Gift 5 (see Figure 2.5) is composed of a 3-inch cube divided into twenty-one 1-inch cubes, six triangular ½-inch cubes, and 12 triangular ¼-inch cubes. Gift 5 represents a larger cube and incorporates more pieces and variety than Gift 3. The half cubes and quarter cubes also introduce a triangular prism shape. The gift should be presented to children first as a whole object as it is taken out of the box, before the object is shown being separated into smaller cubes. This helps the child see the whole before the part.

Gift 5

Forms of Nature: Because triangular prisms are introduced in this gift, there are more possibilities for the child to create more realistic interpretations of buildings with roofs. The stories about the buildings that the children make up are just as important as the creation of the building, because the process gives more insight into each child's thinking.

Forms of Beauty: Children can complete symmetrical, asymmetrical, and radial designs. Symmetry is the exact reflection of a form on opposite sides of a dividing line or plane. Symmetry can be used with many figures. An interesting approach would be to rearrange the trapezoid into a parallelogram and ask the children which one is symmetrical. The children can be taught or encouraged to modify rather than destroy and rebuild another design. Other principles of design, such as balance, patterning, scale, emphasis, and unity can also be discussed. Quilts or pictures of quilts can be used to demonstrate the complex symmetries.

Forms of Knowledge: Angles such as right, acute, and obtuse can be discussed as well as solid shapes, such as triangular prisms and rectangular prisms. There can be a discovery of other geometric shapes, such as polygons, quadrilaterals, pentagons, and hexagons. Fractions, such as ½, ⅓, ¼, and ⅕, can be introduced. The gift can be viewed as three cubed. The larger 3-inch cube is composed of twenty-seven 1-inch cubes (although some are triangular prisms). The Pythagorean theorem could also be used ($a^2 + b^2 = c^2$) with this design according to Froebel, although this is a difficult concept for kindergartners and is not normally used in kindergarten. All previous concepts can be taught.

Form of Nature

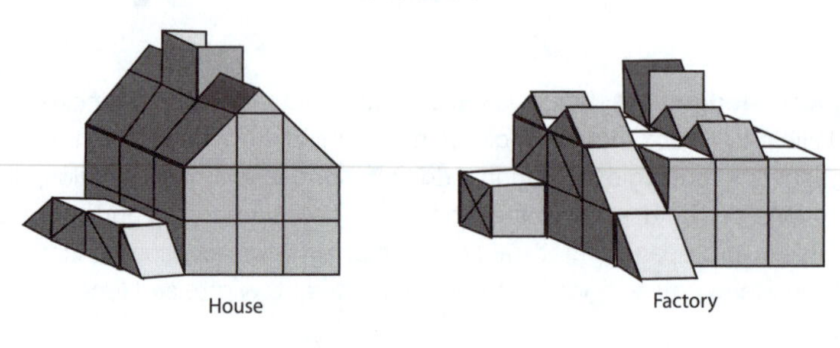

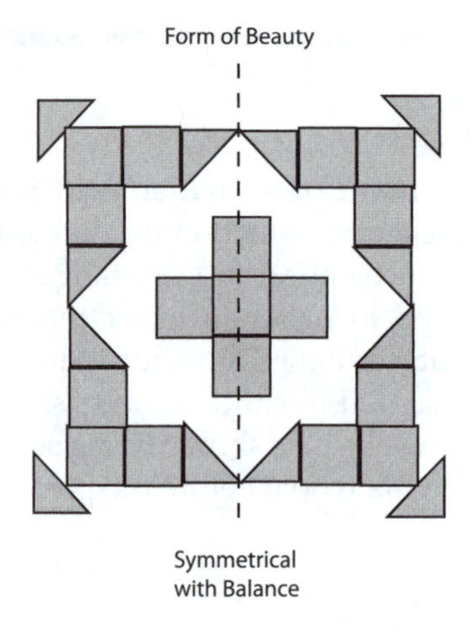

Form of Knowledge

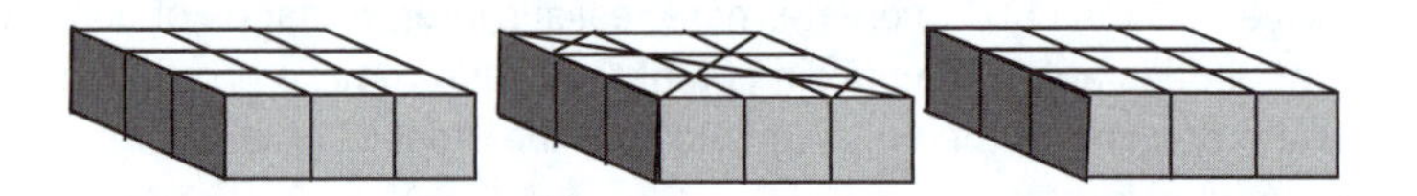

Angles: Right, Acute, and Obtuse
Triangular Prisms and Rectangular Prisms
Quadrilaterals, Pentagons, and Hexagons
Subtracting 27 - 9
Multiplication 3 x 9
Division 8 ÷ 2
Fractions $^1/_2$ $^1/_3$ $^1/_5$
Composing and Decomposing

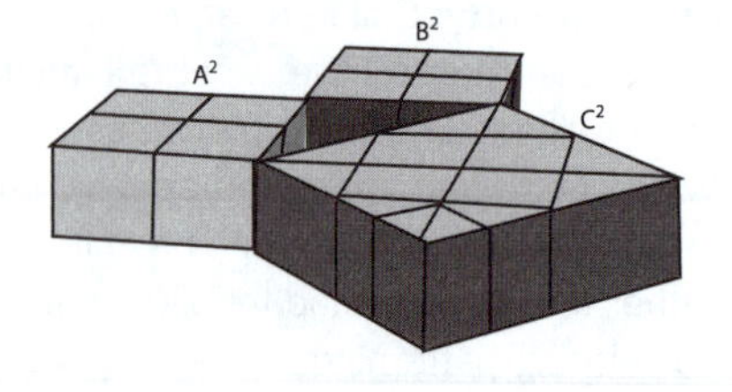

Figure 2.5. Gift 5.

Gift 6: Large Wooden Cube Divided into Multiple Smaller Pieces

Gift 6 (see Figure 2.6) is a 3-inch cube that is divided into 18 oblong blocks, 12 flat square blocks, and 6 narrow columns for a total of 36 pieces. This is a further extension of Gift 5. Froebel says that with the addition of the sixth gift, the child can duplicate all of the architectural forms of Egypt, Greece, and Rome (Osborn, 1991). Gift 6 continues the concept of the form of the 3-inch cube introduced in Gift 5. The gift should again be presented to children as one large block before showing the children that the gift can be divided into smaller blocks. This shows the whole before the parts. There are many reproductions of Frank Lloyd Wright's buildings similar to these blocks.

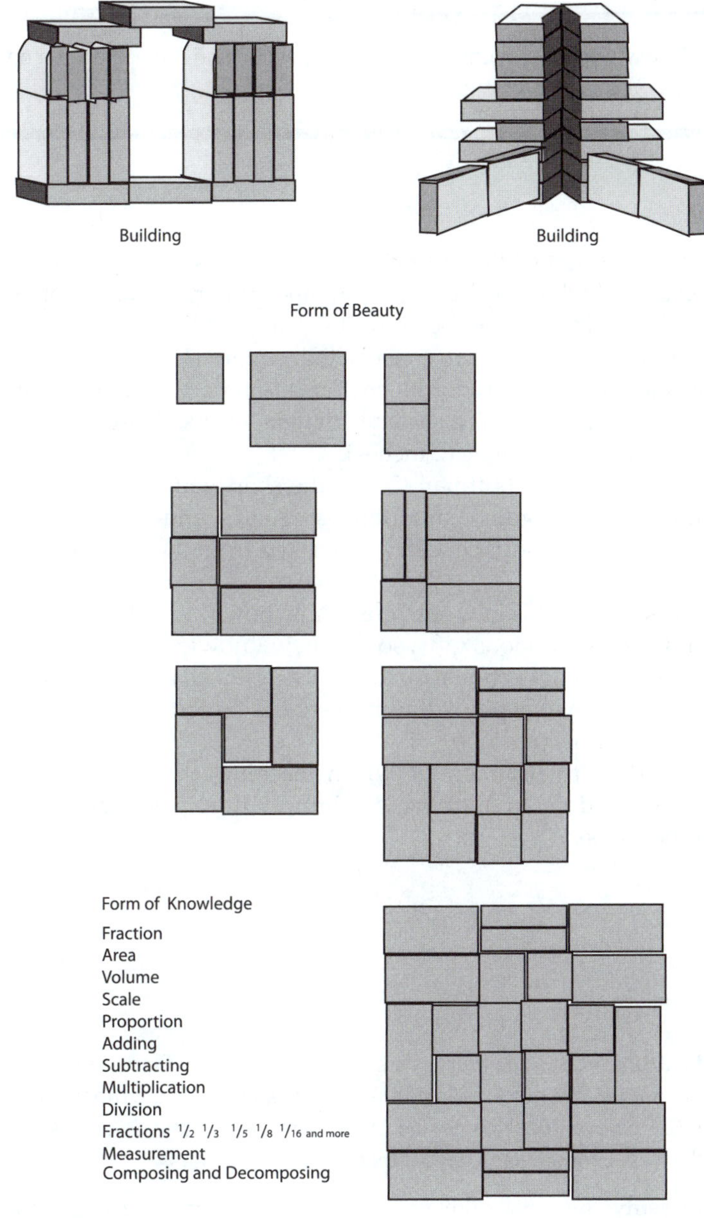

Figure 2.6. Gift 6.

Gift 6

Forms of Nature: Buildings are especially instructional at this stage, and children can create different types of buildings such as churches, skyscrapers, and houses.

Forms of Beauty: Symmetrical designs, which use principles of balance, rhythm, radial balance, and symmetrical balance, can be introduced.

(continued)

Gift 6 *(continued)*

Forms of Knowledge: Fractions, area, volume, scale, and proportion can be discussed as well as all previous concepts.

Gift 7: Series of Colored Shapes Gift 7 (see Figure 2.7) is a series of colored square tablets, circular shapes, and triangular tablets about 1 inch in diameter. Children should be around 4 years old before they use this gift. In all, the following shapes are constructed: square (1 inch and 2 inches), equilateral triangle (1 inch and 2 inches), right-angled isosceles triangle (1 inch and 2 inches), right-angled scalene triangle, obtuse isosceles triangle, circle (2 inches), and a half circle (2 inches).

In the design by Bultman (2000), the shapes are in complementary colors, and there are large and small circles, squares, and triangles. The gift helps the child move to a surface. Gift 7 is derived from the surfaces of the first six gifts.

In presenting this gift, one must show how the surface portion is part of the solids of the previous gifts, so that new knowledge is based on previous knowledge and connections are made. The gifts change from concrete to abstract thought. By this point, the child should be able to place a 1-inch square on the side of a 1-inch cube.

According to Bultman (2000), in teaching, the instructor shares each shape one at a time. In so doing, it is important to pay attention to the qualities of the shape.

Gift 7

Forms of Nature: Forms of nature represent objects in life. Flat surfaces sometimes do not represent forms in nature as well as the three-dimensional gifts in Gifts 1–6. However, designs can be made to represent real objects, such as buttons, flowers, cheese, flags, tiles, box of paints, and kites.

Forms of Beauty: If an even number is used, usually symmetry can be observed. Windmill symmetry and radial symmetry can be seen. The tiles can be joined to create patterns, such as a square or a rectangle (or a trapezoid, parallelogram, or rhombus). Children can build on what they have designed by creating their own patterns. Creations are never destroyed, just transformed. Again, quilt patterns can be used for demonstration of symmetrical designs.

Forms of Knowledge: Squares and all types of triangles (scalene, right, acute, obtuse) can be used. The right-angled isosceles triangle and the right-angled scalene triangle as well as the equilateral triangle can be discussed. The square and circle can be discussed, using fractional parts.

Figure 2.7. Gift 7.

Gift 8: Sticks and Rings Gift 8 (see Figure 2.8) consists of 24 pieces of 2-inch sticks and 12 each of 1-inch, 3-inch, 4-inch, and 5-inch sticks. This gift also consists of 2-inch-diameter rings, 2-inch-diameter half rings, 1½-inch diameter half rings, 1-inch-diameter rings, and 1-inch-diameter half rings. According to Bultman (2000), Froebel used these as part of his gift system, although the work related to this gift was not done until after his death. In teaching, it is recommended that children play with the lines (sticks) and rings before moving to Gift 9, the points. Similarly, it is important to facilitate play with the straight lines before introducing children to the curved line; the straight lines are easier to see and understand.

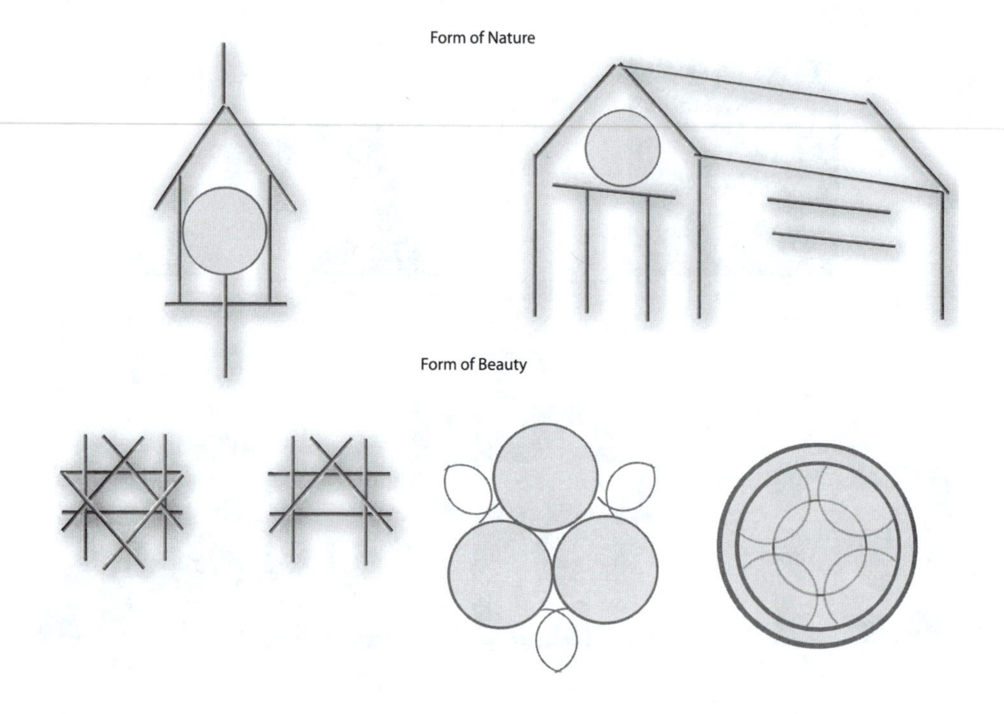

Form of Knowledge

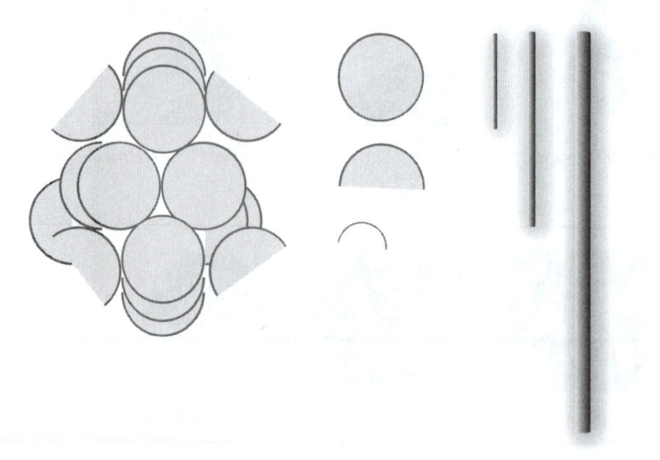

Whole
Half
One Fourth
Diameter
Circumference
Fraction
Scale
Proportion
Adding
Subtracting
Multiplication
Division
Fractions $^1/_2$ $^1/_4$
Measurement
Composing and Decomposing

Figure 2.8. Gift 8.

Gift 8

Forms of Nature: Children should be allowed to take the objects they want and then construct something out of them. Examples of forms of nature using circles are bracelets and necklaces. Children should be allowed to pick from containers of the same type of material, graduating from small amounts to larger amounts. Questions to ask the children may include: What does a half circle look like? What does a whole circle look like? What did you see on the way to school that reminded you of this shape?

Forms of Beauty: Begin with just a few pieces that the children choose, and see what different patterns, lines, shapes, and designs evolve. Designs can be modified by moving each design. After children have worked with just a few pieces, more pieces may be added so that more refined designs can be formed. Children can start with a central design and modify the external pieces. Rings can be used to introduce the quarter, half, and whole circle. Many different designs can be made with the circle. One ring, then a larger ring, and then a much larger ring can be used. Patterning can be used by developing circle, half circle, quadrant, quadrant and repeating this pattern.

Forms of Knowledge: Whole, half, one-fourth, diameter, circumference, as well as other forms and concepts can be used for demonstration purposes.

Gift 9: Points and Lines Gift 9 (see Figure 2.9) consists of points or wooden circles that if placed next to one another form a line. Gift 9 continues the progression from the solid gifts of Gifts 1–6 to the surface gift of Gift 7 and the line gift of Gift 8. It promotes the study of where lines form points. With Gift 9, a point now has no dimension, only position.

Gift 9

Forms of Nature: Children can begin making objects from their environment using a small number of pieces first. Lines can be used to represent asparagus, leeks, tree trunks, palm leaves. Points in nature can be represented as chestnut burrs, thorns, holly leaves, thistles, or a woodpecker beak. It is useful to observe that lines form points.

Forms of Beauty: The gift should be used with a grid so that symmetrical, asymmetrical, and radial patterns can be seen more readily with straight lines. Stripes can crisscross with other stripes to make a pattern. Dots can make patterns, too.

Forms of Knowledge: Emphasize that a line is made of extended points, and allow children to discover that points form a line and that they can make vertical and horizontal lines. All basic geometric figures can be observed. Children can make angles form the points that extend into lines. Sorting, ordering, addition, subtraction, multiplication, and division can be taught in conjunction with points and lines.

Gift 10: Framework for Points and Lines Gift 10 (see Figure 2.10) creates a framework for using points and lines. The gifts are presented sequenced from the solid form to the abstract idea of the point. The gifts complete the full circle of going from the solid to the surface to the line and to the point and back to the skeletal form of the solid. Originally, Froebel did not craft Gift 10; it was an activity with peas and toothpicks. Froebel soaked dried peas overnight until they were soft enough to put on toothpicks. He did so because he felt it was important to limit the amount of materials given to the children at the very beginning. In the 21st century, there are many toys that

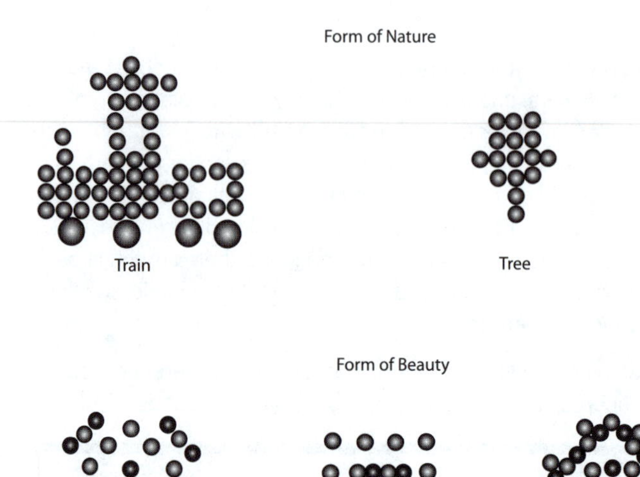

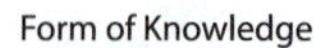

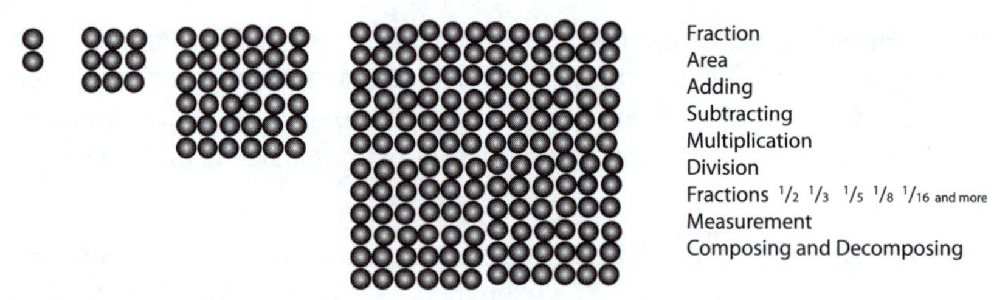

Figure 2.9. Gift 9.

can be used to substitute for toothpicks and peas. Tinker Toys, Erector Sets, and K'NEX are the best known; however, many more toys on the market are similar to these and can serve the same function. See Appendix D of this volume for other related toys.

Gift 10

Forms of Nature: A prism is a three-dimensional figure with length, width, and height and a base forming a polygon. There are four parts of a prism: face, edge, vertex, and base. Prism names such as triangular, quadrilateral, pentagonal, hexagonal, heptagonal, and octagonal can be used. Pyramids are named by their base and have a polygon for their base and triangular sides that meet at a common point. In teaching, it can be pointed out that the base has four points at the

Form of Nature

Mushroom

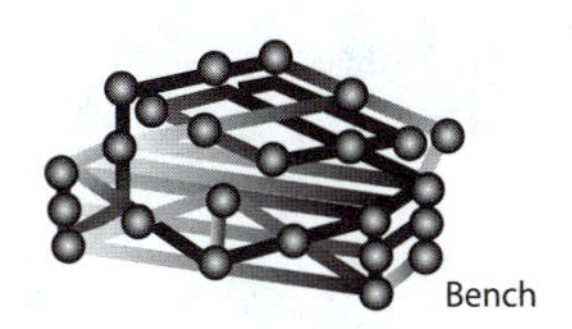

Bench

Form of Beauty

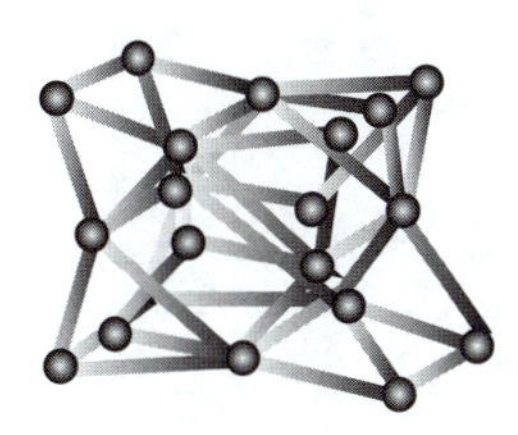

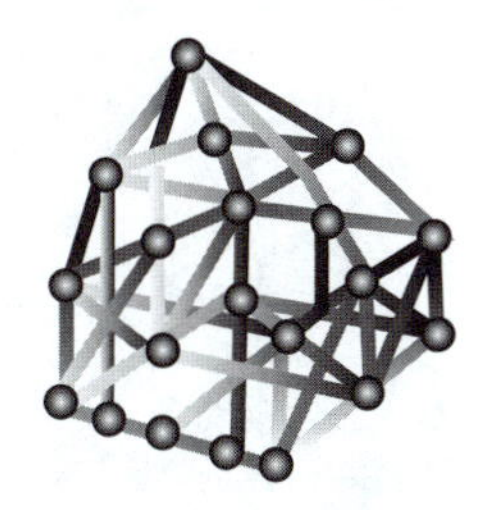

Form of Knowledge

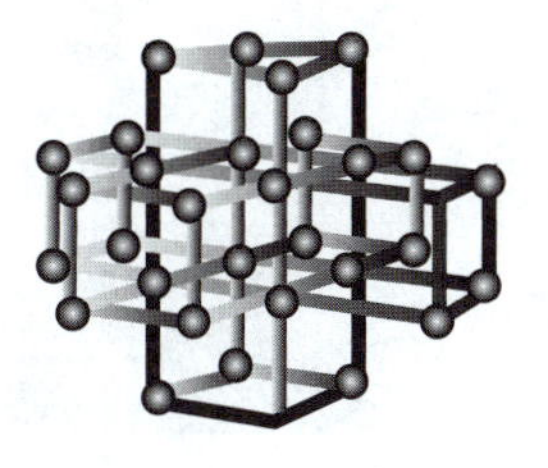

Whole
Half
One Fourth
Scale
Proportion
Adding
Subtracting
Multiplication
Division
Fractions $\frac{1}{2}$ $\frac{1}{4}$
Measurement
Composing and Decomposing

Figure 2.10. Gift 10.

bottom. The lateral faces are the triangular surfaces, whereas the faces are the base and lateral surfaces. The edges are segments formed by the intersection of two faces. The vertices are points formed by the intersection of three edges or three faces.

Forms of Beauty: The forms of beauty would be the lines of symmetrical, asymmetrical, and radial balance of the figures.

Forms of Knowledge: Children can measure perimeters of base, lateral faces, and determine shapes. They can measure lines. They can determine if lines are horizontal, vertical, or oblique and discuss fractions.

Dr. Barbara Corbett, Director of the Froebel Education Centre, Mississauga, Ontario, Canada, taken in 2007.

Using Froebel's Gifts

Examples of how certain gifts can be integrated into the child's day and the manner in which some of the gifts can be used are described below. These lessons were observed by the author at the Froebel Education Center in Ontario, Canada, the only Froebelian school in North America, in April 2008. For more information on integrating the gifts into the curriculum, see Appendix A.

Using Gift 3: Wooden Cube Divided into Eight Smaller Cubes Children who were 5 years old at the Froebel Education Centre were asked to make a building that they were familiar with by using Gift 3. Children were asked to turn the box over very carefully so that only a cube (the whole of the object) appeared. The whole was subdivided into eight cubes, and the children then separated these cubes into various buildings. Many buildings were made. A discussion of the buildings took place. One child built a structure that would withstand earthquakes. He said that the structure would sway. One child created the CNN Tower in Toronto. Another child showed how, in his building, there was a dog who was looking out the window. The teacher immediately sang "How Much Is that Doggie in the Window," reinforcing the concept of *window* with a song. Children also demonstrated how combinations of triangular prisms could make a square and how the prisms could be placed another way to produce a butterfly.

Using Gift 6: Large Wooden Cube Divided into Multiple Smaller Pieces Gift 6 was used in a second-grade class at the Froebel Education Centre to produce a scene from a book that the children had been reading. One child made a truck to bring a dog home. Another showed a scene in which the main character came back hauling trees along the road.

Gift 6 was also used by a third-grade group to construct a town. Children discussed the zoning laws, placement of the buildings, parking, and the height of the buildings. The children discussed what went into constructing a town. Children's constructions included a church, a theater, an outdoor theater, a hospital for animals, residential apartments, and a large mall. The children then measured the heights of their buildings by units and discovered the mean, mode, median, extremes, and ranges of their buildings.

Using Gift 8: Sticks and Rings The last group of children observed by the author were studying Friedrich Froebel himself. This group of 4-year-old children used sticks and rings to construct something that they had learned about Froebel. The children constructed Froebel as he was looking out the window, a birthday cake with candles for Froebel, and a wall similar to the wall behind Froebel's house against a sky covered with raindrops. One child made a happy robin in a nest because Froebel liked nature, and the teacher and class sang a song about robins. In keeping with the nature theme, another child made a forest going up a hill and baby birds. When the teacher asked what the baby birds were singing, the group then sang a bird song, again reinforcing the concept of bird through a song. Yet another child constructed Froebel observing flowers. Another child said Froebel felt very sad for stepping on the beetles and she made a huge exaggerated boot to illustrate her point. After the lesson, one child went around the table telling the story she had just heard from all the students about Froebel. She was able to do so using the vocabulary of the children in the group, thus reinforcing language development.

Summary In summary, Froebel gifts were used in a variety of ways at the Froebel Education Centre. Froebel gifts can be useful in developing and reinforcing concepts the teacher is teaching as well as in the traditional ways Froebel recommended.

Froebel's Influence on Art and Architecture

This section will look at ways in which Froebel's ideas have continued in places that value the integration and unity in nature, design, and knowledge.

His work can be seen in certain pockets that emphasize freedom of thought and trust in the teacher's self-efficacy to implement both the integration of the curriculum and unity in the world.

Froebel's Influence on Frank Lloyd Wright

> When you are truly creative in your attempt to design, this thing that we call good design begins and never has an end.
> Frank Lloyd Wright

In 1876, the concept of kindergarten was a new import to America, and there was a display of Froebel's gifts and educational philosophy at the Centennial Exposition in Philadelphia. Mrs. Anna Wright, mother of the famous architect Frank Lloyd Wright, was so impressed that she purchased a set of Froebel's blocks, and she went to classes on how to use them with her child. The kindergarten did not evolve from the traditional structure of the public school. Like the exhibits at the Philadelphia Centennial celebration, it was also an invention. It was a precursor of things to come in art, architecture, engineering, and math.

Frank Lloyd Wright (1932) once said that he began his interest in the architecture profession while using Froebelian blocks. Believing that organic architecture blends in and harmonizes with nature (Hart, 2007), Wright used both two- and three-dimensional objects in his work to demonstrate his great respect for nature, which was similar to Froebel's respect for nature. Wright showed in his designs his respect for nature by complementing the land with his sense of unity. He often used materials that were found near the site of the structure. He would abstract or simplify forms seen in nature, similar to what Froebel did in designing according to the forms of nature. Wright would reduce materials to the simplest geometric shapes. When Wright decided on a shape, he would repeat it in the furniture, the shape of the room, the windows, the ceilings, and many parts of the room. This repetition of shape is found in many of his architectural creations. Wright felt repetition gave a unified whole to the structure (Hart, 2007). This same transformation can also be seen in many of Froebel's gifts.

Only recently has science discovered that the forms seen in nature that were once thought of as random are governed by geometry and other forms of math. Many people have tried to unravel the geometric equations. Leonardo Da Vinci and Albert Einstein are just two examples of persons who spent a lifetime studying certain aspects of nature and developing formulas in line with nature. The elements of nature, design, and math are all similar. Wright thought that the shapes of things in nature were determined by their function. The branches were natural to a tree. The petals of flowers were natural to the flower.

Froebel's gifts and occupations are the framework for all toys developed in the toy industry for construction purposes. Although Froebel's work could be very abstract, one can understand how self-initiated activity was the basis of learning.

Froebel's Influence on the Bauhaus Movement

After visiting Bauhaus museums in Weimar and Berlin, the author could see the strong connection of Froebel's work to the Bauhaus design movement started in Germany in the early 1900s. The Bauhaus movement was a movement that used geometric shapes in art and industrial design.

In the beginning of the Bauhaus movement, Walter Gropius, head of the movement, instituted a laboratory in art and design, very similar to the design work and discussion that took place in the Froebelian kindergarten. Teachers and students worked together to solve design problems and formulate new ideas for the machine age. Gropius wished to train artists and architects in an apprenticeship setting. The training, which enabled students to use their talents most effectively, was the basis for the Bauhaus philosophy. The members of the Bauhaus design movement rejected traditional forms of beauty and created beauty from shapes, emphasizing teamwork and social responsibility as well as the function of whatever they were designing. Just as Froebel encouraged a small group of children to talk as they worked with a gift and then to share any observations they might have, the Bauhaus design movement encouraged its artists to share their ideas and inventions.

Oskar Schlemmer was one of the painters in the Bauhaus movement along with Josef Albers, who was well known for his pure squares of different colors. Hungarian Laszlo Moholy-Nagy and the Swiss painter Paul Klee also were artists of the movement. Although there were only 200 students, the Bauhaus artisans and architects were far reaching in their ideas because of publications. Unfortunately, the movement was banned by the Nazi government. Members of the Bauhaus movement escaped to other countries to carry on their work, and their ideas flourished globally. Gropius became head of the School of Architecture at Harvard University in 1937. In summary, the Bauhaus movement allowed deep exploration of shapes and forms whereby analytical thinking and creative designing took place in the context of a small group of people.

Froebel's Influence on Cubism and Other Movements

After the Bauhaus movement was dismantled, other movements sprang up that emphasized the uses of shapes. Cubism made use of shifting viewpoints. As children in Froebel's kindergarten made different objects out of the cube, the Cubist painter attempted to capture this on canvas. Georges Braque and Pablo Picasso have been associated with this movement. Later, Cubism inspired other movements such as Suprematism, Futurism, and Neoplasticism. *Suprematism* was a movement led by Russian artist Kasmir Malevich. It was geometric and often colorless, similar to Froebel's blocks. *Futurism* was an Italian movement that was characterized by its aggressive celebration of modern technology, speed, and city life. The movement of the car and the experience of acceleration were more significant to Futurists than the car's shape or appearance. Futurism is represented by the art of Giacomo Balla. The movement could be represented by many of the designs in the gifts and occupations developed by Froebel. *Neoplasticism* refers to black horizontal and vertical lines on an off-white background to which are added blocks of primary colors (blue, red, and yellow). An example of this style is the work of Piet Mondrian. The line and shapes that were combined in Froebel's kindergarten were similar to Neoplasticism. The Neoplasticist work represented the spiritual order underlying the endlessly changing appearance of the world. Again, Froebel's work represented a spiritual unity and change using the line and the shapes of the gifts. This was demonstrated by the lines of the gifts, particularly Gift 8.

Buckminster Fuller, inventor of the geodesic dome, has stated that he remembered the toothpicks and dried peas that his kindergarten teacher brought for him to make structures (Museum of Contemporary Art, Chicago, 2009). Many others would also master the abstract symbolism that was part of the kindergarten. Brosterman (1997) thoroughly and meticulously researched how Froebel's educational system may have influenced the course of art and architectural history. He used artistic examples from Georges Braque, Piet Mondrian, Wassily Kandinsky, Frank Lloyd Wright, and Le Corbusier as well as artistic designs from Froebel kindergartens to show how Froebel's work may have influenced geometric abstraction.

Froebel's Influence on Education

Froebel's Influence on Education in Germany

The author's visits to the Froebel Museum in Oberweissbach and a second Froebel Museum in Bad Blankenburg, Germany (where Froebel founded the first kindergarten), showed many examples of how forms of nature, forms of beauty, and forms of knowledge can be used. These museums are visited by many people from all over the world. They have many examples of children's work. At schools located in Bad Blankenburg and Rudolstadt, Germany, the methods are still being used. Teacher trainers are going out from Rudolstadt to the former Soviet countries to instruct teachers in Froebelian methods.

Froebel's Influence on Education in North America

There is only one Froebelian school in North America, and it is located in Mississauga, Ontario, Canada. This school was founded more than 25 years ago and has used Froebel's philosophy in depth since it opened. The current director of the school, Dr. Barbara Corbett, has written two books on this topic: *A Century of Kindergarten Education in Ontario* (1989) and *A Garden of Children* (1979). These books, along with the Froebel Society, an international society of educators devoted to preserving the work of Froebel, have helped to perpetuate the work of Froebel in North America.

Froebel's Influence on Education in Asian Countries

There are Froebelian schools in Korea as well as in Japan and China. Dr. Barbara Corbett and two other staff members of the Ontario school went to Seoul to visit the departments of Korea-Froebel Co. Ltd. This affluent and highly educated region has embraced Froebelian education for its children. The kindergarten at Pai Chai University in Korea was observed by Scott Bultman of the United States using the Froebelian gifts.

Summary

The Froebelian gifts helped children learn how science and math (knowledge), design (beauty), and the physical world (nature) are interrelated. This belief was held by many noted scientists and philosophers. Germany has maintained examples of Froebel's gifts for all to observe. Students of early childhood, math, artistic design, architecture, and nature are amazed at the creative use of geometric abstractions of the blocks.

Spatial Development Throughout the Curriculum

Spatial Development and Math

The Trends in International Mathematics and Science Study (TIMSS) is an assessment that compares the performance of U.S. students (at the end of fourth and eighth grade) with students of other countries. The TIMSS in 2007 assessed six major content areas of mathematics (number sense, geometric shapes, data display, knowing, applying, and reasoning) and six content areas in science (life science, physical science, earth science, knowing, applying, and reasoning). The TIMSS was offered in 1995, 1999, 2003, and 2007. In 2007 the average U.S. fourth-grade mathematics score was higher than those of 23 of the 35 other countries; it was lower than those of 8 countries, all in Asia or Europe (U.S. Department of Education, Institute of Education Sciences, 2009). The TIMSS provides the most reliable assessment available from an international perspective. In the 1999 test, U.S. students ranked 27th of 38 countries, testing below average in geometry. Chinese children outperformed U.S. children of the same socioeconomic background in spatial and geometric knowledge by 30%, while Chinese children outperformed U.S. children by only 15% in number sense (Starkey et al., 1999). However, the United States performed above the average in fractions and number sense, data representation, analysis and probability, and algebra.

Compared with 1995, the average mathematics scores for U.S. fourth graders was 16 points higher in 2007. Furthermore, in light of the scores in math, many believe there should be more emphasis on teaching geometric

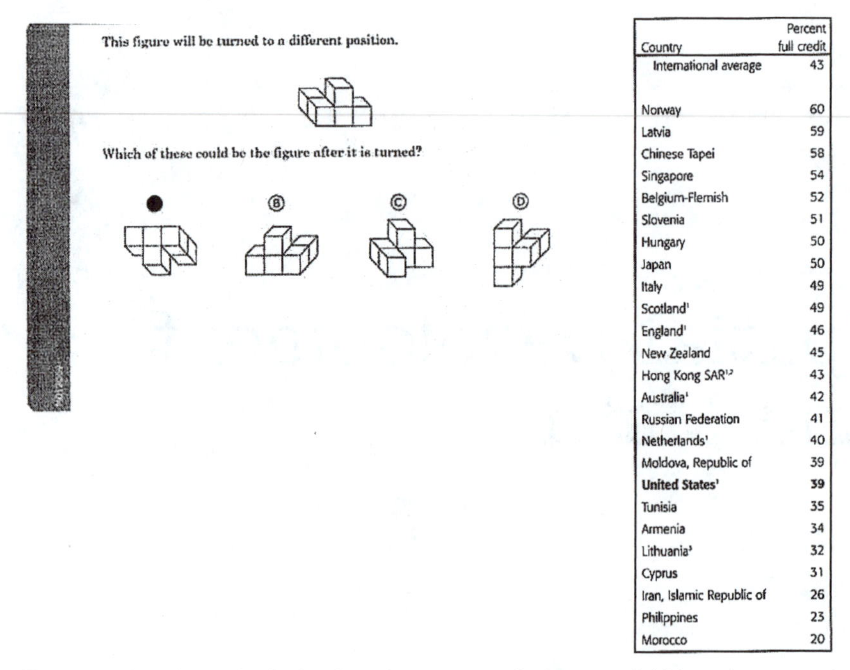

Country	Percent full credit
International average	43
Norway	60
Latvia	59
Chinese Tapei	58
Singapore	54
Belgium-Flemish	52
Slovenia	51
Hungary	50
Japan	50
Italy	49
Scotland[1]	49
England[1]	46
New Zealand	45
Hong Kong SAR[1,2]	43
Australia[1]	42
Russian Federation	41
Netherlands[1]	40
Moldova, Republic of	39
United States[1]	**39**
Tunisia	35
Armenia	34
Lithuania[3]	32
Cyprus	31
Iran, Islamic Republic of	26
Philippines	23
Morocco	20

Figure 3.1. Sample question for fourth-grade geometry and percentage of children who answered correctly, 2003. (*Source:* From Trends in International Mathematics and Science Study [TIMSS], 2003.)

and spatial thinking, and teachers should be able to express geometric concepts. The lowest score in 2007 was in the area of geometry. For some examples of questions from the TIMSS, see Figure 3.1, Figure 3.2, and Figure 3.3 for 2003 and Figure 3.4 and Figure 3.5 for 2007.

Math Standards and Spatial Thinking

In order to understand the relationship between spatial and geometric development and overall math, one should understand the structure of the math standards. The National Council of Teachers of Mathematics (NCTM) Standards are built around five content standards—number and operations, algebra, geometry, measurement and data analysis, and probability. There are also five process standards—problem solving, reasoning and proof, communication, connections, and representation (NCTM, 2000).

Only the geometry standard employs the language of spatial thinking. Geometry uses two and three dimensions, shapes, relationships, locations, and spatial reasoning. The following are the geometry standards for K–4 from the NCTM:

- Analyze characteristics and properties of two- and three-dimensional geometric shapes and develop mathematical arguments about geometric relationships
- Specify locations and describe spatial relationships using coordinate geometry and other representational systems

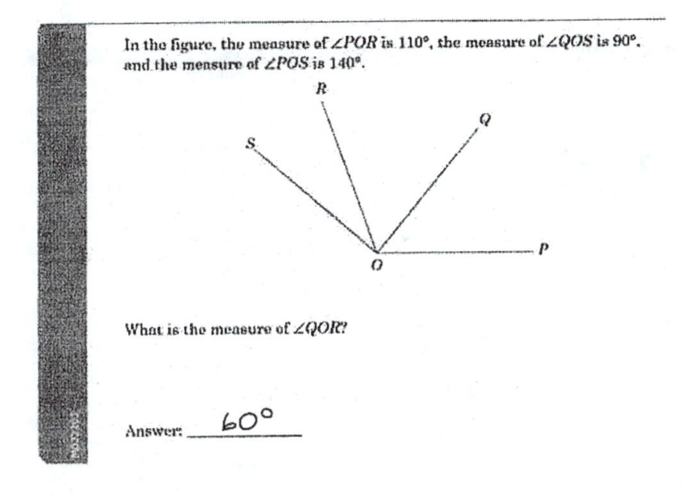

Country	Percent full credit
International average	28
Korea, Republic of	64
Japan	60
Singapore	58
Hong Kong SAR[1,2]	57
Chinese Taipei	49
Hungary	44
Norway	41
Russian Federation	40
Armenia	39
Latvia	37
Belgium-Flemish	36
Estonia	36
Slovak Republic	36
Serbia[3]	35
Bulgaria	34
Romania	34
(Israel)	32
Malaysia	32
Moldova, Republic of	32
Netherlands[1]	28
New Zealand	28
Lithuania[4]	27
Australia	26
Lebanon	26
(Macedonia, Republic of)	26
Italy	25
Slovenia	25
(United States)	**22**
Cyprus	21
Sweden	20
Tunisia	19
Scotland[1]	17
Bahrain	16
Indonesia[3]	16
Palestinian National Authority	16
Egypt	15
Jordan	14
Iran, Islamic Republic of	11
(Morocco)	11
Philippines	11
Chile	10
Botswana	9
Saudi Arabia	6
South Africa	4
Ghana	#

Figure 3.2. Sample question for eighth-grade geometry and percentage of children who answered correctly, 2003. (*Source:* Trends in International Mathematics and Science Study [TIMSS], 2003.)

- Apply transformation and use symmetry to analyze mathematical situations
- Use visualization, spatial reasoning, and geometric modeling to solve problems

Research on Math and Spatial Visualization

Spatial visualization—building and manipulating mental representations of two- and three-dimensional objects and perceiving an object from different

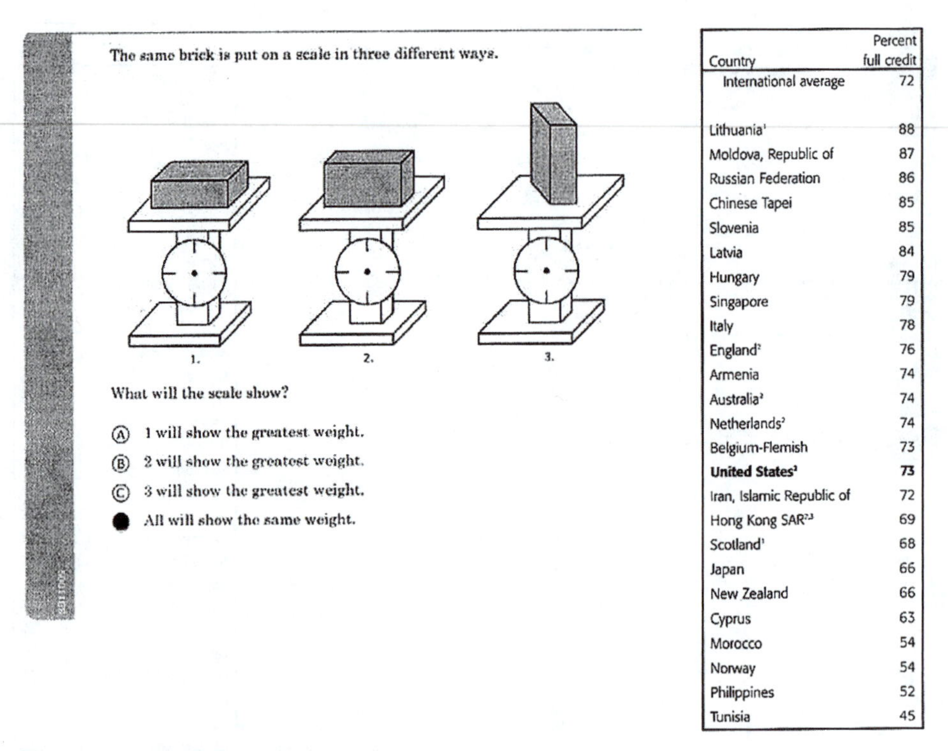

Country	Percent full credit
International average	72
Lithuania[1]	88
Moldova, Republic of	87
Russian Federation	86
Chinese Tapei	85
Slovenia	85
Latvia	84
Hungary	79
Singapore	79
Italy	78
England[2]	76
Armenia	74
Australia[2]	74
Netherlands[2]	74
Belgium-Flemish	73
United States[2]	**73**
Iran, Islamic Republic of	72
Hong Kong SAR[2,3]	69
Scotland[1]	68
Japan	66
New Zealand	66
Cyprus	63
Morocco	54
Norway	54
Philippines	52
Tunisia	45

Figure 3.3. Sample question for fourth-grade physical science, forces and motion, and percentage of children who answered correctly, 2003. (*Source:* Trends in International Mathematics and Science Study [TIMSS], 2003.)

perspectives—is an NCTM Standard. The NCTM Standards address the geometric and spatial skills needed in math in the area of geometry.

Teacher knowledge of geometry is important. Teachers should be able to communicate the content to students as well as develop students' cognitive skills, which include spatial visualization. However, teachers, especially teachers of young children, are often not prepared to do so (NCTM, 2006). Most teachers of young children have limited knowledge of mathematics, including geometric and spatial knowledge (Clements, 2009; Clements, Copple, & Hyson, 2002; National Research Council, 2009).

Culture may play a role in understanding geometry: in the TIMSS, American students scored 55% compared to 84% for Chinese students (Starkey et al., 1999). This may be due to the fact that Chinese word characters are more complex than the English alphabet and many geometric tasks such as tangrams and paper folding are used in Chinese classrooms. However, children in the United States can build spatial abilities as Chinese children do by working to have more detailed visual representation in their drawings, developing more complex origami projects, and working with visual spatial activities such as tangrams and blocks. See Figure 3.6 and Figure 3.7 for examples of spatial visualization tasks on the National Assessment of Educational Progress (NAEP).

Content Domain: Geometric Shapes and Measures

Description: Identifies two triangles with the same size and shape in a complex figure.

The square is cut into 7 pieces. Put an X on each of the 2 triangles that are the same size and shape.

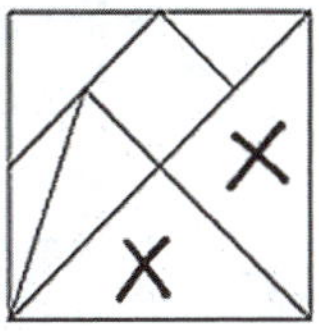

X X

The answer shown illustrates the type of student response that was given full credit

Country	Percent Full Credit	
Hong Kong SAR	91 (1.2)	○
Slovenia	91 (1.3)	○
[1] Lithuania	89 (1.3)	○
[†] Denmark	88 (1.8)	○
[†] Scotland	88 (1.4)	○
England	88 (1.4)	○
Singapore	88 (1.4)	○
Japan	87 (1.4)	○
Italy	87 (1.5)	○
Sweden	86 (1.6)	○
Australia	85 (1.9)	○
[2 †] United States	85 (1.0)	○
Slovak Republic	84 (1.9)	○
Norway	84 (1.9)	○
Czech Republic	83 (1.8)	○
Austria	82 (2.1)	○
Chinese Taipei	81 (1.9)	○
Hungary	81 (2.1)	○
[1] Latvia	81 (2.1)	○
Russian Federation	81 (2.6)	○
New Zealand	81 (1.4)	○
[‡] Netherlands	79 (2.0)	○
[1] Kazakhstan	77 (2.2)	○
Germany	76 (1.8)	○
Armenia	74 (2.2)	
International Avg.	72 (0.3)	
Ukraine	67 (2.3)	▽
Colombia	59 (2.8)	▽
[1] Georgia	59 (2.9)	▽
Iran, Islamic Rep. of	58 (2.7)	▽
El Salvador	50 (2.6)	▽
Algeria	44 (2.3)	▽
[ж] Kuwait	40 (2.5)	▽
Morocco	39 (2.3)	▽
Tunisia	38 (2.2)	▽
Qatar	32 (1.5)	▽
Yemen	13 (1.5)	▽
Benchmarking Participants		
[2 †] Minnesota, US	90 (2.6)	○
[2] Ontario, Canada	90 (1.7)	○
[2] British Columbia, Canada	86 (1.7)	○
[2] Massachusetts, US	85 (2.6)	○
[2] Alberta, Canada	83 (1.9)	○
[2] Quebec, Canada	80 (2.3)	○
[ж ‡] Dubai, UAE	67 (2.6)	

Percent significantly higher than international average ○
Percent significantly lower than international average ▽

Figure 3.4. Sample question for fourth-grade geometry and percentage of children who answered correctly, 2007. (*Source:* TIMSS 2007 International Mathematics Report, p. 97.)

Research on Number Sense

Although number sense plays a central role in mathematical content, research in Israel and in the United States shows that early spatial and geometric work leads to higher mathematics achievement, higher writing skills, and higher IQ scores (Clements & Sarama, 2007c; Razel & Eylon, 1990). According to the National Research Council report on mathematics learning in early childhood (2009), the greatest emphasis among states has been on the teaching of number and operations, while geometry and measurement receive less emphasis. To rectify this, the NCTM Focal Points (2006) were written to have preschool, kindergarten, and first grade place more emphasis on spatial development, and to delineate specific concepts to emphasize in geometry and spatial visualization at different grade levels. Specific concepts were also recommended in number, measurement, and data analysis for pre-K through third grade. Before the Focal Points were developed, there were only the geometry standards from kindergarten through grade 4 that were listed at

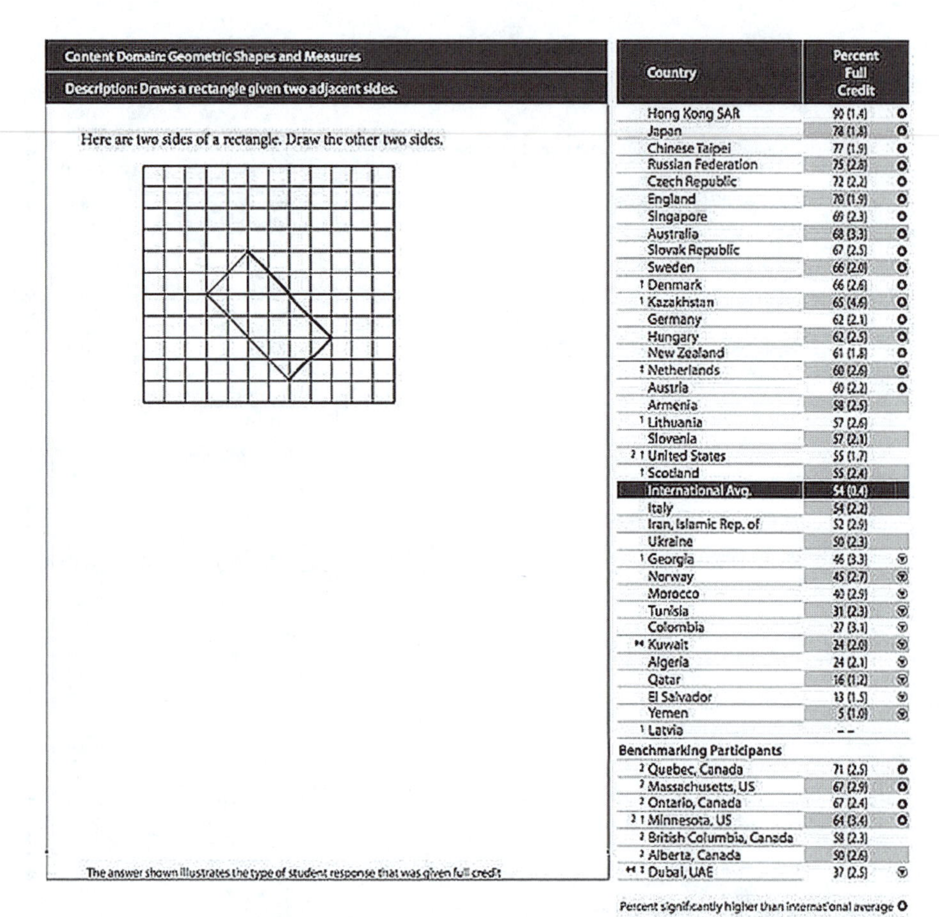

Country	Percent Full Credit	
Hong Kong SAR	90 (1.4)	○
Japan	78 (1.8)	○
Chinese Taipei	77 (1.9)	○
Russian Federation	75 (2.8)	○
Czech Republic	72 (2.2)	○
England	70 (1.9)	○
Singapore	69 (2.3)	○
Australia	68 (3.3)	○
Slovak Republic	67 (2.5)	○
Sweden	66 (2.0)	○
† Denmark	66 (2.6)	○
1 Kazakhstan	65 (4.6)	○
Germany	62 (2.1)	○
Hungary	62 (2.5)	○
New Zealand	61 (1.8)	○
‡ Netherlands	60 (2.6)	○
Austria	60 (2.2)	○
Armenia	58 (2.5)	
1 Lithuania	57 (2.6)	
Slovenia	57 (2.1)	
2 † United States	55 (1.7)	
† Scotland	55 (2.4)	
International Avg.	54 (0.4)	
Italy	54 (2.2)	
Iran, Islamic Rep. of	52 (2.9)	
Ukraine	50 (2.3)	
1 Georgia	46 (3.3)	⊙
Norway	45 (2.7)	⊙
Morocco	40 (2.9)	⊙
Tunisia	31 (2.3)	⊙
Colombia	27 (3.1)	⊙
ψ Kuwait	24 (2.0)	⊙
Algeria	24 (2.1)	⊙
Qatar	16 (1.2)	⊙
El Salvador	13 (1.5)	⊙
Yemen	5 (1.0)	⊙
1 Latvia	--	
Benchmarking Participants		
2 Quebec, Canada	71 (2.5)	○
2 Massachusetts, US	67 (2.9)	○
2 Ontario, Canada	67 (2.4)	○
2 † Minnesota, US	64 (3.4)	○
2 British Columbia, Canada	58 (2.3)	
2 Alberta, Canada	50 (2.6)	
ψ 2 Dubai, UAE	37 (2.5)	⊙

Percent significantly higher than international average ○
Percent significantly lower than international average ⊙

Figure 3.5. Sample question for fourth-grade data analysis and percentage of children who answered correctly, 2007. (*Source:* TIMSS 2007 International Mathematics Report, p. 91.)

the beginning of this chapter, and it was unclear how these standards could be used at certain grade levels. Specific content standards for the pre-K through grade 2 Focal Points are provided in Appendix E of this volume.

Research on Shapes

Concepts about shapes do not develop from just looking at shapes and naming them. Children need to touch, manipulate, draw, and represent shapes in various ways (Clements, 1999). The resources that can be used to promote learning about shapes include, but are not limited to, combining two shapes to make another shape, constructing origami figures, cutting, drawing, cookie cutting, or representing shapes on the computer.

Shapes are generally introduced to preschool children in very rigid ways, and these stereotypes can last throughout their schooling (Burger & Shaughnessy, 1986; Fuys, Geddes, & Tischler, 1988). Copley (2000) found that, even though 3- and 4-year-old children can recognize a triangle in a variety of orientations, the rigidity of some teachers who do not show geometric

14. A cow is tied to a post in the middle of a flat meadow. If the cow's rope is several meters long, which of the following figures shows the shape of the region where the cow can graze?

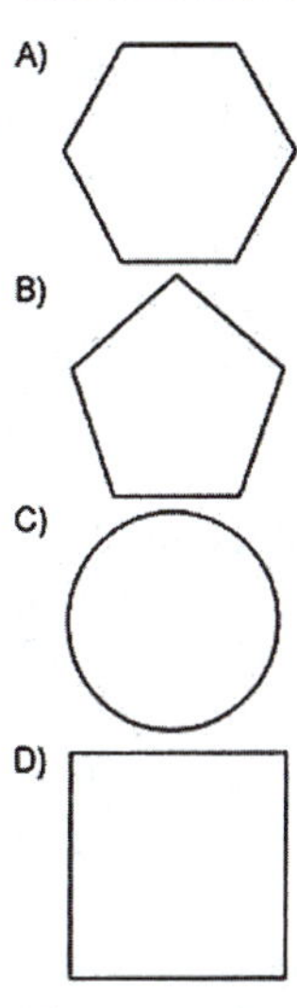

Figure 3.6. Sample question from National Assessment of Educational Progress related to geometry, 2003. (*Source:* National Center for Education Statistics, 2005.)

shapes from different perspectives can prevent children from recognizing different types of shapes as they get older. For example, children may only be exposed to a triangle with the horizontal base early in life; these children may not realize that different triangles can have different types of lines and angles and face different directions. They only recognize the triangle shape in one orientation.

The same problem of shape recognition can occur with rectangles and squares. The teacher usually demonstrates that rectangles are twice as long as they are wide, and other types of rectangles are not shown as examples. It

5. The figure above is shaded on the top side and white on the under side. If the figure were flipped over, its white side could look like which of the following figures?

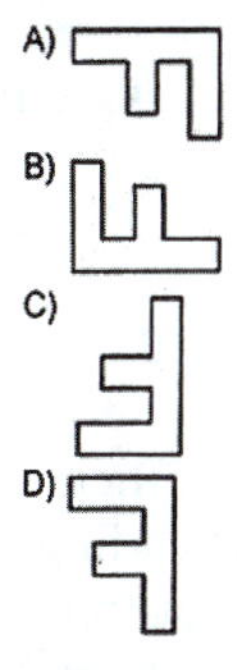

Figure 3.7. Sample geometry spatial visualization tasks. (*Source:* National Center for Education Statistics, 2005.)

is also important for teachers to show that when a square is turned a certain way, this shape becomes a diamond.

Children need to be given many examples of shapes, nonexamples of shapes, and precise language related to the concept of a particular shape. Much discussion needs to take place for children to recognize the number of sides and angles of shapes, and whether they are open or closed. Many young children also give plane figure names for solid figures (Carpenter, Coburn, Reys, & Wilson, 1976). For example, many young children may incorrectly classify a triangular prism as a triangle. Thus there is a confusion between surface shapes and three-dimensional shapes.

van Hiele (1986) has written about levels of shape recognition. van Hiele said that children at Level 1, the visual level, can only recognize shapes as wholes. A figure is a rectangle because it looks like a door. Children do not think about attributes or properties at this level, nor do they become descriptive and analytic. At Level 2, the child can recognize shapes by the properties. Children have to experience many different types of the same class of figures in order to reach this stage. They think about attributes, or any characteristic of the shape or properties in this stage, and they become descriptive in their language and analytic in their comparisons. They learn that a triangle is a figure with three sides, and they should be exposed to many experiences with triangles, where no sides are equal, two sides are equal, three sides are equal, right angles in the triangle, and rotations of these. The children need examples, nonexamples, and other distracters in order to see the attributes. Many children do not experience this if they are given only a certain type of triangle and are not exposed to other types of triangles. Children must analyze and synthesize properties of shapes, including sides, angles, and rotations of figures. It is up to the teacher to enhance the learning of shapes by using clear wording in her guidance of young children.

Research on Angles

Many children, when copying figures, have difficulty making the angles. According to Clements and Battista (1989), children have many different ideas about what an angle is. Children may describe the angle with such words as *corner, turn,* or *tilted line*. However, many preschoolers do use angles intuitively in their block playing. In one study, 5-year-olds were able to judge for congruency of angles (Beilin, 1984). As children progress to primary school, some children distinguish angles based on size. Helping children see turns, corners, and directions in everyday life develops spatial skills needed to understand angles and more difficult problems.

Understanding Spatial Awareness

Spatial awareness begins with children becoming aware of their bodies. An awareness of space outside of the body involves comprehending directions (e.g., *left* and *right, up* and *down*), understanding the projection of oneself in space, and judging the distances between objects. To aid understanding of geometry, it is important to provide children with a grid for the placement of geometric figures as a way to see how the geometric figures relate to each other. There is some evidence, mainly from my observation in museums and of Froebel's early work, that grid work was important to Froebel. Many wooden desks that Froebel used had grids on them. Appendix B of this book provides a grid that could be used when teaching spatial awareness. Children can use the grid to record their movements in space by recording how many spaces across and up they go.

Understanding Three-Dimensional Shapes and Figures

Not so much is known about concept learning in three-dimensional shapes and figures. Preschool children can have a hard time describing three-dimensional figures (Lehrer, Jenkins, & Osana, 1998; Nieuwoudt & van Niekerk, 1997). Many preschoolers use plane figure names for solid figures (Carpenter, 1997). It has been found that block playing builds general reasoning skills (Kamii, Miyakawa, & Kato, 2004) and that if specific terminology is used for three-dimensional blocks, geometric terms can be learned by young children (Nieuwoudt & van Niekerk, 1997). See Chapter 8 of this book for more research on understanding three-dimensional shapes and figures through block playing.

Activities Specifically Designed to Connect to the Focal Points in Geometry

There has been a large body of research to support geometric and spatial thinking levels. However, according to many authors (Clements & Sarama, 2009; Sarama & Clements, 2009; van Hiele, 1986), these developmental levels have not been used in teaching. These trajectories of spatial understanding have been explained in detail in the work of Clements and Sarama (2009) The NCTM has synthesized some of the extensive age-level research on mathematical development in young children in its Focal Points (2006). NCTM's book, *Curriculum Focal Points* (2006), explains the need for more specific emphasis of concepts at certain levels. The math content areas of the Curriculum Focus Points and Connections to the Focus Points are being used in all grade levels to develop consistent state standards throughout the country. Explicit information is given to teachers for each grade level, and teachers can also see an increased emphasis on geometry, particularly in the preschool and early grades. The emphasis in early childhood should be just about the same for geometry as the emphasis on number sense.

The following sections will present concepts of Jean Piaget related to spatial development, information on the NCTM's Focal Points in geometry by grade level in early childhood, and ideas to promote more geometric and spatial development specifically by grade level activities in order to promote the Focal Points in geometry.

Piagetian Thoughts on Preschoolers' and Kindergartners' Spatial Development

Preschoolers and kindergartners are in the *preoperational stage,* according to Piaget (1959). They are still bound to their perceptions and usually see things from only one perspective. They like to focus on only one aspect of a thing, so they can be deceived by appearances. Preschoolers and kindergartners have not yet learned to conserve space in the preoperational stage of Piaget (Piaget, 1959; Piaget, Inhelder, & Szeminska, 1960). When six cars are represented in a parking lot spread out on a 10-inch × 10-inch lot, a typical preschooler or kindergartner says that there are more cars than if the cars are shown close together on the same size parking lot. When the child is asked by the teacher, "Is there more cement on the lot with the cars spread out or more with the cars close together?" the child usually answers that there is more cement when the cars are close together. This child cannot conserve number or space. According to Piaget (1959), in the preoperational stage, children are still using intuitive thought rather than logic. This intuitive thought is prevalent in young children's thinking about spatial development. The good news is that, with teacher guidance, the child can progress to a higher degree than was once thought. The following activities will support children in their enhancement of spatial skills:

Geometry Focal Point for Preschool: Identifying Shapes and Describing Spatial Relationships

Children develop spatial reasoning by working from two perspectives on space as they examine the shapes of objects and inspect their relative positions. They find shapes in their environments, and describe them in their own words. They build pictures and designs by combining two- and three-dimensional shapes, and they solve such problems as deciding which piece will fit into a space in a puzzle. They discuss the relative positions of objects with vocabulary such as *above, below,* and *next to.* (NCTM, 2006, p. 23)

1. Children can work with cubes or rectangular prisms. They identify these shapes and can create an actual design on grid paper, such as a fence for a pet, or they can design a pen for a zoo animal. Children can also put the cubes on paper, and then discuss what they have created. Then they can see them from different perspectives.
2. Children can investigate shapes with playdough. The teacher can help the children touch the outline of the shapes and describe them by the type of line, number of lines, the number of points, and what they look like when transformed.
3. Children can find many shapes in the environment, and describe them in their own words. Children can look for shapes on the floor, the wall, the door, the ceiling, their clothing, walls, fences, or cars. Children should go further than naming a triangle, a rectangle, and a square.

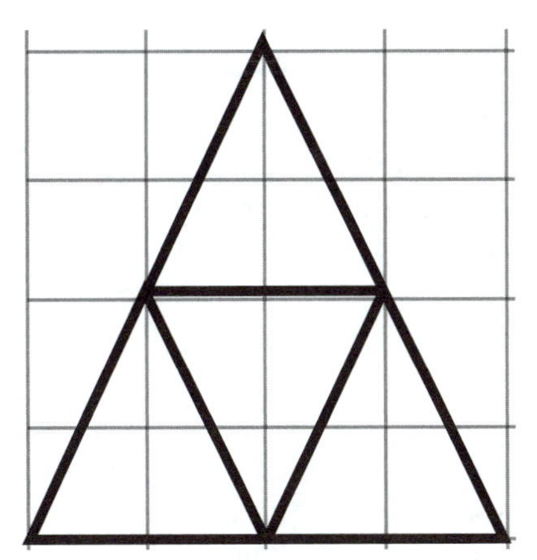

Figure 3.8. Find three triangles in one triangle.

They should see that not all triangles are equilateral and discuss in depth the attributes of the shapes so that language development is taking place and explanations are precise. The teacher needs to describe, for example, the roundness of the bird's nest, the round peas, and the round cherry. The teacher describes the triangle mountain tip, the triangle shark's fin, and the triangular ear of the cat. The teacher asks the children what they can build with two triangles. The teacher then asks the students to name three shapes they can build with three triangles. The students decide what shape fits into a space.

4. The teacher asks the children to fold a square in half. The teacher then asks the children what shape they have created. The teacher asks the students what kind of origami animal could be made with three triangular folds. This beginning origami is very difficult for children in preschool. Folding from one point to another is rather difficult for most preschoolers in the United States because they have not had much experience in paper folding. Children from Asian countries have many origami projects that they learn at home and school. I observed young children in Japan performing this activity with ease. The children can easily fold the square into a rectangle. It might be helpful to demonstrate how a square can be turned into two triangles.
5. The teacher can have students play a game called Guess What the Shape Is at circle time and bring the shapes out of an apron. Play this with three-dimensional shapes and with flat shapes.
6. The teacher can ask the students to find three triangles in one triangle (see Figure 3.8).
7. The teacher can ask the students to build different things with two triangles.
8. Students can be asked to find smaller circles in larger circles. Make a 10-inch circle on paper, and let children use paint with cans and place circles within the large circle. Repeat this with other two dimensional shapes.

9. The children can discuss the relative size of the objects using simple adjectives, such as large, big, small, and little. Using buttons that are large and round and small and round, and large and square and small and square, they can complete an activity helping a teddy bear find its buttons. The teacher can ask the following question: "Can you help the teddy bear find one large button and one small button?" Even though sorting by color is the first way most preschoolers learn, sorting by color sometimes takes away from the spatial sense of words because children focus on the color.

10. Using a grid, such as the one in Appendix B in the back of the book, the children can visualize what is happening with cubes, rectangles, triangles, and prisms as they place them on the grid. The grid helps the children structure their learning and later can lead into learning about coordinates.

11. Students can sort three-dimensional figures by size, number of sides or vertices, and weight, and precisely describe the characteristics. Weight and graphs should be related to extensive language in math whereby size, shape, and quantity can be described (connection to data analysis).

12. Students can determine how many sides a shape has (connection to number and operations).

13. Students can develop simple sequential patterns, such as triangle, triangle, and square (AAB) or triangle, square, and square (ABB) (connection to algebra).

14. Students can play with puzzles of all types, starting with small puzzles of two or three pieces and moving into complex puzzles. The teacher's role is to give some guidance if needed but not to show exactly how to perform the activity. After using picture puzzles, the children can work on shape puzzles using various shapes to make a picture.

15. Many books, such as *All About Where* and *Over, Under and Through and Other Spatial Concepts* by Hoban (1973) can be used to discuss position words and phrases, such as *under, above, below,* and *next to.* There are other books on position words in Appendix F.

Kindergarten Focal Points in Geometry: Describing Shapes and Space

Children interpret the physical world with geometric ideas (e.g., shape, orientation, spatial relations) and describe it with corresponding vocabulary. They identify, name, and describe a variety of shapes, such as squares, triangles, circles, rectangles, (regular) hexagons, and (isosceles) trapezoids presented in a variety of ways (e.g., with different sizes or orientations), as well as such three-dimensional shapes as spheres, cubes, and cylinders. They use basic shapes and spatial reasoning to model objects in their environment and to construct more complex shapes. (NCTM, 2006, p. 24)

1. Children should be able to recognize basic geometric shapes of circle, triangle, square, rectangle, rhombus, and ellipse. Children should also be able to recognize examples of three-dimensional geometric shapes such as cylinder, cube, triangular prism, and rectangular prism. It should be noted that materials should include different types of triangles—not just equilateral triangles, because the equilateral triangle with the point up and horizontal base is the most common way children identify triangles. It is important to make sure to use different types of triangles such as the right triangles with one right angle, the equilateral triangle with all sides equal, the isosceles triangle with two congruent sides and two congruent angles, the scalene triangle with no congruent sides, the acute triangle with three acute angles, and the obtuse triangle with one angle greater than 90 degrees and two angles less than 90 degrees. They should be rotated to present different viewpoints. The rectangles should include all sizes of rectangles—not just twice the size of a square.

2. Children can sort three-dimensional figures by size, number of sides or vertices, or weight, and precisely describe the characteristics. Weight and graphs should be related to extensive language in math where size, shape, and quantity can be described (connection to data analysis).

3. Using large round and small round buttons, and large square and small square buttons, children can play a game where they help a teddy bear find its buttons. The teacher can ask the students the following question: "Can you help the teddy bear find one large square button and one small round button?" Classifying by size and shape is harder than classifying by one property, and kindergartners need to start thinking in this way.

4. Children can sort three-dimensional objects that roll, three-dimensional objects with flat sides, three-dimensional objects with slanted sides, three-dimensional objects with flat and slanted sides, three-dimensional objects with and without points, three-dimensional objects with square surfaces and/or rectangular surfaces, and three-dimensional objects that can and cannot stack easily. A Venn diagram could be used to represent some of these ideas.

5. Teachers can teach children space concepts, such as position words (*on, off, on top of, below, beside, in front of, in back of, by, next to, between*), direction words (*up, down, around, through, to, from, toward, away from, sideways, across, forward, to the right, to the left*), distance words (*near, far, close, far from*), and organization and pattern words (*place in a row, AB pattern, ABA pattern, ABBA pattern*). Learning about these concepts can also lend itself to having children perform movement activities with their bodies. By performing movement activities, children can integrate their understanding of geometry, measurement, and number by using the grid to go from one place to another and discussing how many steps to take to the left, how many to take to turn right, and how many steps to go forward. Then children can use the grid in Appendix B in the back of this book to show this because this prepares children to use coordinates on the grid.

6. As children progress to using blocks as objects to make real structures in the environment, they can make houses, buildings, and furniture with

unit blocks. The teacher needs to help them use technical language in block playing. For more specific information on block playing and vocabulary, see Chapter 8.

7. The teacher can have students make up shape and location pictures. The students can make a picture so that a triangle is over a square and a circle is under the square.
8. There are numerous books, such as *Changes, Changes* (Hutchins, 1987) and *Round Trip* (Jonas, 1984) that help children with different orientations toward objects in the environments. These books help the child with visualization. *It Looked Like Spilt Milk* (Shaw, 1947) helps children see shapes in clouds. See Children's Literature List in Appendix F for more books on spatial development.

Piagetian Thoughts on First and Second Graders' Spatial Development

By the end of the first grade, children are in the *concrete operational* stage, according to Piaget (1959). As children approach age 7, their thinking becomes more logical. They mentally organize their thoughts. In the concrete operational stage, children can usually understand the concept of *conservation of space* problem written above (Piaget, Inhelder, & Szeminska, 1960). The child at this stage also understands conservation of matter; for example, they can tell clay is the same when it is pulled out from a pretend hamburger into a pretend hot dog. Most children of this age can also conserve length, which gives them the opportunity to understand measurement. For example, most children can see that four toothpicks that are in a straight line are the same length as four toothpicks that are in a wavy line. They can categorize and sort things, such as triangles, rectangles, and squares. With practice, children should also be able to compose and decompose geometric figures.

First-Grade Focal Points in Geometry: Composing and Decomposing Geometric Shapes

Children compose and decompose plane and solid figures (e.g., by putting two congruent isosceles triangles together to make a rhombus), thus building an understanding of part–whole relationships as well as the properties of the original and composite shapes. As they combine figures, they recognize they form different perspectives and orientations, describe their geometric attributes and properties, and determine how they are alike and different, in the process developing a background for measurement and initial understandings of such properties as congruence and symmetry. (NCTM, 2006, p. 26)

1. Children need to be constantly putting things together and taking them apart, because composing and decomposing is important to this first-grade Focal Point. Children should be able to take apart three-dimensional and

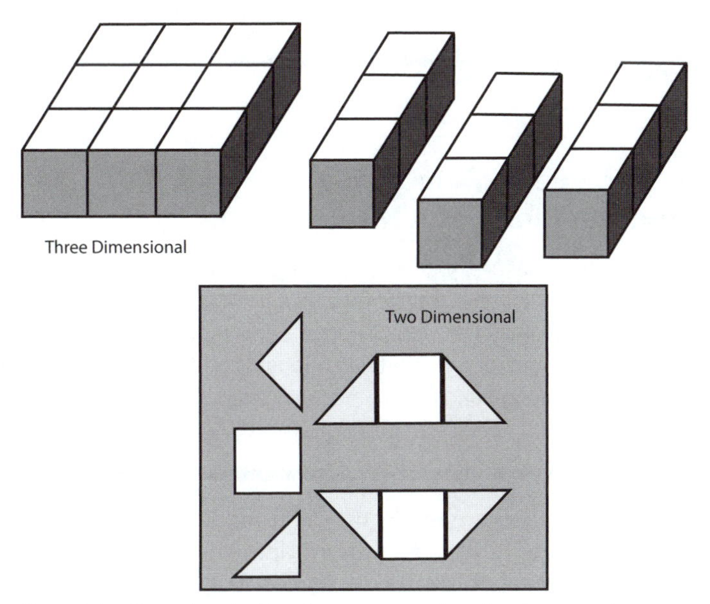

Figure 3.9. Examples of taking shapes apart and putting them together.

two-dimensional shapes and put them back together. Examples of children taking things apart and putting them together are seen in Figure 3.9.

2. The grid can help children see part–whole relationships using the eight 1-inch cube blocks as in Froebel's Gift 3 (see Chapter 2 for more information on Froebel's gifts) and showing how they can be taken apart and placed back together.

3. The grid can be used with parquetry blocks or simply cut-out figures (similar to Froebel's Gift 7; see Chapter 2) with squares, right isosceles triangles, obtuse isosceles triangles, equilateral triangles, scalene triangles, circles, and half circles. Blocks and cut-out figures are especially useful when demonstrated on a grid (see Appendix B of this volume for a grid sample). Children can show how two small equilateral triangles can make a square and how triangles attached to a square can make different figures.

4. Children can learn area by composing and decomposing smaller shapes that are part of a larger shape, beginning with a square. This skill leads into fractions. A possible activity to teach this skill could be to have children look at a sandwich. The children can determine how many ways you can look at sandwiches and determine how many ways you can cut a sandwich into four parts. The teacher can make four sandwiches out of white paper or other materials. Then the teacher can cut one into four equal parts by cutting it in half and then in half again. Let the children think of other ways to cut the sandwich into equal parts, such as by cutting diagonals or four long strips. Another way is to cut it in half down the middle and then cut diagonals down each of the other two sides.

5. After folding a piece of paper in half, the children can make figures, such as a cross, and notice that the cross is symmetrical on both sides.

Children can learn composing and decomposing geometric shapes by using origami.

Second-Grade Focal Points in Geometry: Geometry and Measurement

Children estimate, measure, and compute lengths as they solve problems involving data, space, and movement through space. By composing and decomposing two-dimensional shapes (intentionally substituting arrangements of smaller shapes for larger shapes or substituting larger shapes for smaller shapes), they use geometric knowledge and spatial reasoning to develop foundations for understanding area, fractions, and proportions. (NCTM, 2006, p. 28)

1. In second grade, there is a connection made to measurement. Children measure lengths at first by nonstandard measurement and then move into standard measurement with inches, feet, and yards, and millimeters, centimeters, and meters.
2. Gifts 3–10 of Froebel (see Chapter 2 for more information on Froebel's gifts) can be used for composing and decomposing shapes at this level. They can be used to lay the foundations for understanding of area, fractions, and proportions.
3. Three rectangular pieces of paper can be used to teach fractions. The teacher can let children divide the rectangular pieces into four parts, but none of them can be divided in the same way. The teacher can let children come up with their explanations.
4. The teacher can ask children to cut a pie into four, six, and eight pieces, and then discuss what happens.
5. The teacher can have the students use the grid sheet in Appendix B by designing the 20 squares as seats in different ways on the grid sheet. They might be in groups of two, four, five, or ten. The teacher can have the students describe the shapes and why they placed them in the design that they used.

Summary

It is important that early childhood and elementary school teachers become trained in teaching geometry to students so students can become familiar with the precise language of geometry and the importance of visualization. It appears that elementary students are taught math more in terms of number sequence and less in terms of stages of spatial development and geometry. Research has concentrated on number sense, sometimes to the exclusion of geometry, which is the area that students in the United States still need improvement on, according to the TIMSS. Recent developments brought about by research in spatial development, as well as the low international test scores in geometry, have encouraged the NCTM to devote more emphasis to geometry at earlier grades, beginning in preschool, and also to make connections to other areas of mathematics.

4

Spatial Development and Art and Literature

The visual arts provide many ways of promoting spatial development, including creating art and analyzing the creations of artists. Research has shown that cognitive skills, such as spatial development and language skills, are increased when children have teachers who are knowledgeable about the arts and about how to discuss art media and elements of art with children (Althouse, Johnson, & Mitchell, 2003; Douglas & Schwartz, 1967; Hogg & McWhinnie, 1968). However, teachers need a better understanding of how to bring about an appreciation of spatial images. Research by Harlan (1996) found that preservice and in-service elementary teachers viewed art as an opportunity for free self-expression or as a craft. Teachers in this study did not view art as a way to bring about better spatial understanding for students.

Therefore, there is a need to help teachers bring about an appreciation of spatial images. For teachers to use art media to promote spatial understanding appropriately, a theoretical background is needed to understand how to better have collaborative expressions with the media. The Reggio Emilia approach, founded in Italy after World War II, has emerged as a leading curriculum in creative and spatial education for preschools because of its philosophy supporting multiple experiences in the arts as extensions of thinking and spatial understanding. Children study in depth a topic and produce many versions of their topics in art media based on their observations and questioning. The theoretical background of Reggio Emilia is based on the work of Jean Piaget (1952, 1974), Lev Vygotsky (1962, 1978), John Dewey (1934, 1938), and Socrates.

Theoretical and Research Background: Piaget, Vygotsky, Dewey, and Socrates

This section will explain the theories of Piaget, Vygotsky, and Dewey, and the philosophy of and the questioning technique of Socrates, as they relate to the promotion of cognitive thinking, which in turn promotes spatial thinking in the arts. Piaget stressed social interaction with peers as students work with objects. He believed that children construct their own knowledge as they work with peers with objects. Piaget theorized that children were learning to see another viewpoint as they constructed knowledge with their peers (Piaget, 1952, 1974). A student assimilates knowledge and accommodates that knowledge by creating a new schema to produce action, or in the case of art, to produce an artifact (Walling, 2000).

Vygotsky (1962, 1986), on the other hand, emphasized that children learn from a more socially competent peer or teacher using the concept of *scaffolding*. The major ideas of Vygotsky were based on children watching and interacting with adults or more advanced peers to help them understand thought and concepts. He felt that children need to make discoveries not only on their own but also from the experience of others. Children can perform at a higher level by being guided by a peer or adult. According to Vygotsky, most learning takes place when children are challenged to their potential developmental level.

The teacher should be comfortable explaining some information about a subject, as long as it honors the child who is the co-creator. By making the effort to see just a little bit more in everything, a child and a teacher use their gifts; the more they experiment with the media, the more they are open to new ideas and spatial development.

In order to connect children to the higher level of understanding in creating an art masterpiece, discuss different aspects of media, the elements of art, and the principles of design. Draw from the sociocultural milieu in the classroom to promote the arts, because the environment of the classroom includes family, cultural, linguistic, racial, and economic diversity. Richness of social diversity promotes a richness of diversity in art forms and spatial figures.

A third theorist whose work should be included in early childhood art experiences is John Dewey. His work emphasized integrating art into the curriculum. He theorized that art should not be a separate course but should be taught as a part of all subjects. It should be integrated into the classroom throughout the day. Dewey (1934, 1938) wrote the book *Art as Experience* to show the importance of art and its place in the formation of intelligence in young children.

Socrates believed the teaching environment should emphasize discussion. The teacher asks questions related to the media, the elements, the subject matter, and the design. The children also ask questions. A discussion takes place. This type of teaching, according to Glickman (1998), is the "pedagogy of democracy." The discussion of media enhances the child's understanding of the media and it helps the teacher understand the spatial thinking of the child.

In general, the works of theorists and educators, as well as the Socratic method, have provided the inspirations that are needed for creative use of media and the enhancement of inspiration and spatial development. The fuel of all creative art is the invisible force to express in a unique way what is seen. The inspired child notices details, and wants details pointed out by the teacher and others. "Stopping to smell the roses" is not enough. The child must enter the rose, or media, and become part of it; many highly creative people have experienced and spoken of this concept in the literature. The sources for inspiration for creative spatial development are in the media itself, in nature, in books, in other children's work, as well as in seeing famous works of art.

Art is really an extension of the thinking of the child. The Reggio program in Reggio Emilia, Italy, emphasizes the theories of Piaget, Vygotsky, Dewey, and Socrates in order to help children think cognitively and spatially through art media. It is a model of excellence in the arts, and in collaborative teaching strategies for children and teachers throughout the world.

Spatial Development Through Elements of Art

As artists try to express their feelings and their ideas, they must instinctively use elements and principles of design. Elements of art include line, shape, form, color, and texture. Elements such as line and shape and form are especially important to young children in understanding space and form.

Types of Lines

Line in art is a way of making something become visible. Lines vary in width, emphasis, and direction. In width, they can be thick or thin. In direction, they can come together or converge, radiate from the center, twist, run parallel to each other, or curve. Artists use many different tools such as pencils, pens, markers, paint brushes, crayons, and even fingers. Lines can be curvy or straight, zigzagging or looping. They can make shapes and show feeling.

Lines in Nature Lines in nature are everywhere. Lines are in leaves, on the bark of a tree, on the tree itself, on bushes, and on flowers. Teachers need to understand the expressions made by lines in nature and the impact they have on art. Different lines mean different things when they are analyzed.

Vertical lines may express tallness, power, and importance. A way to demonstrate this is by showing what a man looks like when he is stooped over versus when he is standing straight. Horizontal lines may express calmness across a painting or piece of art; for instance, a sunset spread across the horizon induces a feeling of tranquility. Diagonal lines, on the other hand, may express speed as they dart across a picture or sculpture. Zigzag diagonal lines may express danger when they are associated with natural dangers such as lightning. Curved lines may express softness because, like zigzagging lines, they are associated with natural materials in the world—for example, water and the ocean. The teacher is responsible for identifying the lines as children make them, so that they become aware of the lines they have created.

Lines in Famous Works of Art Lines start with a dot and extend to a line. Many of Vincent van Gogh's paintings and drawings, such as *Street in Saintes-Maries,* show dots and lines. Some lines are straight (horizontal and vertical), some are curved, some are zigzagged, and some just wiggle. Paul Klee uses many lines and shapes in his work. In the painting *Farbtafel,* for example, Klee uses horizontal and vertical lines in a grid to create squares of various vibrant colors.

Van Gogh's painting *The Bedroom* may easily inspire children to draw their own bedrooms. But the most famous of van Gogh's paintings, *Starry Night,* can be introduced by asking students to make observations of the painting. The teacher can ask the students, "How do you think the artist is feeling?" The teacher can have the students point out the swirls and colors the artist is using. The teacher can let the students explore swirls and lines with movement using paints or other media. It is important to also emphasize the flowing strokes. Jackson Pollock made lines with wiggles and splats in his painting entitled *One.*

Children may be inspired to represent all the kinds of actions that athletes do in the Olympics by representing movement with lines. In *Comedians' Handbill,* Klee used lines to represent motion. Matisse made curvy lines in all of his forms of art. Children may experience making thin lines using pencils; show them thin-penciled drawings by famous artists. Viewing Georgia O'Keeffe's works can allow children to understand the use of thick lines in paintings. Her *Evening Star* series of paintings use very thick lines. Children may enjoy making thick lines using crayons, markers, and finger paints.

Lines in Children's Literature Many children's books demonstrate an artistic use of lines. In Goble's *The Girl Who Loved Wild Horses* (1993), the galloping horses and thunder are shown through lines. In the book *Ben's Trumpet* (Isadora, 1997), sound is represented through lines. Sendak's classic, *Where the Wild Things Are* (1964), features detailed line drawing, and Yenawine's book *Lines* (1991) helps children look at lines and then discuss the thoughts and feelings that lines convey.

Types of Shapes

Shapes are created by lines that touch or intersect to form a point. The shapes can take many forms. Shapes can be flat and two-dimensional or three-dimensional.

There are three ways to classify shapes: by simple and compound shapes, by geometric or free-form shapes, or by sorting flat surfaces and three-dimensional shapes.

1. **Classification by simple and compound shapes:** Simple shapes are shapes such as a rectangle, triangle, square, oval, diamond, semicircle,

heart, spiral, crescent, pentagon, hexagon, or octagon. Include all types and transformations of these shapes in the classification. Compound shapes are shapes composed of more than one shape. For instance, a house might be composed of a rectangle and a triangle. Children can use simple shapes to make realistic objects.

2. **Classification by geometric or free-form shapes**: Geometric shapes are shapes such as a triangle, rectangle, and square. Free-form shapes are amorphous, or formless; they do not have names.
3. **Sorting by flat forms or three-dimensional forms**. Shapes can be sorted by the geometric forms or flat forms previously mentioned or by three-dimensional forms, which are the pyramid, cube, sphere, cylinder, and cone.

Shapes in Nature Ideally, the teacher first allows the children to explore artifacts in nature on their own, and he or she supports and enhances the child's exploration and discovery of art through vivid descriptions. Introducing the varying shapes of objects in nature is important to enhance children's understanding of the world and how this understanding can be incorporated into their art. Shapes of different trees, such as the weeping willow, the redwood, the pine, and the oak, may be discussed to help children comprehend the shapes in nature that can be displayed in their artwork. Flower shapes found in a garden, such as the sunflower, snapdragon, tulip, daffodil, and daisy, represent different shapes as well as shapes within shapes. Seeds from these flowers may easily be planted in separate containers in the science area, so children can observe the growth of the shapes of the flowers; this activity integrates science with art.

As children grow in their viewing and appreciation of flower shapes, the teacher may want to introduce them to other aspects of the garden. Herbs, for instance, can be introduced by displaying them, allowing children to touch them, smell them, and even eat them. Some kindergartens have used smelling such things as herbs to set up a sensory learning experience. Rosemary, basil, chives, and parsley are distinctive, and these herbs can be easily identified by their shapes. Rosemary has a long, thin shape and distinctive odor; chives have a long, grasslike look; basil has a leaflike appearance; and parsley may be identified by its irregular edges.

It is most important to allow children to observe nature and discover the simple shapes in nature on their own. The teacher can show kindergartners pictures or video of the sea, and see if they can recognize a star of a starfish, a circle on the eyes of fish; or a semicircle on the top of a jellyfish. The teacher can ask the children, "Can you see a heart shape on certain fish, triangles on a shark's teeth, and a spiral on the snail?" The teacher may also show a picture of the mountains or take a field trip to the mountains to enable children to see the mountains firsthand. It is important for the children to notice that the mountain itself is a triangle, a rock is a sphere, a pond as an oval, and pinecones have a cone shape. The teacher can also show the children pictures of the moon in the night sky, showing the changing shapes of the moon over time. The moon can be shown to be a full or circle moon, or the moon can also be shown as variations of a crescent shape. Changes in the shape of the moon can be graphed, thus integrating art with mathematics.

Shapes in Famous Works of Art In Mondrian's *Composition 1921* and his *Composition with Red and Yellow,* one can see shapes in color, and at the same time, see abstract painting. Aline Wolf's book *Mommy, It's a Renoir!* (1984) suggested that matching identical pictures is a first stage for children to appreciate art; the second stage is to see the difference in similar pictures by the same artist.

Paul Klee paints trees as simple shapes in *Park Near Lucerne,* an abstract representation of a park. Some of the shapes are curved and some of the shapes bend, while others are very tall. Klee had to study nature just as thoroughly as someone who paints a realistic picture of a park in order to represent the park in this way. Young children will benefit from seeing Klee's painting because he painted trees as simple shapes.

Picasso used transformed shapes in his work, such as in his *Maya in a Sailor Suit,* which shows how he rearranged shapes in unique ways. His rearrangement of shapes is helpful for children to view, because many children have difficulty seeing shapes from a different perspective, particularly children under the age of 7.

Children can examine Cezanne's *Apples and Oranges* and talk about the shapes, specifically the circles used in the pictures. The children can make circles and see them in a famous work of art. The teacher can bring in real apples, oranges, and tomatoes for the children to see and feel. They can then expand to other round shapes in the room. Children can then draw the shapes of these objects.

Shape in Children's Literature Children explore shapes of clouds in *The Cloud Book* by DePaola (1975) and *It Looked Like Spilt Milk* by Shaw (1947) and they can go outside to continue their exploration of clouds and what they see in the clouds. They can explore sea shapes in *Sea Shapes* by MacDonald (1994), find the star in the starfish, the circle in the whale's eye, the semicircle in the jelly fish, as well as the triangle teeth of the shark. Multiple shapes can be explored in *The Shapes of Things* by Dodds (1994) by discovering how many shapes can be embedded in the shape of one item. Both *Changes, Changes* by Hutchins (1987) and *Round Trip* by Jonas (1984) help children with transformations and seeing things from different perspectives, as well as the age-old folktale told in *Grandfather Tang's Story* by Tompert (1990), a book about Grandfather Tang and Little Soo who were sitting under a tree, playing a game with their tangram puzzle.

Summary

The visual arts are an excellent way of promoting spatial development. However, early childhood teachers need better methods of helping children understand their spatial world through the arts. The Reggio Emilia preschools have set the standard for spatial understanding in their long-term projects with extensions of the child's thinking by using the theories of Piaget, Vygotsky, Dewey, and Socrates. Further understanding of the elements of art, particularly the elements of line and shape, is accomplished through using nature, famous works of art, and children's literature to show children spatial relationships.

Spatial Development and Social Studies

Today's young learners need social science skills to succeed. Social studies has probably not been given as much emphasis as other subjects because social science is not tested on the National Assessment of Educational Progress (NAEP), and it has not been deemed worth the same attention as math, literacy, and science, which are tested on the NAEP. Spatial thinking is an important part of geography, one of the social sciences, because map reading is essential in understanding geographic concepts. Academics define modern geography as having six essential elements, addressing such topics as world in spatial terms, places and regions, physical systems, human systems, environment and society, and uses of geography (Grosvenor, 2007).

America is falling behind in geographic knowledge. The United States scored second to last in overall geographic literacy in the 2002 Roper poll commissioned by the National Geographic Education Foundation (2002). It trailed Canada, France, Germany, Great Britain, Italy, Japan, and Sweden. Perhaps understanding the world in spatial terms will help children develop better geographic knowledge. Students in the United States travel less frequently to other countries than children in Europe, according to the National Geographic report (2002) and have less chance to develop experiential geographic literacy. Children in the United States need to have more experiences in seeing how the world is spatially organized so that they can progress in their understanding of geographic knowledge. This includes learning to read maps and develop spatial thought in relation to the world.

Research on Mapping and Spatial Development

Several views have guided the teaching and learning of maps. One view, coming from a Piagetian perspective (Piaget, Inhelder, & Szeminska, 1960), is that mapping abilities appear slowly over the years, so these skills should not be taught in an elementary school classroom. In this view, 1-year-olds can use movement to explore their space. Later they can progress to map reading at various levels. Another view is that mapping knowledge is innate, and therefore does not need to be taught. Because of these differing views, school experiences in mapping can be somewhat limited and their connection to other subjects can be even more so, according to Muir and Cheek (1986). However, recently there has been recognition of a need for more information on how children learn mapping, because of its importance in geography, math, science, and technology. There has been more effort to show that practice and high-quality explanation from adults are important in helping children understand maps (Baenninger & Newcombe, 1989, 1995; Huttenlocher, Levine, & Vevea, 1998).

Piaget, Inhelder, and Szeminska (1960) and Stolzman and Goolsby (1973) have shown how a developmental sequence of spatial stages have substantially complemented the Expanding Horizons curriculum, in which a child learns first from his immediate environment or his family, then his school, neighborhood, state, country, and world. In addition, Muir and Cheek (1991) found that assessment of spatial abilities is integral to designing instruction for children in making or reading maps. Other scholars have also found the need to have systematic training in map-reading skills (Rice & Cobb, 1978). Evidence indicates that children possess complex spatial information and can abstract information from symbols (Liben, Moore, & Golbeck, 1982), and they can learn cardinal directions as early as kindergarten (Lanegran, Snowfield, & Laurent, 1970).

Liben and Downs (2001) and Blades, Spencer, Plester, and Desmond (2004) found that, with assistance, children can create models of spaces; with input by the teacher, this can lead to spatial growth in the understanding of maps (Baenninger & Newcombe, 1989, 1995; Huttenlocher et al., 1998; Liben & Downs, 2001). Mapping is usually transmitted through interactions with other children and through the use of Vygotsky's (1986) approach, whereby scaffolding takes place for cognitive spatial development.

Movement and Spatial Development

At age 1, if children walk around a display of objects instead of being carried over them, the children are more apt to remember what is in the display (Acredolo, Adams, & Goodwyn, 1984). This leads one to realize how important movement is to spatial development. Infants should be allowed to crawl, and toddlers should be allowed to touch and feel their environments. Toddlers and preschoolers should be allowed to explore their environments, and parents or teachers should discuss their environment and the spatial features with them as they move from place to place with them. Teachers need to use terms such as *on top of, above, below, next to, beside,* and *inside* as they move. Filippaki and Papamichael (1997) found that when preschool children tutor others in spatial directions in school and outside and there are frequent discussions of spatial subjects (e.g., putting things under the table or over the table, finding the way home after going on a trip), then they build spatial concepts necessary for mapping. Children can be walked to the lunchroom, outside, and on a field trip, and given specific features to remember. Activities that require children to move their bodies and deal with concepts of space and shape help children learn abstract thought (Pica, 2000). An extensive movement program using the elements of movement in space helps children orient themselves in space.

Representation and Symbolization

Children need to understand that one thing represents something else in map reading. At 4 years old, children may recognize that a rectangle can represent a piece of furniture but, at the same time, may not realize that colors on a map represent something (Liben & Myers, 2007). Liben and Myers (2007) found that children as young as age 3 have determined that one thing can represent something else. Children as young as age 3 can build models of familiar spaces with different objects, although these children usually do not do this very well until they are about 6 (Blades et al., 2004). From the inconsistencies in the research, it is believed that much needs to be done to help children represent symbolically, understand that a map represents a place, and carefully help children construct knowledge of their own maps.

Directional and Positional Words

Froebel emphasized the importance of using directional and positional words when presenting his gifts to children (see Chapter 2 for more information on Froebel's gifts). Directional words promote direction, such as *left* and *right,* while positional words show where something is located, such *over, under, in,* or *off.* Piaget and Inhelder (1967) suggested that preschoolers understand topological concepts such as *in, on, over, next to, under, between, open,* and *closed.* These words can be expanded for preschoolers to include such sentences as "Place the doll between the door and the window," or "Place the doll next to the box." Many preschoolers can also understand how the letter *U* is different from the letter *O,* but they have a hard time understanding a different point of view from a side opposite to their own.

As children progress to kindergarten, directional words, such as *up* and *down,* can be taught by singing songs like "Riding Up and Down in the Little Red Wagon" and "The Noble Duke of York." Concepts of *left* and *right* can be taught by asking children to find which one of their hands has the letter *L* in it when they extend their thumbs away from their forefingers. Songs such as

"Hokey Pokey" or "Here We Go Looby Loo" can be sung, or directional games such as "Simon Says" and "Follow the Leader" can be played. When teachers lead a class, they should use precise directional terms such as "We will turn left at this stop sign" instead of "We will turn left here" or "Let's go this way," because it gives children a visual reference point. Even though a very early study (Lord, 1941) said that children do not understand cardinal directions until adulthood, another study found that when children were taken outside and shown directions in relation to the sun in the morning and the sun in the afternoon, they were able to correctly answer more questions related to cardinal directions (Howe, 1969). From this it was shown that precise teaching was important in learning cardinal directions. The teacher can say, "The classroom is always sunny in the east because it faces the east." Taking the class outside gives the teacher many ways of showing cardinal directions and what happens to the sun during the day using shadows. Children can make a connection between the direction of the shadow and location of the sun. The teacher can explain that a shadow happens when a person or object gets between the sun and the surface of the earth and help the children observe changes over time. If the sun is behind the child, the child will see his shadow in front. If the sun is shining in front of him, he will see his shadow behind him.

Maps

According to Seefeldt, Castle, and Falconer (2010), research has not demonstrated the exact developmental sequence of children's understanding of maps. It is important, however, to build a foundation for maps and map reading. Gauteux (2001) and Mosenthal and Kirsch (1991) think that experiences with maps should be simple, based on the child's experiences in preschool. A teacher can draw a pathway in the room to different learning centers, and then let children place photographs of the dramatic play center, the blocks center, the science center, the math center, and the literacy center on the map. Children can follow a map with pictures on the playground. Preschoolers also need to see the teacher reading maps; having an adult model map reading gives the child the impetus to read the maps.

In kindergarten, there should be a globe and map in the classroom. Children need to understand that maps and globes use symbols; pointing out signs in the environment, such as centers in a room, and then labeling them on a map, prepares them for using maps. It is important for children to understand many symbols that they see in their environment. Symbols in the room such as "exit" and "entrance" as well as labels on their buildings can be used in block play. Children need to understand that blocks represent real objects or furniture in the environment. Oblique maps, which show legs on chairs or tables, help preschoolers comprehend a bird's-eye view of items on a map because some representation is made (Liben & Yekel, 1996).

As children reach early primary school, they need to understand that when looking at a map they are looking at it from a bird's-eye view (see Figure 5.1). The concept of scale can be taught by showing children a photograph of children in the classroom. The teacher can explain that the photograph is much smaller than the children but that it still represents the children in the

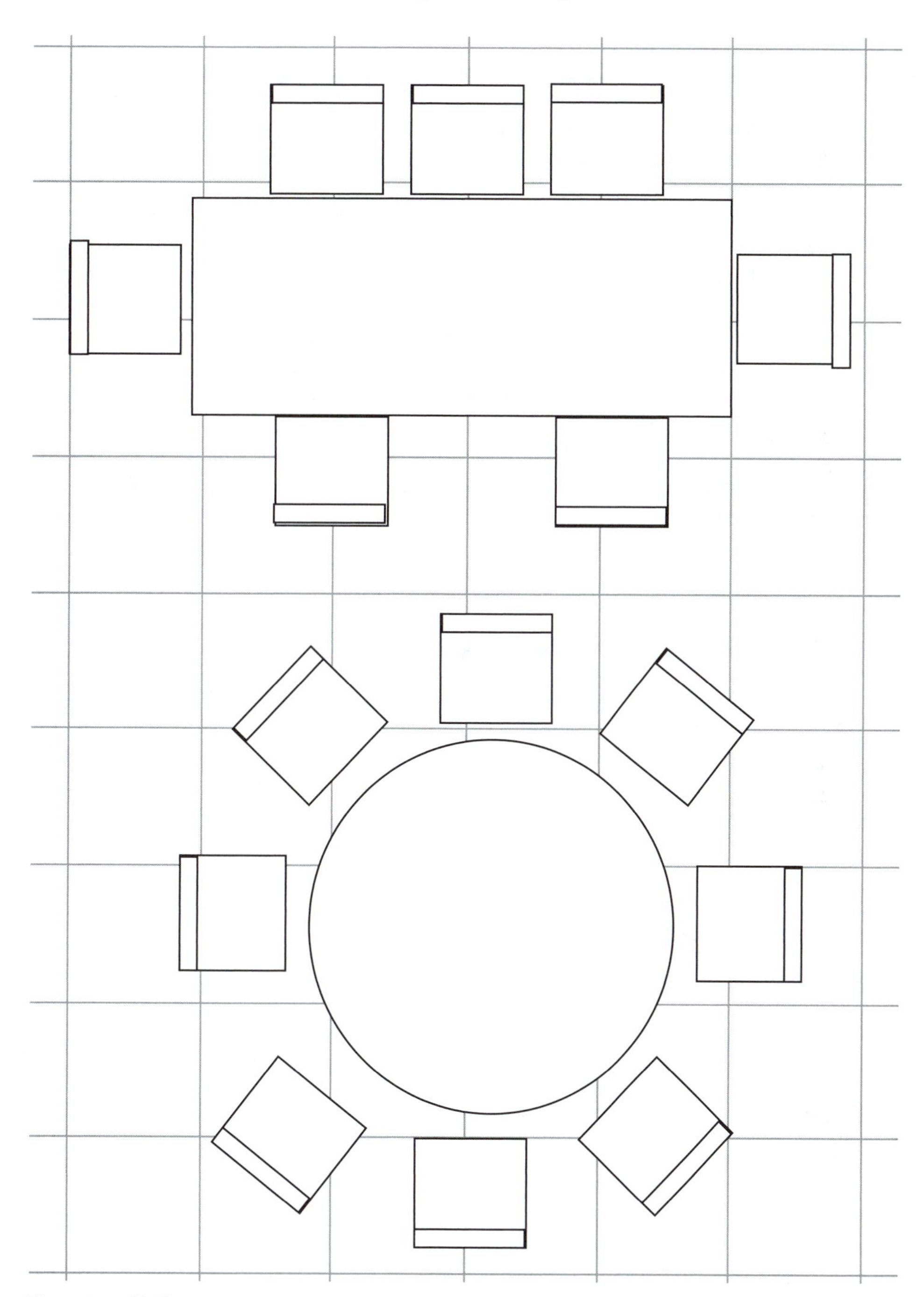

Figure 5.1. Bird's-eye view of tables.

class. The teacher then compares this concept to a map representing a particular place. In early primary grades the children can be introduced to the children's book *As the Crow Flies* (Hartman, 1991), which shows perspectives of a map of a city from the view of an eagle, rabbit, horse, crow, gull, and the moon. The children in early primary school can begin to see perspective in this way.

Materials for Mapping

A map is a representation or a small picture of a much larger place from a bird's-eye or aerial view. Maps help people position themselves on the earth. Mapping must begin with the experiences the children have had in order to build a foundation.

Materials for mapping should go from the most concrete to the most abstract. For instance, unit blocks should be used to reproduce a house or the child's classroom in a kindergarten class. Boxes, sticks, and paper with cutouts, relief maps, grids, and other drawing materials should also be used progressively, because they represent a continuum from concrete to abstract. Boxes or blocks, the most concrete of objects, could be used in preschool to represent houses. The classroom is usually the first location to be represented on a map. Children can then progress to their school, playground, route to school, and their towns. Examples of this are discussed in Chapter 8. Today, software programs such as Snyder's Neighborhood MapMachine provide line drawings that can be printed out, cut, folded, and glued together to form three-dimensional models of buildings with different shapes.

Children's Literature and Mapping

Children's literature should be an additional source for understanding mapping. Discussing the sequencing of characters walking to various places and repeating that walk by drawing a map is important for spatial literacy. Teachers can help children use concrete objects and clay maps to help develop spatial skills. A recipe for creating map models is provided here.

Recipe for Map Modeling

Materials:

1 part salt	food coloring or paint
1 part flour	heavy cardboard
⅔ part water	bowl

Process:

1. Mix salt and flour in bowl.
2. Add enough water until the consistency is like thick frosting.
3. Stir.
4. Add food coloring before molding, or mold and paint when dry.
5. Draw map on heavy cardboard.
6. Spread mixture on cardboard, adding hills and valleys.
7. Dry (dries in 1 to 2 days).
8. Paint if desired.

Useful for box dioramas, building free-form designs, and making fantasy maps of imaginary towns, islands, or worlds.

Maps depicting the routes taken by the main character of the books listed as mapping literature in Appendix F can be made by the teacher and some form of symbolization of the landmarks that were passed by the main character can be made for the child to recreate the story and play the main character.

Standards

Understanding the world in spatial terms is a geography standard (National Geography Standards, 1994). The understanding of this standard can start with children as young as age 1. One-year-olds can use movement to explore their space. Later they can progress to map reading at various levels of difficulty, beginning with their immediate environment and moving to the neighborhood, city, state, nation, and the world. Teachers need to understand how a child's comprehension of space develops so that the teacher will be able to see how things are organized spatially. Google Earth, MapQuest, TopoZone, and global positioning systems (GPS) in cars, planes, and boats have given maps an important and pervasive place in our society. With Google Earth and MapQuest, a primary teacher can zoom in and locate schools, houses, and baseball fields to teach spatial concepts.

In order to help students understand new technologies in navigation, teachers need to prepare students in high-quality spatial representation and reasoning. Spatial layouts and understanding verbal descriptions of spatial material are very important for students to learn.

Summary

This chapter reviewed the research on spatial development and its usefulness in promoting the geographic standard of understanding the world in spatial terms. The importance of movement exploration, representation and symbolization, directional words, and using maps was emphasized. Research repeatedly demonstrated that practice and high-quality, precise explanations from adults can increase spatial and navigational skills in mapping for young children. The chapter concluded with literature on mapmaking and literature emphasizing spatial concepts necessary for further understanding of mapping.

6

Spatial Development and Science

Sandra Phifer

If one thinks of science as a systematized study based on facts, principles, and methods derived from observation, one might conclude that, as very young children start observing and trying to make sense of their environment from a very young age, the study of science begins early. Children use all of their senses to observe and make observations about their environment; these learning processes are included in the scientific processes and standards. Spatial awareness and spatial discrimination of objects is inherent in all young children; shape, size, and location of objects provides information to help children discriminate between objects in the environment.

Pattern recognition is inherent to all learning. In addition to color, size (e.g., large, small, thick, thin), two- and three-dimensional shapes, and relationships of objects to other things are variables children use in determining and describing patterns. Recognizing and describing these variables can begin in the preschool years, and gradually pattern recognition skills can become more complex. Individuals vary in their expertise, depending on the quality and frequency of their experiences and the integration of language with the experiences.

Research on the Importance of Spatial Development and the Sciences

The Committee on Support for Thinking Spatially, which includes advisers from the National Academy of Science, the National Academy of Engineering, and the Institute of Medicine, takes the position that spatial thinking is a skill that can and should be learned by everyone (Downs et al., 2006). The development of spatial thinking, like all thinking, depends on an individual's experience, education, and practices. Because spatial thinking is included in many domains, the committee recommends that spatial thinking, like reading and writing, "be integrated throughout the school curriculum, so that students may achieve a deeper understanding of spatial thinking in addition to more insightful thinking about other subject areas. Including spatial thinking as a fundamental part of grades K–12 education will help equip the next generation to live and work in the 21st century" (Sarama & Clements, 2009).

Geometry is a very visual component of mathematics and promotes visual thinking. A number of scientists, including Albert Einstein, Michael Faraday, Sir Francis Galton, James Watson, and Buckminster Fuller, have credited visual thinking as playing a dominant role in their lives (Shepard, 1978a, 1978b). Geometry plays a basic role in physics and engineering, and in other areas with strong aesthetic connections to art, dance, and sports. Zal Usiskin (1997), a researcher and developer in mathematics, argued that geometry must be learned from earliest years because of the interrelationships of math to other domains. Geometry 1) connects math with the real, physical world, 2) studies visual structures and patterns, 3) represents phenomena whose origin is not visual or physical (e.g., graphs, networks), and 4) uses the same language to describe space in these areas.

Standards and Spatial Development

Science is more than factual information; the science curriculum also includes the processes of scientific investigation and helping young students learn to "think like a scientist." Science is not static, as the "facts" are continuously evolving and changing with more current knowledge. The National Science Education Standards (National Research Council, 1996) includes basic knowledge in life science, physical science, and earth–space science. Science standards also include technology, science in personal and social perspectives, and the history and nature of science. Elementary teachers and students do not need to master a huge number of facts about science, but they do need to understand basic concepts and patterns of science. It is more important for children to learn how to "do" science to construct their own conceptualizations that are essential for survival in the real world.

Learning to "do" science focuses on the processes of the science standards, including observing, classifying, communicating, measuring, predicting, inferring, identifying and controlling variables, formulating and testing hypotheses, interpreting data, defining operationally, experimenting, and constructing models. These processes are similar to the methods used by scientists (Crawford, 1998). Scientists do not follow a script or a set process; instead they begin with observations, reflections, and questions—much like young children do as they attempt to figure out all the "whys" of their world. Learning the processes of science really provides the framework for being a thinker and problem solver and can empower individuals to engage in the active process of being learners.

Integrating Science with Spatial Development in the Learning Program

Science is studied as systems, or organized groups of related objects or components. This systems approach to the study of science helps students understand relationships so that they can develop basic laws, theories, and models that explain their world. Therefore, learners need to recognize and describe properties of objects before they understand changes in the objects.

The broad scope of the science standards almost seamlessly integrates science with other content areas. It has already been noted that science and math process standards are closely aligned, and almost all areas of mathematics are utilized in understanding and describing science properties, relationships, and changes. Literacy components are all needed to describe, communicate, and share understandings—including the use of technology to research, communicate, and develop models. Social studies components are included in the history and social aspects of science, and maps and other social studies methods are used to document the relationship of time and space in our world.

Actually "doing" science and integrating math helps young learners make the connection between the subject areas. Using children's literature in varying genres, for example, offers the opportunity to present and discuss mathematical and science concepts in the context of a story with familiar language. Johnson and Giorgis (2001) postulated that using children's literature nurtures curiosity and wonderment and invites readers to discover new concepts. Furthermore, the clear visuals spark interest for discussion and help young learners make connections and applications to their real-world experiences.

Integrating Spatial Concepts with Science Content Areas

Spatial concepts are integrated in all areas of science content, including biology, astronomy and aerospace science, physics, engineering, earth science, and science in personal and social perspectives. Spatial concepts included within the science content areas are noted next.

Biology: Students can identify characteristics of organisms, life cycles, and the environment. Students can also identify plant and animal life from shapes and sizes.

Astronomy and Aerospace Science: Students can identify shape, size, time, and location relationships of objects in the sky. Students can also identify weather conditions and patterns.

Physics: Students can identify properties of objects and materials, position and motion of objects, light, heat, electricity, magnetism, building with blocks, figuring out how to get "big" things from one place to another. Concepts of balance can be identified.

Engineering: Students can create planning and constructing activities using the principles of physics.

Earth Science: Students can identify properties of Earth materials and changes in Earth systems and Earth history.

Science in Personal and Social Perspectives: Students can identify types and changes in populations, resources, environments, technology, and science as human beings affect changes.

Examples of Spatial Science Activities

Some specific spatial science activities will be noted in the next sections. These activities integrate spatial and geometric aspects of mathematics and science. All activities will require learners to apply the scientific and mathematical processes to observe, organize, problem-solve, measure, model, and interpret mathematical and scientific ideas through the use of real-life applications and literature.

Biology

Biology requires a high degree of spatial understanding. Children should be able to identify organisms in their environment by the shapes and patterns.

Shape Walks Shape walks can focus on any specific purpose of observation; for example, students could observe and identify manufactured objects such as buildings and signs, or the teacher could require students to observe only "natural" objects such as trees, leaves, rocks, and flowers. Documentation of student observation can be varied to fit the developmental abilities of the students.

A digital camera can be used to record shapes the children find. Multiple copies of photographs can be made for follow-up organization. A grid can be provided (either on a clipboard or on a tagboard necklace) for students to draw and label shapes they observe on their walk.

Follow-up activities can include sorting and graphing the shapes, creating a group mural or bulletin board of shapes in their environment, or using technology to create a visual depiction of the students' observations.

Math/Science Processes Students can observe and analyze attributes of geometric shapes and apply mathematical ideas to other contexts.

Math Concepts Students can recognize geometric shapes in the everyday world and identify patterns of shapes in everyday objects.

Science Concepts Students can identify the characteristics of everyday organisms.

Literature Connections

Hoban, T. (1986). *Shapes, shapes, shapes.* New York: Greenwillow Books.

MacKinnon, D. (2000). *Eye Spy shapes.* Watertown, MA: Charlesbridge.

Rotner, S., & Kerisler, K. (1992). *Nature spy.* Columbus, OH: Macmillan/McGraw-Hill.

Seuss, Dr. (1997). *The shape of me and other stuff.* New York: Random House.

Seymore, D., & Britton, J. (1990). *Introduction to tessellations.* Palo Alto, CA: Dale Seymore.

Stevens, P. (1974). *Patterns in nature.* Boston: Little, Brown.

Tompert, A. (1990). *Grandfather Tang's story.* New York: Crown Publishing.

Internet Resources

National Council of Teachers of Mathematics, Illuminations: http://illuminations.nctm.org/ActivityDetail.aspx?ID=24. This web site allows children to investigate line symmetry with mirrors.

National Library of Virtual Manipulatives: http://nlvm.usu.edu/en/nav/topic_t_3.html

Virtual tangrams can be manipulated to fill shapes or manipulate freely.

Assessment/Documentation

Assessment tools and strategies (Focus issue). (2004, September). *Science and Children, 42(1).*

National Research Council. (2000). Classroom assessment and inquiry. In *Inquiry and the national science education standards: A guide for teaching and learning* (pp. 74–85). Washington, DC: National Academies Press.

Spider Webs Students should have background knowledge in differences in characteristics of spiders and insects and on spider's habitat needs and common prey. The focus of this lesson will be on observing spiders' spinning threads and designs. Teacher should provide collections of pictures of spider webs (or take their own pictures with a digital camera) so students can view the base and "sticky" lines of the spider webs.

Math/Science Processes Students can observe and analyze attributes of geometric shapes and apply mathematical ideas to other contexts.

Math Concepts Students can recognize geometric shapes and structures in the environment and build and draw geometric objects (including lines and angles, if appropriate).

Figure 6.1. Spider web.

Science Concepts Students can identify relationships between organisms (e.g., spiders, insects) and their environment (e.g., nature).

Literature Connections

Carle, E. (1984). *The very busy spider.* New York: Philomel Books.

White, E.B. (1952). *Charlotte's web.* New York: Harper Row.

Internet Resources

Backyard Nature, Spider Silk: www.backyardnature.net/spidsilk.htm
This web site gives examples of spider webs, with differences by species.

PhotoVault, Arachnid Museum: http://www.photovault.com/Link/Orders/EntomologyInsects/SpidersAraneida/OESVolume01.html
This web site provides pictures of spiders and their webs.

Assessment Documentation Depending on the age or ability of the students, a web can be drawn with chalk on black paper, or constructed with thread and glue. If appropriate, students can identify geometric shapes and concepts used, including measurement of angles (see Figure 6.1).

Astronomy and Aerospace Science

Many aspects of the solar system are related to mathematics. These include the identification and relationships of the objects in space and their relationships to each other. Some activities that address these relationships are noted in the following sections.

Moon Phases The moon's appearance changes during the month. Students will investigate the differences in how the moon appears and the reasons for these changes in the moon's appearance. Students can monitor and draw the moon's appearance over the course of the moon cycle (see Figure 6.2).

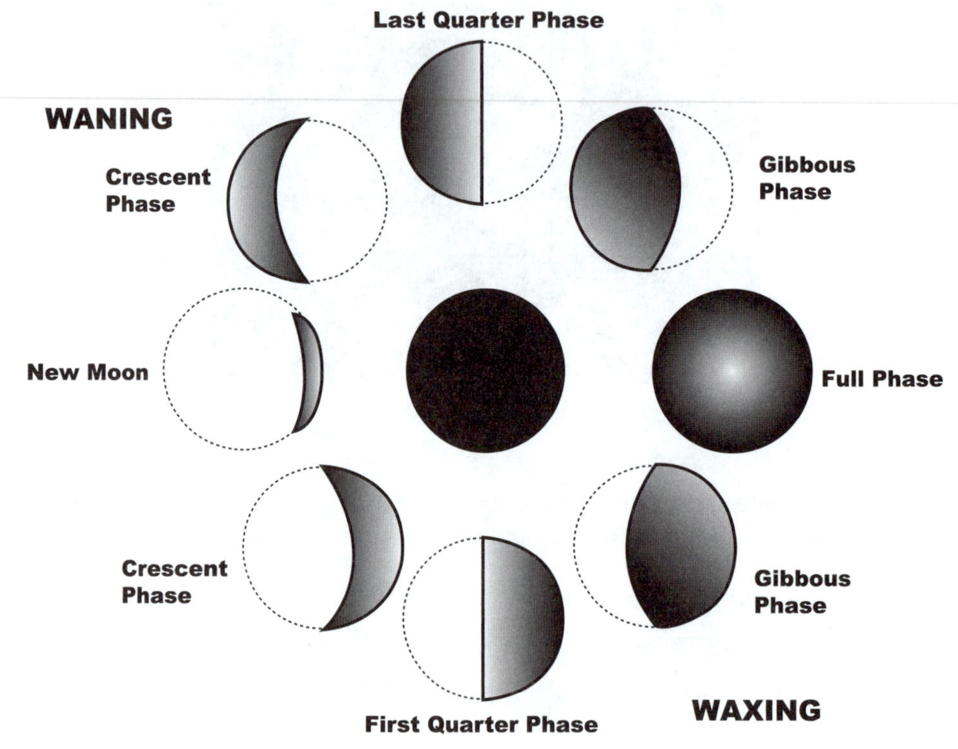

Figure 6.2. Phases of the moon.

To demonstrate that one can see the moon only when light is reflected, the following activities can be performed:

1. Darken the room, and use a flashlight to shine on a reflecting object. Use a mirror or bicycle reflector to demonstrate that the moon (reflector) does not give off its own light. It simply reflects light from the sun (flashlight).
2. To have children observe the phases of the moon, position a light up high; place a shiny ball (you can cover a ball with foil) so the light shines on the ball. Make certain that there is space in the room so children can walk around the ball slowly and observe how much of the ball is reflecting the light as they travel around the moon (ball).

Math/Science Processes Students can observe and classify objects in space (e.g., the moon). Students can observe and collect data about the moon.

Math Concepts Students can learn about collecting data from the moon. Students can also learn about the idea of parts and whole in relation to the moon's changing shapes and about the relationships between the sun, planets, moons, and stars.

Science Concepts Students can identify the patterns of the moon cycles and how these changes can affect their own personal lives.

Literature Connections

Brandley, F.M. (1987). *The moon seems to change.* New York: HarperCollins.

Coats, L.J. (1986). *Marcella and the moon.* New York: Macmillan.

Fowler, A. (1992). *So that's how the moon changes shape!* New York: Scholastic.

Gibbons, G. (1997). *The moon book.* New York: Holiday House.

Internet Resources

Can-Do, Phases of the Moon: http://www.can-do.com/science/moonphases/moonphases.html
This is an interactive site with which to order the moon phases.

Moon Connection, Phases of the Moon: http://www.moonconnection.com/moon_phases.phtml
Colorful diagrams provide an explanation of moon phases.

StarDate Online, Moon Phase Calculator: http://stardate.org/nightsky/moon/
This site will provide the moon phases for any given month.

Assessment Documentation Assessment documentation can include drawing the changes in moon reflections, making a moon phase flip book, or developing an electronic description of the moon phases.

Constellations Constellations are groups of stars that appear to form figures or shapes in the sky. People have looked at the stars for centuries, have given names to 88 constellations, and have made up stories about the figures in the sky. Due to the rotation of the earth, constellations will not always appear in same place. Before machines and technology were developed, the constellations were one of the guides for mariners, shepherds, and others exploring open seas and lands. Here are some activities involving constellations:

1. Visit a planetarium to learn about the constellations and changes during the seasons. A map or chart of the night sky would be an alternative to the planetarium. Look for shapes in the constellations. Encourage vocabulary development of the correct terminology of shapes and angles. Students can draw the constellations and connect the lines between the stars to show the shapes. Punch holes for the stars, glue or tape over a cylinder (e.g., oatmeal box), and shine a light through to represent the constellation at night. Students could also create a large mural of the night sky on black paper with white crayon or chalk (or create on individual black papers, and then connect papers) and hang it in the classroom.
2. Read Native American legends about the constellations. Create a class constellation and have children write myths about the constellation.

Math/Science Processes Students can observe and classify constellations. Students can observe and collect data about constellations and planets.

Math Concepts Students can learn about relationships between constellations, the moon, and planets.

Science Concepts Students can identify the patterns of the constellations.

Literature Connections

Barner, B. (2002). *Stars! Stars! Stars!* San Francisco: Chronicle Books.

Driscoll, M. (2004). *A child's introduction to the night sky.* New York: Black Dog & Leventhal.

Love, A., & Drake, J. (2004). *The kids' book of the night sky.* Tonawanda, NY: Kids Can Press.

Mitton, J. (1998). *Zoo in the sky: A book of animal constellations.* Washington, DC: National Geographic Society.

Sasaki, C. (2003). *The constellations: Stars and stories.* New York: Sterling.

Turnbull, S. (2003). *Usborne beginners: Sun, moon, and stars.* New York: Scholastic.

Internet Resources

Kids Astronomy: http://www.kidsastronomy.com/

Interactive and fun resources for kids to explore astronomy and space-related topics.

University of Wisconsin, Madison, Department of Astronomy, The Constellations and Their Stars: http://www.astro.wisc.edu/~dolan/constellations/constellations.html

Site provides sky charts and information about constellations.

NASA: http://www.nasa.gov

NASA home page contains pictures and links to information on space and objects in space.

NASA, The Space Place: http://spaceplace.nasa.gov/en/kids/st6starfinder/st6starfinder.shtml. Fun site to check out games, projects, and facts about Earth and space.

Assessment Documentation See other resources about documenting learning through pictures, charts, and science logs.

Physics and Engineering

Engineering is applying scientific knowledge to practical use, particularly in planning, designing, and construction of machinery, roads, bridges, buildings, and so forth. Physics is the science of the properties, changes, and interactions of matter and energy, so it has a natural interconnection with engineering. Young children, given the opportunity to work with building materials—both natural (e.g., sticks, rocks, sand) and manufactured (e.g., boxes, blocks, LEGOs)—naturally design and construct objects. These often serve as "sets" for creative play and interactions. Repeated opportunities to plan, build, and rebuild provide insight into both how shapes go together to form other shapes (geometry) and how to make the constructions meet other building variables (e.g., strength, stability, durability).

Simple Machines Levers, wedges, inclined planes, and pulleys are examples of simple machines that make work easier. A *lever* is a bar that pivots on a fixed point called a *fulcrum.* Sometimes the fulcrum is between the object being moved and the force (e.g., scissors, pliers, seesaw); some levers have the object between the fulcrum and the force (e.g., wheelbarrow, nutcracker) and others have the force between the object and the fulcrum (e.g., tweezers, shovel).

A *pulley* is a simple machine of a wheel with a rope moving around it to raise objects. An *inclined plane* (ramp) is a slanting surface on which to push, rather than lift, heavy objects, and a *wedge* is used to spread or raise an object (e.g., crowbar). Activities to help children understand the types and purposes of simple machines found in daily life are included in the next sections. The following are some activities involving simple machinery:

1. Invite a carpenter to visit the class with his or her tools and demonstrate how tools make work easier. Have students draw and label tools and relate them to simple machines.
2. Find an inclined plane (ramp); explore the difference in pushing a heavy object up the ramp versus lifting the object to the top.
3. Use a thick board (i.e., a lever, such as a leaf from an old table or a wooden board) and a brick (fulcrum). Place the brick at one end; the teacher stands at the other end. Then the teacher challenges the students to find a way to "lift" the teacher. Appoint certain students as "board standers," and use other students as spotters. Remind the students (if necessary) about which components of the lever can be altered.
4. Create a pulley with empty thread spools and twine, or you can use one of the LEGO pulley kits. Attach the pulley to a support by threading twine through the middle of the spool. At one end of the twine, attach a heavy weight; put the twine up over the pulley (spool). Attach the other end to a paper clip, which is then hooked through a rubber band. Attach the rubber band to a stable object (like a measuring stick). Pull on the measuring stick; measure the amount of "stretch" the rubber band takes to lift the weight.
5. Students can identify all the simple machines they see in their everyday world. They can also identify jobs or careers that use machines to facilitate the work.

Math/Science Processes Math and science processes include observation, classifying, comparing, contrasting, and then completing tests to answer questions about the effects of tools on work, and asking students to communicate their observations and thinking to others.

Math Concepts The math concepts being integrated would naturally include geometry and measurement. Because children are testing and gathering data, they would also be using the mathematical concepts of gathering and organizing data to be able to make conclusions about their science experiments.

Science Concepts Students will be investigating how machines affect effort and work, and how tools are used in everyday life. In the engineering and construction, they will be discovering how shapes affect strength of structures, and how shapes are used together to make new shapes and structures.

Literature Connections

Aliki. (1981). *Digging up dinosaurs.* New York: Harper Trophy.

Barton, B. (1987). *Machines at work.* New York: Thomas Y. Crowell.

Burton, V.L. (1976). *Mike Mulligan and his steam shovel.* New York: Houghton Mifflin.

Khalsa, D. (1987). *I want a dog.* New York: Clarkson N. Potter

Steig, W. (1982). *Dr. DeSoto.* New York: Farrar, Straus and Giroux.

Internet Resources

www.edtech.kennesaw.edu/web/simmach.html
This site teaches children about simple machines; includes other links.

Edheads, Simple Machines: http://www.edheads.org/activities/simple-machines/
This site includes ideas for teachers and interactive learning activities for children.

Assessment Documentation As with other construction learning, assessment should begin with children explaining their goal, using thought processes to think through their construction, and then documenting what they completed, using correct scientific and mathematical vocabulary. Photos can be taken to document the steps of the scientific process and the final construction. Teachers should provide checklists or rubrics to clarify expectations and to have children use those to assess their own learning.

The next step in assessment would be to have children draw and label their process; results could be organized into charts or graphs. Students would then be expected to state and write conclusions about their process and results. Checklists and rubrics should clarify expectations for both students and teachers to use in the assessment process.

Architects, Engineers, Construction, Properties of Materials

Humans and other animals have always built structures. These structures may be a form or house or building, a bridge, or abstractions for beauty or play. Strength and durability are two of the fundamental needs of structures.

Structures have changed over time, partly due to new options for building materials and tools. Other variables include weather and climate needs, and philosophical and cultural attitudes and beliefs about beauty and play. Here are some activities involving architects, engineers, construction, and properties of materials:

1. Go for a structure walk (looking at, e.g., houses, barns, fences, play equipment), with the objective of comparing and contrasting the structures by shapes, materials, structural frames, and beauty or ornate qualities. The walk could be a real neighborhood walk, or a picture or video walk. Look for dates and types of materials used as sources for comparison.
2. To determine which shapes are strongest, use any of the rods and connectors listed below to construct an enclosed shape (such as a house). Test strength by seeing how many same-weight books the structure will hold.
   a. Straws and string
   b. Cotton-tip swabs and rubber cement
   c. Tooth picks and peas, cranberries, or raisins
3. Using rolled newspaper and masking tape, construct a bridge across a gorge or water as in the story of the *Three Billy Goats Gruff.* Stress finding a shape that will not bend and buckle under weight and pressure.
4. Create a building using food items such as crackers and peanut butter or frosting, vegetable pieces, and toothpicks. Use knowledge about strength to determine how to put shapes together for strength.
5. As raw materials become more scarce, builders are looking at recycling materials for building. Research and create new building materials from junk items.
6. Use building blocks, attribute blocks, or any other building materials in the classroom to design a new zoo with animal houses and recreation areas.
7. Using any building materials available, construct a new playground or fun park. Remember that structural durability and safety are key factors in this design.

Literature Connections

Burton, V.L. (1942). *The little house.* Boston: Houghton Mifflin.

Dorros, A. (1992). *This is my house.* New York: Scholastic.

Holberman, M. (1978). *A house is a house for me.* New York: Viking.

McDonald, M. (1990). *Is this a house for a hermit crab?* New York: Orchard Books.

Wilder, L.I. (1932). *Little house in the big woods.* New York: Harper Collins.

Wilder, L.I. (1935). *Little house on the prairie.* New York: Harper Collins.

Wilder, L.I. (1937). *On the banks of plum creek.* New York: Harper Collins.

Folk Tales (multiple retellings and interpretations): *The Three Little Pigs* and *The Three Billy Goats Gruff*

Internet Resources

http://www.fastq.com/~jbpratt/education/thems/construction.html
This site includes ideas for activities and literature to integrate with construction ideas.

Assessment Documentation See earlier section on Physics and Engineering for assessment ideas.

Teacher Resources

Caney, S. (2006). *Steven Caney's ultimate building book.* Philadelphia: Running Press.

LEGO Educational Division. *Simple machine kits*. Enfield, CT: LEGO System Inc.

American Forest Foundation. (2007). *Project learning tree: Pre-K–8 environmental education activity guide.* Washington, D.C.: Author.

Council for Environmental Science. (2005). *Project wild: K–12 curriculum and activity guide.* Houston, TX: Author.

Summary

Geometry lies at the base of biology, astronomy, aerospace science, physics, engineering, and architecture. It should be learned in the early years because of its interrelationships with the sciences. The activities discussed in this chapter show how science and math process skills as well as science and math concepts have a synergic effect on each other when geometry is used as a base. The early childhood curriculum should give children the tools needed to thrive in the future by providing opportunities to develop spatial and geometric skills through the sciences.

Spatial Relationships and Technology

Today's children have grown up watching television and are highly oriented to visual learning. Children from birth to 8 years have a need to engage in visual spatial relationships, and such relationships sometimes help make visualizations become a reality. The National Council of Teachers of Mathematics (NCTM) and the National Association for the Education of Young Children (NAEYC) issued a joint position statement, *Early Childhood Mathematics Education: Promoting Good Beginnings,* which says that technology is a tool that is "essential to teaching and learning mathematics; it influences the mathematics that is taught and enhances students' learning" (2002, p. 3). Newer computer technologies, if developmentally appropriate, can enhance spatial development and visual spatial skills if used in conjunction with manipulatives to produce artistic designs and mathematical concepts.

While computers have enriched lives, they do not replace the tactile experiences and important interactions that can take place with media and blocks. Some computer programs have simulated the tools of the artist. These computer programs can be used to reinforce learning about media, the elements of art, and other spatial art concepts. Nevertheless, computer programs should never replace for children the tactile experience of experimenting with art media. Moreover, according to NAEYC standards for early childhood professional preparation (2001), teachers should be able to demonstrate knowledge about how to combine appropriate software with other teaching tools to integrate and reinforce learning of computers.

Some critics have stated that computers hinder creativity, but others argue they can enhance creativity. Sabbeth (1998) utilized the computer in combination with "hands on" experiences in her book of art activities for children ages 4 to 8. She says that a "cyber masterpiece" does not have to disappear when the off-switch is hit. When technology is used well with manipulatives and as a tool in the curriculum, technology can enhance creativity (Haugland, 1999, 2000). Many teachers also believe that certain software programs not only help children learn language but become a form of language (Clements & Sarama, 2003). The children in Reggio Emilia (see Chapter 4) use the computer as a form of language (Edwards, Gandini, & Forman, 1998).

Using a computer program such as Kid Pix Deluxe and other similar programs allows learners to see many designs through such maneuvers as cut, shrink, paste, mirror, blur, superimpose, symmetry, enlarge, terrace edges, magnify, rotate, and twirl. These skills are essential to spatial development.

Research on Virtual Manipulatives and Geometry

The computer aids the metacognitive aspects of spatial activity and can foster a deeper conceptual thinking whereby children explore shapes in a playful way and use them similarly to the ways in which they use their play objects (Clements & Battista, 1991; Johnson-Gentile, Clements, & Battista, 1994; Moyer-Packenham, Salkind, & Bolyard, 2005). Children are able to take shapes apart, transform them, and see them from different perspectives. Computers can help children carry out mathematical processes with shapes that they could not otherwise do with paper and pencil. Children might be able to construct symmetrical shapes on the computer, but not with pencil and paper (Clements & McMillen, 1996). Also, children are able to think about their motions while moving objects in computer programs; they do not think about their actions while solving a puzzle, because they do it intuitively. When guided, children can explain their motions (Clements and Battista, 1991; Johnson-Gentile et al., 1994) and use words such as *slide, flip, turn,* and later other words such as *shrink, symmetry, enlarge, magnify, rotate,* and *twirl.* Clements and Sarama (2005, 2008b, 2009) have recommended that actions and graphics be provided in a meaningful context, and that initial adult support and active mentoring be a part of the learning when using computers with young children. If software is to be effective for spatial and geometric development, software should provide as much manipulative power as possible so that the child has control.

According to Clements and Sarama (2005, 2008b; Sarama & Clements, 2002), effective software should provide meaningful context for children, be at the appropriate reading level, give children some sense of independence after the initial help by the teachers, and give some corrective feedback. Software should also provide the potential for the child to invent something new and allow for more than one correct response.

Using software wisely can increase student learning. Although there are many mathematical software programs on the market, most of these fall into the categories of drill work, "edutainment," and exploratory. Although the exploratory type can be beneficial, children unfortunately only explore on the surface level (Sarama & Clements, 2002). The Building Blocks Curriculum by Clements and Sarama (2004), a software-enhanced mathematical curriculum addressing the NCTM Standards (2000), integrates technology activities with off-computer activities. It helps teachers provide a connection between off- and on-computer activities, and there are extensive sections on geometry. It is designed to integrate three types of media: computers, manipulatives, and print.

Online resources for math manipulatives have become readily available. A very effective use of virtual manipulatives that utilizes the National Library of Virtual Manipulatives was demonstrated by Rosen and Hoffman (2009) using construction of houses with three-dimensional objects and then representing the houses through drawing, sorting two-dimensional shapes, and then drawing a house with the two-dimensional shapes on the computer. Using the virtual manipulatives to reinforce sorting shows how a combination of real physical manipulatives (Clements & Sarama, 2003) and onscreen virtual manipulatives is more effective than either one alone and how it reinforces some of the NCTM Focal Point Connections for First Grade (2006):

> Children compose and decompose plane and solid figures (e.g., by putting two congruent isosceles triangles together to make a rhombus), thus building an understanding of part–whole relationships as well as the properties of the original and composite shapes. As they combine figures, they recognize them from different perspectives and orientations, describe their geometric attributes and properties, and determine how they are alike and different, in the process developing a background for measurement and initial understandings of such properties as congruence and symmetry. (NCTM Focal Points, p. 26)

Using Computers in the Classroom to Enhance Spatial Concepts in Math

Many of the tools in two- and three-dimensional geometric forms are now available online through web sites, which are cheaper to use than a purchased computer program. The following are web sites or programs that could be used to demonstrate geometric and mathematical concepts through virtual manipulatives or that can lead to virtual manipulatives in the geometric and spatial areas:

The Eyeballing Game (http://woodgears.ca/eyeball/): The Eyeballing Game works by showing a series of geometries that need to be adjusted a little to make them correct. Children can move lines and shapes and experience transformations and rotations.

Fun Brain (http://www.funbrain.com/numbers.html): This web site offers games for kids and resources for parents and teachers. There are lots of games focusing on various concepts and there are links to other math sites. The site includes lesson plans and a homework relief center. There are geometry sites.

Math Playground (http://www.mathplayground.com/thinkingblocks.html): Thinking Blocks is an interactive math tool developed by classroom teachers to help students learn how to solve word problems. Children have to look beyond the surface to solve problems.

Math-U-See (http://www.mathusee.com): This grades K–12 math program uses visuospatial methods to teach mathematics.

A Maths Dictionary for Kids, by Jenny Eather (http://www.teachers.ash.org.au/jeather/maths/dictionary.html): This is an interactive dictionary word game for kids that includes math examples in geometry.

National Library of Virtual Manipulatives (http://www.nlvm.usu.edu/en/nav/vLibrary.html): This site makes available, at no charge, interactive web-based virtual manipulatives for math instruction, grades K–2. It offers many manipulatives in the five areas of number and operations: algebra, geometry, measurement, data analysis, and probability. Especially noteworthy are the virtual manipulatives related to geometry. There are manipulatives for attribute blocks, attribute trains, congruent triangles, geoboards, pattern blocks, pentominoes, platonic solids, three-dimensional blocks, tangrams, tessellations, and many transformation types of materials.

Northeast and the Islands Regional Technology in Education Consortium (NEIRTEC) (www.neirtec.org/activities/math_portal.htm): This site links educational leaders at the state, district, and school levels and addresses the challenges of putting technology to use. NEIRTEC shows how to get to virtual manipulatives web sites. It has some spatial and geometry sites.

Primary Games Candy Land (www.primarygames.com/downloads/doracandyland/index.htm): This web site includes many puzzles, patterning activities, and shapes.

Primary Games Carnival (www.primarygames.com/math/carnival/start.htm): This site has geometry games.

Shodor Interactivate (www.shodor.org/interactivate/activities): This is a national resource to improve math and science education through modeling and simulation technologies. Shodor Interactivate has more than 155 activities for grades K–12.

Using Computers in the Classroom to Enhance Spatial and Artistic Work

Art software promotes very creative behaviors as well as very mechanical behaviors. The following are good questions to ask before buying software in order to promote creative thinking in the area of art and spatial development:

1. Is there a way for children to experiment?

2. Are children able to expand their knowledge of the elements (line, color, shape, texture) and principles of design?
3. Is the quality of marks unique or unusual so that personal and not stereotypic figures can be drawn or painted?
4. Are the users able to elaborate or extend the visual representations into something of visual complexity or into artistically unique productions?
5. Are children able to problem solve?

There are computerized coloring books, such as Crayola Magic 3D Coloring Book by IBM, that fulfill the need to "fill in" rather than have the child draw and create on his or her own. Others, such as Orly's Draw-A-Story (for ages 5–10 years) from Broderbund, provide animated and highly interactive illustrations. Orly's Draw-A-Story also enables drawing and coloring, which promote creativity. Nick-O-Matic Design Studio (Mattel Media) may be good for craft lovers, but is not conducive to developmentally appropriate art. Because teachers are typically unsure of their own skills, they often do not critically evaluate educational software. Animation, graphics, and music may distract from the objectives that the teacher had in mind. It should be noted that if the purpose is to promote creative art, children should be creating with different media, lines, shapes, and textures. Just because software offers paint or color does not mean that it may be helpful in producing creative behaviors in the child. The software must stimulate creative growth in the child rather than merely enabling the child to make something that looks great. It is most important to keep in mind that computer interactions cannot replace working with real paint or other media. They can, however, enhance the child's learning experiences.

Using Computers in the Classroom to Promote Map Reading

Children can learn to read virtual maps or actually create computer-generated maps. Today, software programs such as Snyder's Neighborhood Map-Machine provide line drawings that can be printed out, cut, folded, and glued together to form 3-D models of buildings with different shapes. Children can actually create neighborhoods and cities using this software. Google Earth, downloadable from www.earth.google.com, will help primary-grades children see spatial features of the earth and look at places anywhere in the world from a bird's eye view. MapQuest, www.mapquest.com, can be used too. Make-A-Map 3D, available from Learning Ladder, will help children make their own virtual map—not just see one. This helps the child experience spatial mapping as it happens.

Software Evaluation

There are many software programs on the market and it is important to evaluate them for high quality and developmental appropriateness. Haugland

and Shade's Software Evaluation Scale (1997) has been used to evaluate developmental appropriateness of software for a number of years. It looks at whether children are active learners while using the software, whether the children are able to successfully use the software, and whether the software is developmentally appropriate.

Other information on how to evaluate developmental appropriateness of software can be found at the following web sites:

SuperKids Educational Software Review (www.superkids.com/aweb/pages/aboutsks.html): SuperKids provides reviews and ratings of educational software, practical and fun educational tools for online and offline use, news about important educational issues, and views of visionaries and policymakers.

Review Corner (www.reviewcorner.com): This site provides comprehensive reviews of the best children's educational products, including computer software, books, music, videos and DVDs, toys, and games.

TEEM (www.teem.org.uk/): This site gives teachers advice and guidance on educational software.

Rate It All! (www.rateitall.com/t-854-childrens-educational-software.aspx): This portion of the site gives a ranked rating for children's educational software on the market. Teachers can post their own rating or give feedback to request that another program be added to the list.

Summary

Computer technology can help children think spatially in the mathematical, geographic, and artistic fields. Children can learn to make spatial figures and maps with many different media. Used in conjunction with concrete objects, computers can increase spatial and geometric knowledge in mathematics and can contribute to the visual world in which children are living. Adult support and mentoring are both important; therefore, teachers should be trained as guides to encourage creativity, problem solving, and correct use of technical language. (See Appendix F for a list of software that promotes challenging learning experiences in the arts.)

Where Are All the Blocks?

Blocks can be used as a tool to integrate a curriculum so that all subject matter can be studied. Blocks have always been a part of preschool and kindergarten, but teachers sometimes do not recognize the value of block play (Wellhousen & Kieff, 2001; Zacharos, Koliopoulos, Dokomaki, & Kassoumi, 2007). It is significant and worth noting that children gain a great deal from block play. MacDonald (2001) listed 29 mathematics and 20 science concepts and skills that children can develop through block playing. Furthermore, MacDonald (2001) as well as Hirsch (1996) showed how block play can contribute to literacy, social development, and learning about art, science, and social studies. Many teachers have a prescribed academic curriculum to teach and do not provide concrete objects like blocks for children to explore cognitive and spatial concepts. This chapter looks at how a teacher can guide children's interest in block play to promote academic achievement.

Research on Block Play

Block-play performance has shown a significant relationship to spatial thinking and mathematical thinking. Wolfgang, Stannard, and Jones (2001) found that children's block-play performance in preschool is a predictor of mathematics achievement in middle school and high school. Golbeck (2005) has studied the complexity of unit-block construction in relation to performance on spatial knowledge and graphic skill in writing and drawing. Block-building skill scores have been related to other measures of spatial thinking such as problem solving, drawing, and writing (Golbeck, 2005). Seo and Ginsburg (2004) have found that preschool children, at least intuitively, use many sophisticated geometric concepts in block play that are usually taught in elementary school. Park, Chae, and Boyd (2008) also found that young children's block play with mathematical tasks promoted math skills, which may lay the foundation for later math learning. Graphics and diagrams can also be used to promote spatial visualization and perspective taking (Szechter & Liben, 2003). Many different types of graphics can be used with LEGO blocks, Cuisenaire rods, and Unifix cubes to promote spatial development. A perusal of the toys shows that most of them do have diagrams or examples that show children how to construct. Clements (2004) and Sarama and Clements (2004) have taken this one step further and have created a math computer program integrating math and pattern blocks.

Research by Clements and Sarama (2007a, 2007c) and Klibanoff, Levine, Huttenlocher, Vasilyeva, and Hedges (2006) has shown that involvement by teachers in a discussion of mathematical ideas during block play can influence the math abilities of children as well as future play of the children. Effective teacher training is also important. Research by Kersh, Casey, and Young (2008) found that teachers should have planned, systematic block building in their curriculum, but many do not do this. When learning trajectories were used and a developmental progression for block-play concepts was followed, more learning took place (Kersh, Casey, & Young, 2008). Research has found that the major difference between children from different socioeconomic backgrounds is not the ability to use blocks or other spatial objects but the ability to solve problems with language and explain their thinking using blocks (Jordan, Huttenlocher, & Levine, 1992; Sophian, 2002). A teacher who recognizes the importance of blocks will provide many opportunities for the child to discuss ideas and clarify thinking while playing with blocks.

Block Building Advocates

Friedrich Froebel, Maria Montessori, and Caroline Pratt were educators who emphasized block building. While Froebel and Montessori had more prescribed ways of using block materials, they both emphasized methods of allowing children's creative self-expression to develop. Caroline Pratt's way of using block materials emphasized free expression. She was known for Pratt's Unit System, a set of blocks based on the proportion of 1:2:4—half as high as they are wide, and twice as long as they are wide. Basic shapes of Pratt's Unit Blocks are shown in Photo 8.1.

How Blocks Are Important

The following vignette illustrates how important blocks are to some children. In this story, the teacher realizes the importance of blocks and is sensitive to the student's work in a pre-K class:

Photo 8.1. Unit blocks provide the most flexibility for building structures. (Photo courtesy of Community Playthings, © 2009; reprinted with permission.)

"Not again," Tyrone said with a sigh when Mrs. Conway told the children it was time to pick up their things and come to the literacy area for a story. Tyrone had been busy creating a beautiful building in the block area and wanted to continue his work. He told Mrs. Conway he was building a new house for his mom and dad to live in. It had many details: bedrooms, a garage, a kitchen. He told her that he had to keep working so his family would have a place to sleep that night.

Mrs. Conway realized how important this building was for this young child, so she asked the class to meet in the block area so Tyrone could hear the story while he worked. He listened intently as Mrs. Conway told a story about how builders know where all the rooms go when they are building. At the end of the day, Mrs. Conway told Tyrone that his building could stay up overnight so he could work on it again the next day. The next day Tyrone got a paper and pencil and went to the block area. He then drew the plans of the house he had built. Next he challenged his friend José to build a house like his by following his drawings. When the second house was built, Tyrone began to understand how builders really build houses.

Mrs. Conway had perceived that by letting Tyrone continue with his work instead of joining a large group, he would be free to express himself creatively. In fact, she even changed her rule of having everyone pick things up when it was time to read a story. Mrs. Conway now only reads stories to those who are interested in joining the story time.

Tyrone and José began to ask the teacher many questions about building. José's father worked in construction, so Mrs. Conway invited Mr. Sanchez into the classroom to answer such questions as why we need a roof on top, what the pipes are for, what the wires are for, and what keeps the house warm. He answered these questions as he helped the children who were working in cooperative groups build complicated houses of blocks.

Given the time and encouragement from mentors like Mr. Sanchez and Mrs. Conway, Tyrone and José grew in their imagination, creativity, and spatial development.

Their houses began to look different and their buildings began to be more creative and imaginative.

In order to enhance her students' learning, the teacher decided to learn more about the history of block building, the stages of block building, and how block building can be integrated into literacy, math, science, art, and social studies. Mrs. Conway also learned how to enhance the language and thought of the children at the block play area. The next section lists some ways to enhance building for children in your classes. Many of these activities could be used with students like Tyrone and José.

Using Blocks

A wide variety of types of blocks and other manipulative materials should be used in the block area to help children represent geometric forms (Clements & McMillen, 1996). Blocks are to be manipulated by children. As the renowned architect Frank Lloyd Wright put it, "Using the smooth, shapely maple blocks with which to build, there was a sense of what to build, a sense of which never afterwards left the fingers: so [that] form became feeling" (1932, p. 11). The quote shows the power of the materials that the artist long remembered. Blocks can be integrated into the disciplines of literacy, math, science, social studies, art, and music. The teacher needs to be aware of how to accomplish this using the skills and content standards. Collaborations with other children can take place in the block area, especially where there are hollow and unit blocks; such collaborations cannot always take place in other learning areas.

Stages of Block Play

Because block play likely has been a part of the child's natural play, it is important for the teacher to guide children in their developmental level of block play. The teacher's role is to carefully observe the children and enhance their play with questions. The seven developmental stages of block play (Johnson, 1966)—carrying, building, bridging, enclosing, making decorative patterns, naming, and symbolizing—are explained in the next sections. Through these seven stages, children are able to master many skills and perform many important building tasks with guidance from the teacher.

Stage 1: Carrying Blocks are carried around by children but not used for construction. This stage applies to the very young child, approximately age 2. In this stage, it is important for the child to experience how the blocks feel. Teachers can ask, "Are they smooth or rough?" Lightly put a block against a child's skin. "Are the blocks heavy?" Put one block in one hand and one in the other. "Which one is bigger? Are they the same or different?" Put blocks in the box and take them out. "Did you put a lot of blocks in the box?" Children can be supplied with boxes or baskets to take blocks from one place to another.

Stage 2: Building Building usually begins at the beginning of age 3. Children make mostly rows, either horizontal or vertical (with much repetition). In this stage, allow children to stack blocks. Stacking can be done in many ways. One way is by stacking blocks vertically. Children can use the same kind of blocks and stack blocks upward, making sure the blocks do not fall down. Children can also stack blocks across on the floor horizontally. This is the beginning of seeing something from another viewpoint. At this stage, children should realize the spatial concept of *on* (Kamii, Miyakawa, & Kato, 2004). Teachers can ask the following questions: "Can you make a long block that is the same size? Are there as many blocks on the ground as there are in the air?" Simple pattern cards can be supplied so children can have ideas for stacking. Words indicating location and position that can be used include *on, off, on top of, over, under, next to,* and *between*.

Stage 3: Bridging *Bridging* is the concept of using two blocks with a space between them connected by a third block to form a roof or a bridge. Helping children move to this stage is important; it occurs around age 3. The teacher may need to put up two vertical blocks, and ask children to put another block on top. Once children master this initial concept, the teacher can let the children experiment by using sidepieces that are larger or smaller. The teacher can see if the children can make the sides of a bridge using two blocks. The teacher can ask the students how high they can make the bridge without it falling down. The student can then create a small space between the vertical blocks. The teacher can ask the students, "What does the bridge look like now? What goes on a bridge? Is the bridge over water or land? Who goes over the bridge? Who goes under the bridge?" The teacher can ask children to construct an arch bridge. The teacher can explain that an arch's beauty comes from its smooth curves. Its strength comes from carrying weight in both directions. The teacher can also ask students to make a tunnel. The teacher can ask children to think about a tunnel they have been in and continue with related questions such as, "Did the tunnel have sides? Did it have a cover? What goes in a tunnel? How is a tunnel different from a bridge?" Pictures of bridges and blue poster paper with boats can be used for props.

Stage 4: Enclosing Enclosures involve placing blocks in such a way that they enclose a space; children start making enclosures when they are around age 4. The concept of *enclosure* is important in understanding space. The teacher can ask students to make a shape with four blocks that are the same size. The teacher should then ask the students to name that shape. Students can be directed to create another enclosed shape with two blocks the same size and two blocks that are longer. Again, the teacher can then ask the students to name that shape. The children can use blocks of many sizes and shapes to make an enclosure, and the children can then make their own enclosure with many different sizes and shapes. The teacher can ask the students to get in and out of their enclosures. The teacher can ask the students the following questions: "Does your enclosure have a door? Can you make the walls higher? Can you change the shape of your enclosure?" Children can also create a shape with three blocks that are the same size. The teacher can provide something to place inside the children's enclosures, such as toy farm animals, zoo animals, cars, or furniture. Spatial words to use include *on, off, on top of, over, under, in, out, into, out of, top, bottom, up, down, forward, near, far, short, long, large,* and *small.*

Stage 5: Making Decorative Patterns In this stage, children at age 4 or 5 make decorative patterns in the structure they are building. They incorporate many different things into the structure. This is the stage when the teacher uses names of shapes, such as *square, rectangle, triangle, pentagon,* and *octagon.* The teacher should allow children to make patterns, both horizontally and vertically. The teacher can also talk about concepts of *long, short,* and *curves,* and help children see transformations, such as having a square turn into two triangles or a having a square made up of four triangles. It helps to show this on paper first. These same triangles can be made into a parallelogram. Can the children make a solid rectangle using both long and short blocks? The child can make an AB pattern, an ABA pattern, and an AABB pattern. The teacher can provide labels to identify what the structure is and large paper to record what the child says about the building. The teacher can also provide books or pictures of famous buildings. Spatial terms that should be identified are *forward, backward, around, through, sideways, across, back and forth,* and *straight*. Also, spatial words that have been previously used should be reviewed.

Stage 6: Naming Naming of structures for dramatic play begins at age 4½. This is where children are thinking of a structure that they would like to build. Some suggestions for structures that children can build are a grocery store, a house, or a McDonald's. The teacher should ask questions such as, "What needs to be added to your building? Do you need to redesign your building to accommodate those changes? What else can you use?" Again, the teacher needs to help children discover two-dimensional and three-dimensional shapes. Four triangles can make a square. Four of the large triangles make a rhombus. A square and two triangles make a parallelogram. The teacher should ask the students, "What can make a trapezoid?" Before this stage, children may have named their structures, but the names were not necessarily related to the purpose of the building. The teacher should ask the students what else can be added to their buildings. Continue to use spatial words.

Stage 7: Symbolizing Children's buildings often reproduce or symbolize actual structures that they know, and this sets the stage for dramatic play at age 5. This occurs when there is group play, and the group negotiates on something to build. The group decides what they are going to build (tall building, stadium, castle, or store). The teacher can ask the group the following questions: "What jobs do people have? Who is the leader? What design do you want to make? Sometimes someone can think of a better idea. Can we listen to the idea? Can we change things to accommodate new ideas? What patterns and shapes do we need? What things do we want in your building (i.e., people, trees, cars, trucks)? Do you need a map? Do you need to make a map or blueprint? Can you tell another group about the structure? Can you write a story about your structure?"

An example of reinforcing this stage was demonstrated by a teacher who had an open house to show off the new building the children had made. She invited parents and had the children share with the parents what they had constructed. In a kindergarten room, where there were morning and afternoon classes, a display of children's work was left up by the morning class for the afternoon class to see and vice versa.

In this final stage, the following architectural terms should be used by students: *beam, angle, arch, area, buttress, circumference, curves, column, plane, tunnel, bridge, door, foundation, ramp, roof, tower, blueprint, steeple, balance, patterns, chimney,* and *window.*

Activities for Blocks

There are many ways blocks can be integrated into the curriculum. A wonderful book to introduce blocks is *Block City* (Stevenson, 2005). It is a poem by Robert Louis Stevenson that has been reproduced in book form and illustrated by Daniel Kirk. It shows a nostalgic but quite wonderful celebration of the imagination of a young boy who creates block cities, mills, harbors, palaces, towers, and ships in his living room. The boy tears down his buildings but remembers them in his mind. The discussion that follows offers activities that can be used with unit blocks, although this does not preclude other types of blocks from being used with the unit blocks. In particular, the activities described in the section on art activities show many types of blocks that can be created from materials already found in the house.

Language Arts Activities

Listening, speaking, reading, and writing can be integrated into block play, and children can naturally learn language and literacy skills as they play with blocks. Blocks can help provide a high-quality educational environment that is purposefully rich in language, books, and writing, thereby integrating the National Council of Teachers of English (NCTE) and the International Reading Association (IRA)'s standards for the English language arts (NCTE/IRA, 2003).

Recreate Parts of a Story with Blocks Teachers can place books on the block shelf for easy reference. If children are building houses, as in the example about Tyrone and José given earlier in this chapter, the teacher can provide informational books such as *How a House Is Built* by Gail Gibbons (1990). This book describes how a house is built with help from architects, heavy equipment operators, carpenters, plumbers, and others. In this book, children are introduced to log cabins, stone houses, adobe houses, cement block houses, brick houses, glass houses, and frame houses as well as the simple shelters of the past including caves, earth huts, bark huts, grass huts, igloos, teepees, and tents. Technical terms for parts of homes can be demonstrated and used as a reference by the teacher.

Children can be exposed to houses from other cultures in *Wonderful Houses Around the World* by Yoshio Komatsu (2004) and in a similar book, *True Book of Houses* by Katherine Carter (1982). All different types of houses from many cultures are described in these books. The teacher can discuss the fact that construction workers help build homes but they also build skyscrapers, schools, hospitals, stadiums, airports, train stations, and other places. Some interesting books to motivate children to build other buildings besides homes are listed in Appendix F. It is important for the teacher to expose children to fiction, informational nonfiction, and biographies of people associated with building, particularly the informational books.

Use Labels Teachers can use labels to identify the structures children are building *(house, church, grocery store, zoo, farm, car wash, drive-in restaurant, boat dock, tall building with tower, rows, patterns, spaces, columns, airport, bridge, train station, skyscraper, castle, city, city of the future, stadium, plane, stop sign).* These labels help the child to see that print represents a physical space.

Create a Language Experience Chart Teachers can have students create a language experience chart with the blocks. The teacher should write out the story that the children tell about the building. Let the children describe what they have built and what the others have built. If possible, the teacher should take a picture of the structure and try to leave it up indefinitely. The next day the teacher can reread the story and keep a collection of the stories of the class.

Make a Blueprint Teachers can have students make a blueprint of the rooms after the children have completed the structure so that they can see it on paper. Discuss the difference between the actual model, the photograph, and the blueprint.

Make Task Cards The teacher can make task cards for children to read. For instance, the teacher can think of an occurrence that just happened in a book that could be recreated in the block area. The teacher can write this on a card. Examples of task cards might include the following: 1) Make a door for your house, 2) Make three windows for your house, or 3) Put a roof on your house. If the children cannot read, the teacher can place a rebus picture above the words. The teacher can suggest that the children recreate the picture with blocks. The teacher should look at the frequently used word list and try to write the words on the chart that are appropriate while pointing to the words as they are said.

Art Activities

The National Visual Arts Standards (National Art Education Association, 1994) can be integrated into block play. The first standard, "understanding and applying media," is obviously addressed in block play because the techniques and processes of using blocks are emphasized. Children can also address the second standard, "using knowledge of structures and functions." They are learning how to use block structures to communicate their ideas.

Make a Design The teacher can have students make a design with the blocks. The students can transfer the design to paper, recreating it using precut pieces of construction paper or by drawing and coloring it.

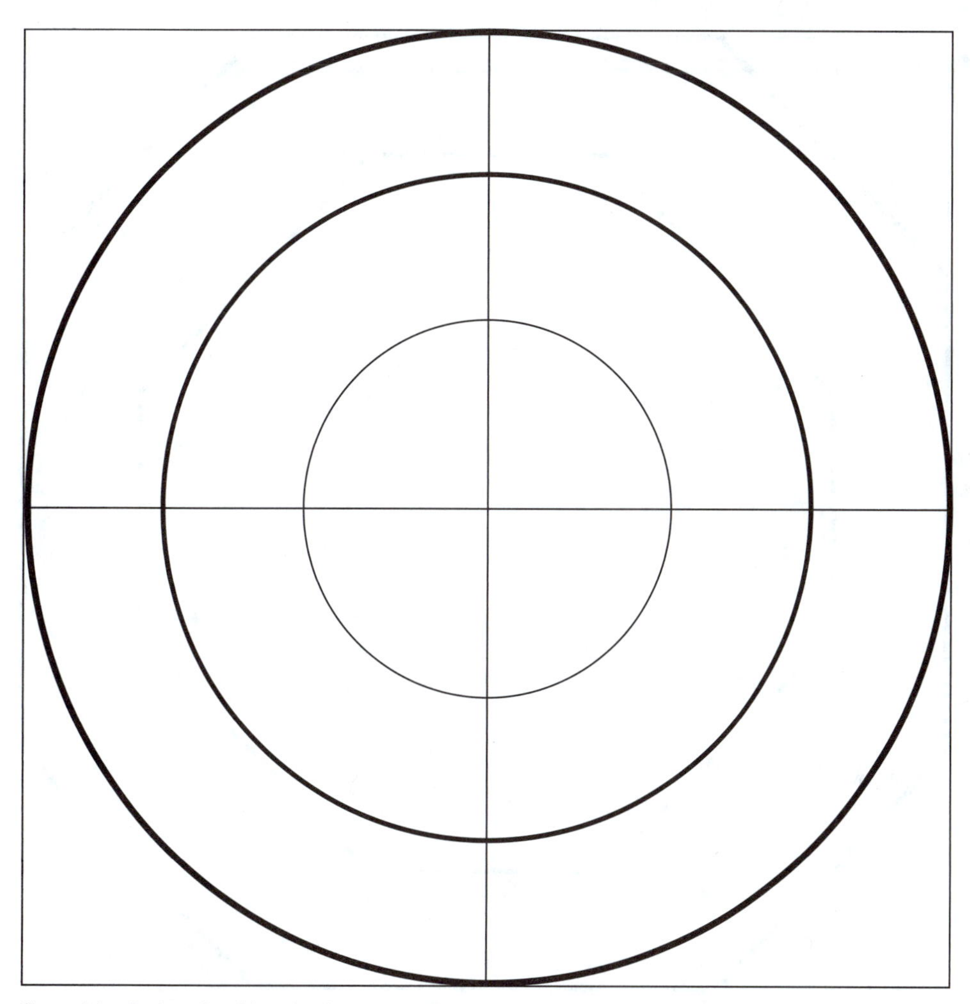

Figure 8.1. Designs for cities: circular.

Promote Construction Art grid work designs can be provided on a sheet to promote construction. (See examples of grid work in Appendix B.) A 5-foot by 5-foot grid work, similar to the small grid works of Froebel, can be used to develop complex cities. Children can design the city around these grid works and develop creative designs for their cities. The teacher should discuss why cities are designed in different ways, such as the circular design of cities shown in Figure 8.1 and the octagonal design of cities shown in Figure 8.2.

Make Blocks Children can make their own blocks by using various sizes of empty milk cartons. The boxes can be covered with construction paper or the teacher can paint them first with acrylic house paint and then let the children paint them with tempera paint. To make giant blocks, children need corrugated boxes that can be modular or arbitrary. These can be used for structures the child can stand in. Other empty boxes of varying sizes (preferably small ones like macaroni boxes) should also be provided. The teacher should supply glue, rubber cement, adhesive tape, masking tape, scissors,

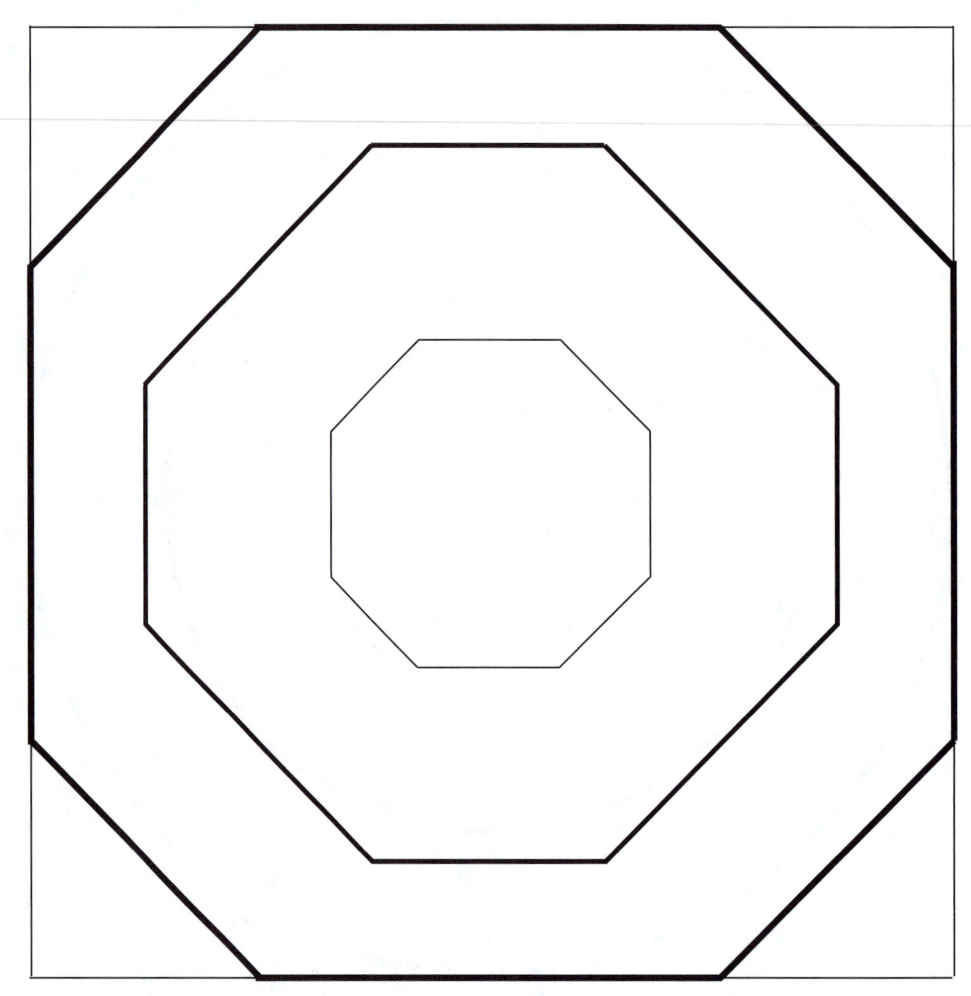

Figure 8.2. Designs for cities: octagonal.

string, and yarn. The children may choose any of the containers they wish and fasten them together however they decide.

Make a Tower Tubes from toilet paper or food wrapping paper can be collected. After children bring in 100 toilet paper tubes and tubes from food wraps, the tubes can be painted or decorated. As tubes are added to a structure, it can taper to a tower on top by using smaller and smaller tubes. If a more permanent structure is wanted, four slits can be made in the sides in exactly the same place to connect the tubes.

Make a Sculpture The teacher can provide wood block scraps and wood glue for the children to make their own sculpture of a building, tower, statue, or furniture. Having a natural medium helps the child experience building with blocks straight from nature.

Match the Shape The teacher can trace around the shape of several blocks and have children match the shape. They can trace and then play games to see who can find the correct block to place in the puzzle. (This activity is good to use with young children learning shape recognition.)

Build a Structure The teacher can have students build a structure using only triangular prisms, cubes, rectangular prisms, or a combination of certain three-dimensional shapes. She can refer back to the three-dimensional shapes they have seen before.

Build a Tower for a Doll Children can build a tower as tall as a doll. After the tower is built, the children can then draw a picture of the tower, and give it to the doll. They can extend this activity to building a tower as tall as a person and seeing if the person is exactly as tall as the tower.

Make a Sequence Children can trace around various blocks that form a sequence. Children can be asked to match actual blocks with the drawn sequence.

***Read* Goldilocks and the Three Bears** The teacher can read the story of *Goldilocks and the Three Bears* to the children. The teacher can have the children build the house in the story by carefully constructing the rooms and the furniture in order to recreate the story.

Take an Architectural Nature Tour The teacher can have children go outside and look at nature. Children can study nature by looking at the curves in nuts (such as walnut shells, smooth pecan shells, the openings in pistachio shells), at the ridges in clam shells, at the curved shells of crustaceans like lobsters and shrimps, and at the shells of eggs. Then they can discover these designs in buildings by going on a second field trip in the community. Lastly, the children can try to construct some of these designs with blocks and accessories. Trace around the blocks to form various animals and habitats. Let the children use the blocks to create the exact design.

The students can also see where animals live. Each animal home has marvelous designs to divulge. The children can look up in the trees for nests and look down in the dirt for ant mazes. The children can also look for the bees' nest with hexagonal shapes and for the spider's web. Some animals in the water, such as snails and turtles, have mobile homes attached to them, which can be observed. The beavers make their homes by cutting down the wood themselves, making a dam, and making fortresses with tunnels for protection. Beavers cut trees, bring the branches to the structure, and pile mortar from mud. They might even have an "architect" who helps design the structure. Children can come back to the block structure to make something similar to what they have seen in nature. For instance, they might make a maze of tunnels like the beaver does, or a mobile home like the turtle or clam have, or a spider web design of a city.

Math Activities

Blocks provide a synergetic effect for promoting the prekindergarten to grade 3 National Council of Teachers of Mathematics (NCTM) Curriculum Focal

Points (2006; see Appendix E), because the blocks enable children to almost naturally understand the concepts of quantity and ordering and to examine shapes and objects and distinguish, classify, and sort them. Children have to think about size, shape, thickness, length, and height. The Curriculum Focal Points (NCTM, 2006) give teachers a consensus for mathematics benchmarks at particular grade levels. A focused curriculum allows the teacher to commit more time to topics that have been deemed important by experts at the national level. Because block building with unit blocks generally involves experimentation, through which children construct their own knowledge, it is imperative that the teacher be versed in both the standards and the focal points at several grade levels. This ensures that he or she can enhance children's knowledge with activities in line with the standards and focal points.

Compare Sets In preschool, children develop the ability to count by using one-to-one correspondence and comparing number sets, an activity that helps children understand numeration. Children can use blocks to develop skill in comparing number sets. For example, a child may have two sets, A and B, with a different amount of blocks in each set. To develop skill in this area, the teacher could ask the following questions: "Are the sets the same? If the sets are not the same, how could you make them equal? How many more blocks does set A have than set B?" Children can also order the number of blocks in the sets from small to large number of blocks. This activity provides skill in numbers and operations.

As children progress in kindergarten, they use both cardinal and ordinal numbers, and develop ways of counting not just "1, 2, 3, 4, 5," but by looking at a set of five and seeing three and counting "4, 5" from the larger of two sets. The teacher demonstrates how to keep track of what has been counted. Ordinal numbers can be used to describe blocks in a tower; for example, the first block in the tower would be the largest one while the sixth block would be the smallest one. Questions that teachers may ask while the children are playing with blocks include "How many blocks did you use? Which side of your house has more blocks? How many blocks did you take away? How many people are staying at your house? How many blocks did you use to build this room? How many more do you need to finish it?"

Find Shapes Children in preschool learn spatial perspective by finding shapes in the environment, describing them, and then constructing them to learn about shape. An appropriate activity is to trace and match shapes from various geometric shapes drawn by the teacher on a piece of poster paper. The child is asked to place a block over the picture, making this a self-checking task for the child. This activity helps children learn geometry and spatial sense.

Provide Sequencing Activities Another activity to help children learn geometric shapes is a sequencing task. Sequencing activities can be structured on prepared poster board with traced shapes. A pattern of block shapes would be repeated once. Then children would continue that sequence by placing the appropriate blocks on the poster board. Using this activity, children learn to recognize particular properties of the blocks and also to focus on a certain attribute the blocks have in common.

Children can combine the three-dimensional shapes such as cubes, rectangular prisms, triangular prisms, and cylinders. They can look at them from different perspectives. The teacher can help children discover how two triangles can be combined to form a rectangle or a square and four triangles can be combined to make a square or how two triangles can become another triangle. The more advanced students can see how two triangles joined to make a square also produce a parallelogram or a trapezoid if transformations are made, or similarly, how two squares and four triangles can produce a hexagon. Children need to see how one-half units make one unit and how four quarter units can make one unit.

Children can make tall buildings and determine why the higher building might not have as many pieces of wood as the lower building even though it is taller. This is demonstrated by the fact that four small triangles make a square. Two squares and four small triangles make a hexagon; and two triangles joined to a square can make a parallelogram or a trapezoid.

Children can learn space position concepts such as the following by using blocks and accessories: *on/off; on top of, over, under; in, out, into, out of; top, bottom; above/below; in front of/in back of; beside, by, next; between.* As they build structures, children can learn direction words such as *up, down; forward, backward, around, through; to, from; toward, away from; sideways; across.* As children build a city with many buildings, they can learn relative distance concepts such as *near, far; close to, far from.* They can learn how to rearrange parts in the block structure until the parts fit.

To develop the concept of transformation, the teacher can ask questions like "Can you make other shapes from these two triangles? What other shapes can you make from these four triangles? What other way could you use these triangles in your building?"

Look at Block Structures from Different Perspectives The teacher can have children look at their block structures from different perspectives and describe what they see. The children can be encouraged to look at the top and side of the structure and recreate it from the bottom on paper.

Take Measurements Children have a difficult time seeing that the length of two identical blocks if placed in different positions remains the same. To understand this, children need to place the blocks in several positions. The process of measurement makes children aware of space that is needed, in terms of height, length, and area. To help children understand the concept of height, they could be asked to construct a tower as tall as they are. The teacher could ask the following questions: "How many blocks did it take to build the tower to your height? Would any of your classmates' towers be shorter or taller, the same length, or as long as yours? Why? Could you make the tower in another way? Can you make a tower the same length using a different number of blocks?"

Blocks can also be used to help children understand the concept of area. Taping off a square for children to fill up with blocks allows them to explore the concept of area.

Make a Pattern Children can identify patterns in their constructions such as ABA or ABBA. To develop the principle of patterns, children can use objects that are the same shape but a different size, or they can use objects that are different shapes but the same size. The teacher should ask questions such as "If a block is missing, could you tell what it is in this pattern? What block goes next in the *triangle, triangle, rectangle, triangle, triangle* pattern?" The teacher should also ask questions about the patterns in the children's buildings.

Group Blocks and Provide Data Analysis Children learn the beginning of data analysis by learning attributes of objects such as rectangular prisms, triangular prisms, or cubes that could be described and used in a graph. To practice this skill, children could graph by the size of blocks, the number of sides or faces of a block, the number of edges of the block, and the vertices of points of the block. Questions that could be asked by the teacher are "What type of block has the most faces or sides?" "What type of block has the most edges?" "What type of block has the most points?"

Science Activities

The process skills of science consist of observing, comparing, classifying, measuring, and communicating. These skills allow students to find new information through concrete experiences and can be sharpened through block play.

Use Visual Discrimination The teacher (or a child) can build a structure in advance, and other children can duplicate it. This is an excellent activity in visual discrimination and spacing. The teacher can talk to the children about the similarities and differences between the structures. This helps children with observation skills.

Build a Maze Mazes develop directing, comparing, measuring, and other skills. The teacher can show children a photo of a maze in a corn field or take children on a field trip to a corn field maze. The teacher can show pictures of elaborate English garden mazes or, better yet, the children can make a maze in an overgrown yard where permission has been obtained. The teacher can let the children plan a maze on paper with straight lines or curved lines and then build it on the floor. All mazes start with an opening on the outside of the perimeter, and twists and turns are necessary. Some mazes have two openings, and some have only one opening. The teacher should explain how it is made. A small animal such as a mouse or hamster can explore the maze, or the children can explore it if the maze is large enough. See Figure 8.3 for an example of a maze.

***Read the Story of* The Three Little Pigs** To demonstrate skills in science children can be encouraged to use blocks to withstand a huge wind. The teacher can read the story of *The Three Little Pigs* and discuss why the Big Bad Wolf could not blow down the house made of brick. Similarly, *The Three Little Javelinas* (Lowell, 1992) sets the story of the Three Pigs in the southwestern United States; in this version, the houses are made of tumbleweed, saguaro rib, and adobe. In the Lowell story (which is unique to the Southwest), the wolf

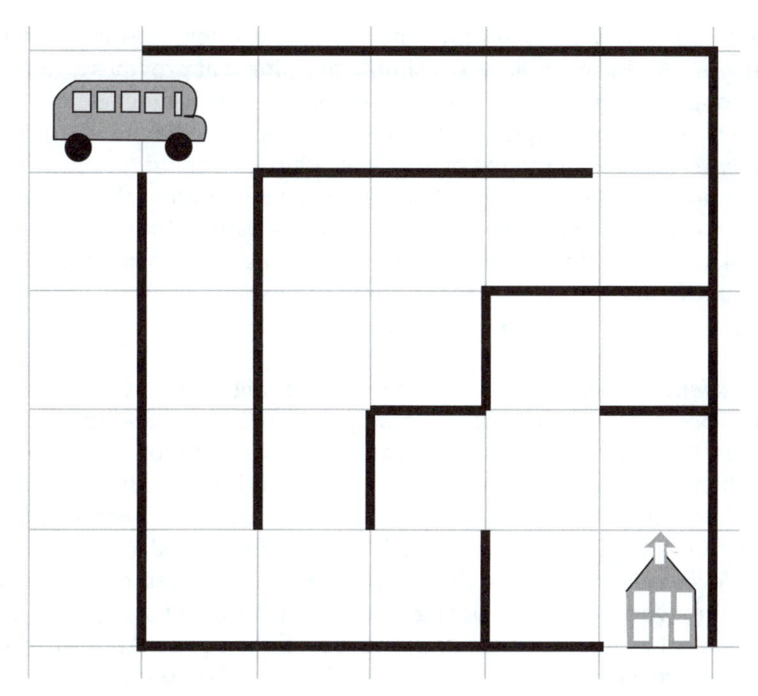

Figure 8.3. Example of a maze.

blows all the houses down except for the adobe house. The teacher should let children decide why certain buildings are stronger than other buildings.

Drop a Block to Demonstrate Gravity Gravity can be taught to kindergarten-age children by giving them a block and having them drop it. The teacher should ask the students, "Where does the block go?" Have each child repeat this activity several times. Each time children drop a block, the teacher can ask a question such as, "Will it fall to the side? What will happen the next time you drop it? What do you think will happen every time you drop it?" The teacher can point out that the object falls to the floor every time, and therefore children can predict that the next time they drop the object, it will fall to the floor. The teacher then discusses the fact that there is a force that pulls everything downward toward the earth, and this force is called *gravity*. The teacher can point out that a structure needs to be built such that it has a strong foundation and a low center of gravity so it does not fall down. Examples of the importance of strong foundations for buildings can be found in the skyscraper books listed in Appendix F. It should be noted that the bigger and the heavier a building is, the more it pushes into the ground beneath it. Because of this, all but the lightest structures must be set on specially prepared supports such as foundations. To demonstrate, the children could try building a tall building on a sponge to see what happens on soft ground. It is also pertinent to talk about why the granite soil of New York City can be more supportive of tall buildings than sandy soil found in other cities.

Move an Object Up an Incline An inclined plane is a slanting surface that connects one level to a higher level. An introducing and guiding question might be, "How can we move the car to the second story of the parking garage?" An inclined plane is a simple machine that provides a gain in force. It should be noted that by moving an object up an incline, we use less force in getting the object up to the higher level than if we had to lift the object directly from the lower to the higher level. One long board (block) can be used to demonstrate how changing board (block) lengths affect the force needed to go up to a given height. Several square blocks that are the same size may first be placed under the midpoint of the board and the board tilted. By using a small toy car that will roll, the children can experiment with different board lengths to see which make the car go faster.

Make a Lever A lever is a rigid bar, straight or curved, that rests on a fixed point called a *fulcrum*. The teacher can talk about the different types of levers that are familiar to children such as a seesaw or bottle opener. The teacher can demonstrate how a lever works and then ask the children to use blocks to make a lever. Children can experiment with what happens when weight is added to one side of the lever. Children can also experiment when one lever is not enough to do the work. The teacher can point out that scissors are two levers that work against each other to cut something, and your fingers act as a lever when gripping a block or pencil. Another example is found in construction, where cranes grab materials and lift them to the top of skyscrapers.

Make a Seesaw to Demonstrate Balance To demonstrate balance, the teacher can inquire whether the children have ever played on a seesaw and ask, "Where do you sit to balance someone heavier than you? Where do you sit to balance someone lighter than you?" Children should be told that they can make a small balance board using the building blocks and it can work like a seesaw. With the balance board, children should be told they may find some surprising ways to balance things.

For another activity with the balance board, have children pile many different objects and balance them on the board, then challenge the children to take away two objects at a time (one on each side) and maintain the balance.

Take a Tour of a Bridge Balance can be demonstrated by having the teacher take students on a tour of a bridge. The teacher can ask, "Is the bridge over water or land? Are the banks rocky or soft? Is the bridge for trains, people, or cars? What materials were used to make the bridge?" The teacher can discuss the history of bridges and point out that some of the earliest bridges were made by people who walked on logs over a river. The teacher can tell children that people learned that if the log or beam is too light for the weight, it will break and that the heavier the beam is, the stronger it will be. Bridges may be very short. In order to build a bridge in modern times, an architect, bridge designer, soils engineer, aerial photographer, traffic expert, and landscape architect are needed. A bridge is like a game of tug-of-war; in tug-of-war, both ends must be weighted equally so that the rope and players are in balance. A bridge is supposed to support the weight of all the cars and other things that go over it. Children can get ideas from the books about bridges listed in Appendix F.

Social Studies

The National Geography Standards (Geography Education Standards Project, 1994) and the National Council for the Social Studies (1994) have identified major themes for the study of geography: 1) The earth is the place we live, 2) Direction and location, 3) Relationships within places, 4) Spatial interactions, and 5) Regions. These themes are incorporated throughout the block-play activities described in the following sections, and they give structure to the activities so that concepts of place and geography are investigated through the study of the child's world.

Map with Blocks The teacher can divide the class into small groups. Each group should be supplied with blocks, small vehicles, and small figures of people. The teacher can ask the students to build a school and several houses. The teacher can have them act out how the children in the houses they built would get to school.

Make a Road of Blocks The teacher can have the students build tracks and roads for small vehicles using blocks. Let them use the roads they have built with small toy cars. Discuss where the cars go and why. Let them build interstate highways and ramps and describe in what directions the cars are going using *over* and *under, left* and *right*.

Visit a Construction Site or Look Through a Book of Homes The teacher can discuss the importance of homes and can talk about how they are built. If possible, the teacher can take the children to visit a construction site. In the classroom, the children can build a house that looks like the ones in which they live, using blocks. Books that show homes throughout history as well as different types of homes in other cultures and in America can be used as teaching tools (see Appendix F for a list of children's books on homes).

Take a Walk Around the Neighborhood The teacher can discuss the different types of homes and places where people work as they take children on a walk around the neighborhood. The teacher should point out the different shapes in the buildings, such as chimneys, steeples, arches, windows, and doors. After the field trip, the teacher can have children construct a model of the neighborhood with blocks. Then, the children can describe what they have built. The children can use a grid of squares to help them construct their ideas.

The teacher can place a large map of a neighborhood on the floor and have the students draw and cut out pictures of houses and other public buildings. The students can tape these pictures to blocks and place them on the map. The children can make rules for living in the block city. Perhaps the grid as mentioned in the previous paragraph could seem to limit the size of the building.

Children and their roles in working can be written out. On a poster, the teacher can make a map of the classroom, tracing around blocks to represent the different pieces of furniture, the chalkboard, bookcase, windows, and door; then the teacher can have the students match blocks to the map.

Parents and Blocks

Parents should become familiar with different types of blocks and should be encouraged to buy some types of blocks that are listed in Appendix D, including unit blocks, large hollow blocks, cardboard blocks, LEGOs, parquetry blocks, and alphabet and picture blocks. Parents can also furnish their children with books that explain building. For example, *The Ultimate Building Book* (Caney, 2006) is a must for parents who want to learn more about building with their children. See Appendix F for further suggestions.

Following are some questions for parents to consider when observing children with blocks:

Use of materials: Is he or she more concerned with neatness or alignment or balance than with creating things that he or she can use? Is he or she selective or haphazard in selecting materials? Does he or she like big structures or little structures?

Adaptability to change: Does he or she often repeat the same designs? Is he or she slow in getting started? Does he or she stick to the task of building?

Self-esteem: Does he or she like his or her own creations? Does he or she attempt more difficult creations, or does he or she stay at the same level?

Quality of relationships: Does he or she build by him- or herself or with others? Does he or she show appreciation of the work of others? Does he or she share his or her blocks with others?

Mathematical learning: Does he or she count blocks? Does he or she know one-to-one correspondence? Does he or she add, subtract, divide? Does he or she show an understanding of spatial relations? Does he or she show evidence of design?

Summary

Blocks have been a part of the early childhood curriculum since their inception, and blocks were particularly important in Friedrich Froebel's curriculum. Maria Montessori continued to use some block play, but Caroline Pratt allowed more free exploration by using blocks that could be placed on the floor. As demonstrated by the examples in this chapter, blocks, particularly unit blocks, still are a viable material with great flexibility that can enhance the curriculum through their emphasis on spatial relations and relationships with others. In addition to building something on the outside, children are building an inner world of their environment. The potential for using blocks not only for learning but also for enjoyment makes them one of the most desirable materials in the classroom. Parents can be keen observers of children with blocks and assessments can be made using standards.

9

Innovation and Spatial Development in the Future

So far, this book has shown how spatial literacy is important for our national well-being and economy; introduced the theories of Friedrich Froebel, a trained architect and mathematician who emphasized spatial development teaching in the 1800s; and shown how spatial development intersects with all areas of the curriculum. It has looked at research on how spatial concepts are formed in young children as well as how to implement a math–science curriculum in early childhood education that utilizes spatial development. It has provided the reader with new perspectives on how to approach spatial literacy in early childhood education using planned, research-based activities. The future of innovation depends on how we help young children learn to be more spatially literate, recognize spatially talented children, and allow them to expand their spatial knowledge to create. This chapter will look at how spatial development is related to innovation.

The recent National Innovation Initiative Summit and Report concluded in their National Survey (2005) that the United States is moving away from global innovation leadership. The United States, according to the report, is now home to only 6 of the world's top 25 most innovative information technology companies. This represents a decline of more than 100% over the last 30 years. The United Nations Educational, Scientific, and Cultural Organization (UNESCO) offers an even more expansive definition of the skills needed to succeed in the global economy:

> Literacy is the ability to identify, understand, interpret, create, communicate and compute, using printed and written materials associated with varying contexts. Our view of literacy must entail much more than reading, writing and math. Literacy involves a continuum of learning to enable an individual to achieve his or her goals, to develop his or her knowledge and potential, and to participate fully in the wider society. (UNESCO, 2004, p. 13)

Innovation involves skills in spatial literacy, so much so that innovation literacy should not be separated from spatial literacy. In other words, any innovative product must have some form of spatial imaging attached to it. Other countries, such as Great Britain in the example in the next paragraph, have picked up on the fact that innovation literacy cannot be separated from spatial literacy.

Innovative thinking must accompany visual design as a meaningful idea in curriculum design. Tim Brown, CEO of the global design consultancy IDEO, said that design thinking should be a part of the K–12 education system in the United States as it already is in Europe (Pethokoukis, 2008) According to Brown, this does not mean art classes; it means teaching kids through projects that are human-centered, creative, and collaborative. Niti Bhan, founder of Bhan LLC, a San Francisco strategy think tank that develops business models for emerging markets, suggests that programs like James Dyson's proposed School of Design and Innovation in the United Kingdom for 16- to 19-year-olds can be set up to educate U.S. high school juniors and seniors about design and innovation as well as science and technology in a series of workshops. Making design education very hands-on in schools, particularly in urban areas, is another powerful approach to innovative learning (Pethokoukis, 2008). Even though this recommendation was made for high school students, this information can be filtered down to primary and preschool students.

Spatial Development and Innovation

How can we use spatial development to innovate for the 21st century? In Frans Johansson's *The Medici Effect* (2004), a book devoted to the breakthrough insights at the intersection of ideas, concepts, and cultures, he says that when you step into an intersection of fields, disciplines, or cultures, you can combine existing concepts into extraordinary new ideas. His book's title refers to the Medici family of Italy, who over the centuries financed the work of artists, scientists, poets, philosophers, and architects, allowing them to learn from one another and create a world based on new ideas. The same thing can be said for spatial and geometric ideas, which converge with many fields of study including movement, math, science, arts, architecture, geography, and technology, to name a few. When different disciplines intersect with spatial development, it is brought to life. What happens is surprising and fascinating, with a "jump" or change in a new direction. Today this intersection is taking place all over the world with the advent of new technologies.

In his book *Mind Set: Reset Your Thinking and See the Future* (2006), John Naisbitt says he expects to see more changes in more places in the next 10 years than in the previous 100. Furthermore, according to Naisbitt, a visual culture is taking over the world, and the Science, Technology, Engineering, and Math (STEM) courses will be adding the arts, changing the acronym to Science, Technology, Engineering, Arts, and Math (STEAM).

Promotion of Spatial Literacy

The following sections provide recommendations for promoting spatial and geometric literacy in our schools.

K–12 and Higher Education

The following are my recommendations for teachers:

- Teach spatial development systematically in our schools from preschool through university in all the areas of the curriculum.
- Make linkages to the early learning standards in pre-K as well as K–12 standards in all disciplines. Learning trajectories need to be built into the standards so that the current research can help teachers develop activities appropriate for the level of the child.
- Spend more high-quality time on planned mathematical, geometric approaches to spatial thinking and measurement, and provide supplemental opportunities to use mathematics during play with blocks, puzzles, manipulatives, and interactive computer software (National Research Council, 2009).
- Reexamine the work of Friedrich Froebel, trained architect and mathematician.
- Use the idea of solids, lines, points, and construction with lines and points to promote architecture, design, and creativity as Froebelian schools did. Discuss with school boards why this model is needed. Develop model charter schools or lab schools using the Froebelian approach or research-based approaches such as the Building Blocks (Clements & Sarama, 2007c).
- If there is no opportunity to develop a model school, then train teachers in the Froebel model using forms of nature, forms of design, and forms of knowledge, in that order. The part–whole in this curriculum should be emphasized, because of the difficulty children have in integrating the part–whole into existence.
- Use long-term projects to promote an in-depth understanding of the integrated approach and the construction of different and spatial design media, as is done in the Reggio Emilia schools in Italy. This approach will help children learn people skills, which then allows teams with different skills and from different cultures to work together.
- Acknowledge the importance of "thinking outside the box": "Design, math, art, and technology produced YouTube and Google," says Thomas Friedman (2007), the author of *The World Is Flat,* a best-selling book describing the future of the 21st century.

- Promote the recommendations of the National Council of Teachers of Mathematics Focal Points, because they lead the way for geometric and spatial trajectories.
- Probe and think further in terms of having children see the differences between triangles, rectangles, and squares. Children should be viewing all kinds of triangles, such as equilateral, isosceles, scalene, right, acute, and obtuse triangles and transformations of the triangles. Spatial and geometric forms should be used in kindergartens initially in the form of blocks—preferably unit blocks rather than other blocks—that emphasize spatial characteristics and not color. Children should examine many different ways of building a tower out of unit blocks. Montessori schools have thoughtfully used materials to emphasize size or volume and kept the same color constant. In this way, space is emphasized.
- Enable students to create with tangrams and the many other versions of tangrams on the market, so that rotations can be seen. In addition, origami can be started earlier.
- Take students on walking field trips and other field trips to understand designs in nature. Fractals should be discussed. Furthermore, children need to discover the marvels of the microscope. The integration of nature, art, and math is a must for innovation and spatial literacy.
- Provide activities for children to examine three-dimensional forms. Young children need to be exposed to three-dimensional shapes beginning with concrete objects, then on paper, and finally on the computer.
- Use gestures to discuss spatial issues, because use of gestures was related to higher scores on spatial tests.
- Teach for visualization. Teachers should promote visualization techniques and models such as grids to represent what is taught.

Community

In *The Creative Spirit,* Goleman, Kaufman, and Ray (1993) look at the ideas of Dean Simonton of the University of California, who has researched 127 twenty-year periods in European history from 700 BC to AD 1839. According to Simonton, creativity depends on exposure to cultural diversity and political fragmentation. Simonton observes that the most creative period in America came after World War II, because of the great diversity of people coming to the United States from various parts of the world to seek opportunities. He says that wealth, geographic growth, a centralized nation, and warfare all failed to show a relationship to creativity, and he found that there was roughly a 20-year lag time in the flowering of creativity. This means that our children are growing the roots of creativity now, and communities should be aware of this. The following are my recommendations for the community:

- Coordinate and make connections among art museums, children's museums, and higher education to promote the enhancement of spatial and innovation issues. Encourage them to provide mathematical opportunities, especially for those who may not have access to high-quality programs.

- Provide a plethora of spatial and art blocks with computer math programs that reinforce concepts.
- Encourage teachers to emphasize the creation of maps using locations in their communities.
- Coordinate with software companies to produce spatial development software that is in line with the school curriculum using three-dimensional objects, patterns, and reinforcement with the computer.
- Coordinate with video game companies to make video games that emphasize spatial development.

Parents

Parents need to become active participants in enhancing spatial literacy. As Frank Lloyd Wright's mother encouraged him to build great buildings by buying Froebelian blocks, so should the parents of today encourage their children in ways that will promote spatial development. The following are my recommendations for parents:

- Be aware of the types of games, technology, and conversations that should take place to enhance spatial literacy.
- Spatial literacy should be a topic of conversation with children similar to math and reading and writing literacy.
- Help children see landmarks and visual aids for directions while in the car.
- Provide books for children that focus on direction, distance, and other spatial concepts.
- Read and discuss with children the biographies of people who were strong in spatial literacy, such as Thomas Edison, Albert Einstein, Leonardo Da Vinci, and Bill Gates. Highlight their hardships in certain areas, such as a weakness in verbal skills, and their strengths in other areas, and discuss how they overcame their hardships.

Summary

In conclusion, spatial literacy is a significant part of nearly every discipline. It is essential for science, technology, engineering, and mathematics as well as many other professions such as art and graphic design. It is important to promote this emphasis early in life in the context of what children are doing by integrating spatial learning into a variety of subject matter. It is essential to promote spatial development in the schools, in the community, and with parents in order to promote innovative development.

References

Acredolo, L.P., Adams, A., & Goodwyn, S.W. (1984). The role of self-produced movement and visual tracking in infant spatial orientation. *Journal of Experimental Child Psychology, 38,* 312–327.

Althouse, R., Johnson, M., & Mitchell, S.T. (2003). *The colors of learning: Integrating the visual arts into the early childhood curriculum.* New York: Teachers College Press.

Ansari, D., Donlan, C., Thomas, M.S.C., Ewing, S.A., Peen, T., & Karmiloff-Smith, A. (2003). What makes counting count? Verbal and visuo-spatial contributions to typical and atypical number development. *Journal of Experimental Child Psychology, 85,* 50–62.

Baenninger, M., & Newcombe, N. (1989). The role of experience in spatial test performance: A meta-analysis. *Sex Roles, 20,* 327–344.

Baenninger, M., & Newcombe, N. (1995). Environmental input to the development of sex-related differences in spatial and mathematical ability. *Learning and Individual Differences, 7,* 363–379.

Beilin, H. (1984). Cognitive theory and mathematical cognition: Geometry and space. In B. Gholson & T.L. Rosenthal (Eds.), *Applications of cognitive-developmental theory* (pp. 49–93). New York: Academic Press.

Beilstein, C.D., & Wilson, J.F. (2000). Landmarks in route learning by girls and boys. *Perceptual and Motor Skills, 91,* 877–882.

Ben-Chaim, D., Lappan, G., & Houang, R.T. (1989). The role of visualization in the middle school curriculum. *Focus on Learning Problems in Mathematics, 11*(1), 49–60.

Blades, M., Spencer, C., Plester, B., & Desmond, K. (2004). Young children's recognition and representation of urban landscapes. In G. Allen (Ed.), *Human spatial memory: Remembering where* (pp. 287–308). Mahwah, NJ: Lawrence Erlbaum Associates.

Blaut, J. (1997). Children can. *Annals of the Association of American Geographers, 87,* 152–158.
Brosterman, N. (1997). *Inventing kindergarten.* New York: Harry N. Abrams.
Bultman, S. (2000). *The Froebel Gifts.* Grand Rapids, MI: Kindergarten.
Burger, W.F., & Shaughnessy, J.M. (1986). Characterizing the van Heile levels of development in geometry. *Journal for Research in Mathematics Education, 17,* 31–48.
Caney, S. (2006). *The ultimate building book.* Philadelphia: Running Press Kids.
Carpenter, T., Carey, D., & Kouba, V. (1990). A problem solving approach to the operations. In J.N. Payne (Ed.), *Mathematics for the young child* (pp. 111–131). Reston, VA: National Council of Teachers of Mathematics.
Carpenter, T.P., Coburn, T., Reys, R., & Wilson, J. (1976). Notes from National Assessment: Recognizing and naming solids. *Arithmetic Teacher, 23,* 62–66.
Carpenter, T.P., Corbitt, M.K., Kepner, H.S., Lindquist, M.M., & Reys, R.E. (1980). National assessment. In E. Fennema (Ed.), *Mathematics education research: Implications for the '80s* (pp. 22–38). Alexandria, VA: Association for Supervision and Curriculum Development.
Carter, K. (1982). *True book of houses.* New York: Children's Press.
Casey, M.B., Erkut, S., Ceder, I., & Young, J.M. (2008). Use of storytelling context to improve girls' and boys' geometry skills in kindergarten. *Journal of Applied Developmental Psychology, 29,* 29–48.
Casey, M.B., Nuttall, R., & Pezaris, E. (1997). Mediators of gender differences in mathematics college entrance test scores: A comparison of spatial skills with internalized beliefs and anxieties. *Developmental Psychology, 33,* 669–680.
Clements, D.H. (1999). Concrete manipulatives, concrete ideas. *Contemporary Issues in Early Childhood, 1*(1), 45–60.
Clements, D.H. (2004). Geometric and spatial thinking in early childhood education. In D.H. Clements & J. Sarama (Eds.), *Engaging young children in mathematics: Standards for early childhood math education* (pp. 267–297). Mahwah, NJ: Lawrence Erlbaum Associates.
Clements, D.H. (2009). *Learning and teaching early math: The learning trajectories approach.* New York: Routledge.
Clements, D.H., & Battista, M.T. (1989). Learning of geometric concepts in a Logo environment. *Journal for Research in Mathematics Education, 20,* 450–467.
Clements, D.H., & Battista, M.T. (1991). Developing effective software. In E. Kelly & R. Lesh (Eds.), *Handbook of innovative research design in mathematics and education.* Mahwah, NJ: Lawrence Erlbaum Associates.
Clements, D.H., Battista, M.T., Sarama, J., & Swaminathan, S. (1997). Development of students' spatial thinking in a unit on geometric motions and area. *The Elementary School Journal, 98,* 171–186.
Clements, D.H., Copple, C., & Hyson, M. (Eds.). (2002). *Early childhood mathematics: Promoting good beginnings. A joint position statement of the National Association for the Education of Young Children and the National Council for Teachers of Mathematics* (Rev. ed.). Washington, DC: National Association for the Education of Young Children/ National Council for Teachers of Mathematics.
Clements, D.H., & McMillen, S. (1996). Rethinking concrete manipulatives. *Teaching Children Mathematics, 2*(5), 270–279.
Clements, D.H., & Sarama, J. (2003). Young children and technology: What does the research say? *Young Children, 58*(6), 34–40.
Clements, D.H., & Sarama, J. (2004). Building blocks for early childhood mathematics. *Early Childhood Research Quarterly, 19,* 181–189.
Clements, D.H., & Sarama, J. (2005). Young children and technology: What's appropriate? In W. Masalski & P.C. Elliot (Eds.), *Technology-supported mathematics teaching and learning* (pp. 51–73). Reston, VA: National Council of Teachers of Mathematics.
Clements, D.H., & Sarama, J. (2007a). *Building Blocks—SRA real math pre-K.* Columbus, OH: SRA/McGraw-Hill.
Clements, D.H., & Sarama, J. (2007b). Early childhood mathematics learning. In F.K. Lester, Jr. (Ed.), *Second handbook of research on mathematics teaching and learning* (pp. 461–555). New York: Information Age.

Clements, D.H., & Sarama, J. (2007c). Effects of a preschool mathematics curriculum: Summative research on the Building Blocks project. *Journal of Research in Mathematics Education, 38*(2), 136–163.

Clements, D.H., & Sarama, J. (2008a). Experimental evaluation of the effects of a research-based preschool mathematics curriculum. *American Educational Research Journal, 45,* 443–494.

Clements, D.H., & Sarama, J. (2008b). Mathematics and technology: Supporting learning for students and teachers. In O.N. Saracho & B. Spodek (Eds.), *Contemporary perspectives on science and technology in early childhood education* (pp. 127–147). Charlotte, NC: Information Age.

Clements, D., & Sarama, J. (2009). *Learning and teaching early math: The learning trajectories approach.* New York: Routledge.

Clements, D.H., & Swaminathan, S. (1995). Technology and school change: New lamps for old? *Childhood Education, 71,* 275–281.

Copley, J. (2000). *The young child and mathematics.* Washington, DC: National Association for the Education of Young Children and National Council of the Teachers of Mathematics.

Corbett, B. (1979). *A garden of children.* Mississauga, Ontario, Canada: The Froebel Foundation.

Corbett, B. (1989). *A century of kindergarten education in Ontario.* Mississauga, Ontario, Canada: The Froebel Foundation.

Crawford, B.A. (1998). The scientific method—a fatal flaw. *Science Scope, 21*(7), 50–52.

Crews, D. (1986). *Ten black dots.* New York: Greenwillow.

DePaola, T. (1975). *The cloud book.* New York: Holiday House.

Dewey, J. (1934). *Art as experience.* New York: Minton, Balch.

Dewey, J. (1938). *Experience and education.* New York: Macmillan.

Dodds, D.A. (1994). *The shape of things.* Cambridge, MA: Candlewick Press.

Douglas, N., & Schwartz, J. (1967). Increasing awareness of art ideas of young children through guided experiences with ceramics. *Studies in Art Education, 15*(2), 2–9.

Downs, R. (1978). *Friedrich Froebel.* Boston: Twayen Publishers

Edwards, C., Gandini, L., & Forman, G. (Eds.). (1998). *The hundred languages of children: The Reggio Emilia approach—Advanced reflections* (2nd ed.). Greenwich, CT: Ablex.

Ehrlich, S.B., Levine, S.C., & Goldin-Meadow, S. (2006). The importance of gesture in children's spatial reasoning. *Developmental Psychology, 42*(6), 1259–1268.

Elliot, J. (1987). *Model of psychological space.* New York: Springer-Verlag

Emmorey, K., Tversky, B., & Taylor, H.A. (2000). Using space to describe space: Perspective in speech, sign, and gesture. *Spatial Cognition and Computation, 2,* 157–180.

Fairweather, H., & Butterworth, G. (1977). The WPPSI at four years: A sex difference in verbal-performance discrepancies. *British Journal of Educational Psychology, 47,* 85–90.

Fey, J., Atchison, W.F., Good, R.A., Heid, M.K., Johnson, J., Kantowski, M.G., & Rosen, L.P. (1984). *Computing and mathematics: The impact on secondary school curricula.* College Park, MD: University of Maryland.

Filippaki, N., & Papamichael, Y. (1997). Tutoring conjunctions and construction of geometry concepts in the early childhood education: The case of the angle. *European Journal of Psychology of Education, 12*(3), 235–247.

Friedman, T.L. (2007). *The world is flat.* New York: Picador.

Fuys, D., Geddes, D., & Tischler, R. (1988). The van Heile model of thinking in geometry among adolescents. *Journal for Research in Mathematics Education Monograph Series, 3.*

Gardner, H. (1983). *Frames of mind: The theory of multiple intelligences.* New York: Basic Books.

Gauteux, S. (2001). Reorientation in a small-scale environment by 3-, 4-, and 5-year-old children. *Cognitive Development, 16*(3), 853–869.

Geary, D.C. (1994). *Children's mathematical development: Research and practice.* Washington, DC: American Psychological Association.

Geography Education Standards Project. (1994). *Geography for life.* Retrieved July 28, 2008, from http://www.nationalgeographic.com/xpeditions/standards

Gibbons, G. (1990). *How a house is built.* New York: Holiday House.
Glickman, C.D. (1998). *Revolutionizing America's schools.* San Francisco: Jossey-Bass.
Goble, P. (1993). *The girl who loved wild horses.* New York: Aladdin.
Golbeck, S.L. (2005). Building foundations for spatial literacy. *Young Children, 60*(6), 72–83.
Goleman, D., Kaufman, P., & Ray, M. (1993). *The creative spirit.* New York: Plume.
Grosvenor, G.M. (2007). The excitement of geography. *Social Studies and the Young Learner, 20*(2), 4.
Harlan, S. (1996). *Exploring early childhood education students' beliefs about art education.* Unpublished doctoral dissertation, Graduate School of Education, Rutgers University, New Brunswick, New Jersey.
Hart, S. (2007). *The Wright space.* New York: Barnes & Noble.
Hartman, G. (1991). *As the crow flies.* New York: Macmillan.
Haugland, S.W. (1999). What role should technology play in young children's learning? Part 1. *Young Children, 54*(6), 26–31.
Haugland, S.W. (2000). What role should technology play in young children's learning? Part 2. *Young Children, 55*(1), 12–18.
Haugland, S.W., & Shade, D.D. (1997). Software evaluation scale. In S.W. Haugland & J.L. Wright (Eds.), *Young children and technology: A world of discovery* (p. 27). Boston: Allyn & Bacon.
Hirsch, E.S. (Ed.). (1996). *The block book* (3rd ed.). Washington, DC: National Association for the Education of Young Children.
Hoban, T. (1973). *Over, under, and through and other spatial concepts.* New York: Macmillan.
Hogg, J., & McWhinnie, H. (1968). A pilot research in aesthetic education. *Studies in Art Education, 9*(2), 52–60.
Howe, G. (1969). The teaching of directions on space. In W. Herman (Ed.), *Current research in elementary school social studies* (pp. 31–43). Upper Saddle River, NJ: Merrill/Prentice Hall.
Humphreys, L.G., Lubinski, D., & Yao G. (1993). Utility of predicting group membership and the role of spatial visualization in becoming an engineer, physical scientist, or artist. *Journal of Applied Psychology, 78,* 250–261.
Hutchins, P. (1968). *Rosie's walk.* New York: Aladdin Paperbacks.
Hutchins, P. (1987). *Changes, changes.* New York: Macmillan.
Huttenlocher, J., Levine, S., & Vevea, J. (1998). Environmental effects on cognitive growth: Evidence from time period comparisons. *Child Development, 6,* 1012–1029.
Isadora, R. (1997). *Ben's trumpet.* New York: Mulberry Books.
Johansson, F. (2004). *The Medici effect: Breakthrough insights at the intersection of ideas, concepts, and cultures.* Boston: Harvard Business School Press.
Johnson, E.S., & Meade, A.C. (1987). Developmental patterns of spatial ability: An early sex difference. *Child Development, 58,* 725–740.
Johnson, H. (1966). *The art of block building.* New York: Bank Street College of Education.
Johnson, N., & Giorgis, C. (2001). Interacting with the curriculum. *The Reading Teacher, 55*(2), 204–213.
Johnson-Gentile, K., Clements, D.H., & Battista, M.T. (1994). The effects of computer and noncomputer environments on students' conceptualization of geometric motions. *Journal of Educational Computing Research, 11*(2), 121–140.
Jonas, A. (1984). *Round trip.* New York: Mulberry.
Jordan, N.C., Huttenlocher, J., & Levine, C. (1992). Differential calculation abilities in young children from middle and low income families. *Developmental Psychology, 28*(6), 44–53.
Kamii, C., Miyakawa, Y., & Kato, Y. (2004). The development of logico-mathematical knowledge in a block-building activity at ages 1–4. *Journal of Research in Childhood Education, 19,* 13–26.
Kersh, J., Casey, B., & Young, J.M. (2008). Research on spatial skills and block building in girls and boys: The relationship to later mathematics learning. In B. Spodek & O.N. Saracho (Eds.), *Mathematics, science, and technology in early childhood education* (pp. 233–252). Charlotte, NC: Information Age.

Kita, S., & Ozyurek, A. (2003). What does cross-linguistic variation in semantic coordination of speech and gesture reveal? Evidence for an interface representation of spatial thinking and speaking. *Journal of Memory and Language, 48,* 16–32

Kitchin, R.M., & Freundschuh, S. (2000). *Cognitive mapping. Past, present, and future.* London: Routledge.

Klibanoff, R.S., Levine, S.C., Huttenlocher, J., Vasilyeva, M., & Hedges, L.V. (2006). Preschool children's mathematical knowledge: The effect of teacher "math talk." *Developmental Psychology, 42*(1), 59–69.

Komatsu, Y. (2004). *Wonderful houses around the world.* Bolinas, CA: Shelter Publications.

Krauss, R.M. (1998). Why do we gesture when we speak? *Current Directions in Psychological Science, 7,* 54–60.

Lanegran, D.A., Snowfield, J.G., & Laurent, A. (1970). Retarded children and the concepts of distance and direction. *Journal of Geography, 69,* 157–160.

Lehrer, R., Jenkins, M., & Osana, H. (1998). Longitudinal study of children's reasoning about space and geometry. In R. Lehrer & D. Chazan (Eds.), *Designing learning environments for developing understanding of geometry and space* (pp. 137–167). Mahwah, NJ: Lawrence Erlbaum Associates.

Levine, S.C., Huttenlocher, J., Taylor, A., & Langrock, A. (1999). Early sex differences in spatial skill. *Developmental Psychology, 35,* 940–949.

Levine, S.C., Vasilyeva, M., Lourenco, S.F., Newcombe, N.S., & Huttenlocher, J. (2005). Socioeconomic status modifies the sex difference in spatial skill. *Psychological Science, 16,* 841–845.

Liben, L., & Downs, R. (2001). Geography for young children: Maps as tools for learning environments. In S. Golbeck (Ed.), *Psychological perspectives on early childhood education* (pp. 220–252). Mahwah, NJ: Lawrence Erlbaum Associates.

Liben, L.S., Moore, M.L., & Golbeck, S.L. (1982). Preschooler's knowledge of their classroom environment: Evidence from small-scale and life-size spatial task. *Childhood Development, 53,* 1275–1284.

Liben, L.S., & Myers, L.J. (2007). Developmental changes in children's understanding of maps: What, when, and how? In J.M. Plumert & J.P. Spencer (Eds.), *The emerging spatial mind* (pp. 193–218). Oxford, England: Oxford University Press.

Liben, L.S., & Yekel, C.A. (1996). Preschoolers' understanding of plan and oblique maps. The role of geometric and representational correspondence. *Child Development, 67*(6), 2780–2796.

Liebschner, J. (2001). *A child's work: Freedom and play in Froebel's educational theory and practice.* Cambridge, England: Lutterworth Press.

Lord, F. (1941). A study of spatial orientation of children. *Journal of Educational Research, 34,* 481–505.

Lowell, S. (1992). *The three little javelinas.* Flagstaff, AZ: Rising Moon.

MacDonald, S. (1994). *Sea shapes.* San Diego: Harcourt Brace.

MacDonald, S. (2001). *Blockplay: The complete guide to learning and playing with blocks.* Beltsville, MD: Gryphon House.

McGuiness, D., & Morley, C. (1991). Sex differences in the development of visuo-spatial ability in pre-school children. *Journal of Mental Imagery, 15,* 143–150.

McLeay, H. (2006). Imagery, spatial ability and problem solving. *Mathematics Teaching Incorporating Micromath, 195,* 36–38.

McNeill, D. (1992). *Hand and mind.* Chicago: University of Chicago Press.

Mosenthal, P.B., & Kirsch, S. (1991). Understanding general reference maps. *Journal of Reading, 34*(1), 60–63.

Moyer-Packenham, P., Salkind, G., & Bolyard, L. (2005). Investigations: Using virtual manipulatives to investigate patterns and generate rules in algebra. *Teaching Children Mathematics, 11*(8), 437–440.

Muir, S.P., & Cheek, H.N. (1991). Mathematics and the map skill curriculum. *School Science and Mathematics, 86,* 284–291.

Mullis, I.V.S., Martin, M.O., Gonzalez, E.J., Gregory, K.D., Garden, R.A., O'Connor, K.M., et al. (2000) *TIMSS 1999 international mathematics report: Findings from IEA's repeat of the Third International Mathematics and Science Study at the eighth grade.* Chestnut Hill, MA: International Study Center, Lynch School of Education, Boston College.

Museum of Contemporary Art, Chicago. (2009). *Buckminster Fuller: Starting with the universe brochure.* Chicago: Museum of Contemporary Art

Naisbitt, J. (2006). *Mind set!: Reset your thinking and see the future.* New York: HarperCollins.

National Art Education Association. (1999). Purposes, principles, and standards for school art programs. Reston, VA: Author.

National Council for the Social Studies. (1994). *Expectations of excellence: Curriculum standards for social studies.* Washington, DC: Author.

National Council of Teachers of English and the International Reading Association. (2003). *Standards for the English language arts.* Washington, DC: Authors.

National Council of Teachers of Mathematics. (2000). Principles and standards for school mathematics. Reston, VA: Author.

National Council of Teachers of Mathematics. (2006). *Curriculum focal points: A quest for coherence.* Reston, VA: National Council of Teachers of Mathematics.

National Council of Teachers of Mathematics & National Association for the Education of Young Children. (2002). *Early childhood mathematics education: Promoting good beginnings.* Reston, VA: National Council of Teachers of Mathematics.

National Geographic Education Foundation. (2002). *Roper 2002 global literacy survey: 16.* Retrieved January 26, 2005, from http://www.nationalgeographic.com/geosurvey2002/

National Research Council. (1996). *National science education standards.* Washington, DC: National Academies Press.

National Research Council. (2006). *Learning to think spatially.* Washington, DC: National Research Council, National Academies Press.

National Research Council. (2009). *Mathematics learning in early childhood: Paths toward excellence and equity.* Washington, DC: National Academies Press.

Newcombe, N.S., & Huttenlocher, J. (2000). *Making space: The development of spatial representation and reasoning.* Boston: The MIT Press.

Nieuwoudt, H.D., & van Niekerk, R. (1997, March). *The spatial competence of young children through the development of solids.* Paper presented at the meeting of the American Educational Research Association, Chicago.

O'Boyle, M.W. (1998). On the relevance of research findings in cognitive neuroscience to educational practice. *Educational Psychology Review, 10*(4), 397–409.

Osborn, K. (1991). *Early childhood in historical perspective.* Athens, GA: Daye Press

Park, B., Chae, J., & Boyd, B. (2008). Young children's block play and mathematical learning. *Journal of Research in Childhood Education, 232*(2), 157–178.

Pethokoukis, J. (2008, January 4). Innovate or else: 6 thinkers' ideas. *U.S. News and World Report,* 48.

Piaget, J. (1952). *The origins of intelligence in young children.* New York: International Universities Press.

Piaget, J. (1959). *The psychology of intelligence.* London: Routledge and Kegan Paul.

Piaget, J. (1974). *To understand is to invent: The future of education.* New York: Viking.

Piaget, J. & Inhelder, B. (1967). *The child's conception of space.* New York: W.W. Norton.

Piaget, J., Inhelder, B., & Szeminska, A. (1960). *The child's conception of geometry.* London: Routledge and Kegan Paul.

Pica, R. (2000). *Experiences in movement.* Albany, NY: Delmar.

Quaiser-Pohl, C., Geiser, C., & Lehmann, W. (2006). The relationship between computer game preference, gender, and mental-rotation ability. *Personality and Individual Differences, 40,* 609–619.

Razel, M., & Eylon, B.S. (1990). Development of visual cognition: Transfer effects of the Agam program. *Journal of Applied Developmental Psychology, 11,* 495–585.

Rice, M.J., & Cobb, R.L. (1978). *What can children learn in geography? A review of the research.* Boulder, CO: SSEC.

Rosen, D., & Hoffman, J. (2009). Integrating concrete and virtual manipulatives in early childhood mathematics. *Young Children, 64*(3), 26–33.

Sabbeth, C. (1998). *Crayons and computers: Computer art activities for kids ages 4 to 8.* Chicago: Chicago Review Press.

Sarama, J., & Clements, D. (2002). Design of microworlds in mathematics and science education. *Journal of Educational Computing Research, 27*(1&2), 1–6.

Sarama, J,. & Clements, D. (2004). Building blocks for early childhood mathematics. *Early Childhood Research Quarterly, 19,* 181–189.

Sarama, J., & Clements, D. (2006). Mathematics, young children, and computers: Software, teaching strategies and professional development. *The Mathematics Educator, 9*(2), 112–134.

Sarama, J., & Clements, D. (2009). *Early childhood mathematics education research.* New York: Routledge.

Schaal, A.G., Uttall, D.H., Levine, S.C., & Goldin-Meadow, S. (2005, May). *Children's gestures provide insight into their representations of space.* Poster session presented at the annual meeting of the Midwestern Psychological Association, Chicago.

Schrank, F.A., Mather, N., McGrew, K.S., & Woodcock, R.W. (2003). *Woodcock-Johnson diagnostic supplement to the Tests of Cognitive Abilities.* Rolling Meadows, IL: Riverside Publishing.

Seefeldt, C., Castle, S., & Falconer, R.C. (2010). *Social studies for the preschool/primary child* (8th ed.). Columbus, OH: Pearson.

Sendak, M. (1964). *Where the wild things are.* New York: Harper & Row.

Seo, K.H., & Ginsburg, H.P. (2004). What is developmentally appropriate in early childhood mathematics education? In D.H Clements, J. Sarama, & A.M. DiBiase (Eds.), *Engaging children in mathematics: Standards for early childhood mathematics education* (pp. 91–104). Mahwah, NJ: Lawrence Erlbaum Associates.

Servin, A., Bohlin, G., & Berlin, L. (1999). Sex differences in 1-, 3-, and 5-year-olds' toy choice in a structured play-session. *Scandinavian Journal of Psychology, 40,* 43–48.

Shaw, C.G. (1947). *It looked like spilt milk.* New York: Harper Collins.

Shea, D.L., Lubinski, D., & Benbow, C.P. (2001). Importance of assessing spatial ability in intellectually talented young adolescents: A 20-year longitudinal study. *Journal of Educational Psychology, 93,* 604–614.

Shepard, R.N. (1978a). Externalization of mental images and the act of creation. In B.S. Randhawa & W.E. Coffman (Eds.), *Visual learning, thinking and communication* (pp. 133–189). New York: Academic Press.

Shepard, R.N. (1978b). The mental image. *American Psychologist, 33,* 125–137.

Sophian, C. (2002). Learning about what fits: Preschool children's reasoning about effects of object size. *Journal for Research in Mathematics Education, 33,* 290–302.

Starkey, P., Klein, A., Chang, I., Qi, D., Lijuan, P., & Yang, Z. (1999, April). *Environmental supports for young children's mathematical development in China and the United States.* Paper presented at the meeting of the Society of Research in Child Development, Albuquerque, NM.

Stevenson, R.L. (2005). *Block city.* New York: Simon & Schuster.

Stewart, R., Leeson, N., & Wright, R.J. (1997). Links between early arithmetical knowledge and measurement knowledge: An exploratory study. In F. Biddulph & K. Carr (Eds.), *Proceedings of the twentieth annual conference of the Mathematics Education Research Group of Australasia, Vol. 2* (pp. 477–484). Hamilton, New Zealand: MERGA.

Stigler, J.W., Lee, S.Y., & Stevenson, H.W. (1990). *Mathematical knowledge of Japanese, Chinese, and American elementary school children.* Reston, VA: National Council of Teachers of Mathematics.

Stolzman, J.P., & Goolsby, T.N. (1973). Developing map skills through reading instruction. *Journal of Geography, 72,* 32–36.

Szechter, L.E., & Liben, L.S. (2003). Parental guidance in preschoolers understanding spatial-graphic representations. *Child Development, 75,* 869–885.

Tompert, A. (1990). *Grandfather Tang's story.* New York: Crown.

United Nations Educational, Scientific and Cultural Organization. (2004). *Education sector position paper: The plurality of literacy and its implications for policies and programmes.* Paris: Author.

U.S. Department of Education, Institute of Education Sciences. (2009). *Highlights from the TIMSS 2007: Mathematics and science achievement of U.S. fourth and eighth grade students in an international context.* Washington, DC: U.S. Department of Education.

U.S. Department of Education National Mathematics Advisory Panel. (2008). *Foundations for success: The final report of the National Mathematics Advisory Panel.* Washington, DC: U.S. Department of Education.

Usiskin, Z. (1997). The implications of geometry for all. *Journal of Mathematics Education Leadership, 1*(3), 5–14.
van Hiele, P.M. (1986). *Structure and insight: A theory of mathematical education.* Orlando, FL: Academic Press.
Voyer, D., Voyer, S., & Bryden, M.P. (1995). Magnitude of sex differences in spatial abilities: A meta-analysis and consideration of critical variables. *Psychological Bulletin, 117,* 250–270.
Vygotsky, L. (1962). *Thought and language* (E. Hanfmann & G. Vakar, Eds. and Trans.). Cambridge, MA: The MIT Press.
Vygotsky, L.S. (1978). *Mind in society.* Cambridge, MA: Harvard University Press.
Vygotsky, L. (1986). *Thought and language* (Rev. ed.). Cambridge, MA: The MIT Press.
Walling, D. (2000). *Rethinking how art is taught.* Thousand Oaks, CA: Sage Publications.
Wellhousen, K., & Kieff, J. (2001). *A constructivist approach to block play.* Albany, NY: Delmar.
Wilson, R.S. (1975). Twins: Patterns of cognitive development as measured on the Wechsler preschool and primary scale of intelligence. *Developmental Psychology, 11,* 126–134.
Wolf, A. (1984). *Mommy, it's a Renoir!* Altoona, PA: Parent Child Press.
Wolf, A.D. (1990). Art, postcards—another aspect of your aesthetics program? *Young Children, 45,* 39–43.
Wolfgang, C.H., Stannard, L.L., & Jones, I. (2001). Block play performance among preschoolers as a predictor of later school achievement in mathematics. *Journal of Research in Childhood Education, 15*(2), 173–180.
Woodcock, R.W., McGrew, K.S., & Mather, N. (2001). *Woodcock-Johnson III Tests of Cognitive Abilities.* Itasca, IL: Riverside.
Wright, F.L. (1932). *An autobiography.* New York: Longman Green.
Xie, Y., & Shauman, K.A. (2003). *Women in science.* Cambridge, MA: Harvard University Press.
Yenawine, P. (1991). *Lines.* New York: Delacorte Press.
Zacharos, K., Koliopoulos, D., Dokomaki, M.A., & Kassoumi, H. (2007). Views of prospective early childhood education teachers towards mathematics and its instruction. *European Journal of Teacher Education, 30*(3), 305–318.

Using the Froebelian Gifts to Promote Further Mathematical Knowledge

This appendix provides specific ways to use the Froebelian gifts (see Chapter 2), employing mathematical concepts instrumental in developing standards. The appendix includes vocabulary that children can learn with each gift as well as activities that children can do involving the gifts. Teachers should be as specific as possible in developing mathematical language with children.

The two grids provided in Appendix B can be used to provide guidelines for structure and thinking about the math concepts being utilized or introduced. It should be noted that many of the tables that children worked on in early Froebelian kindergartens actually had grids carved into them. When used with the gifts, grids provide an added dimension of spatial development.

Gift 1—Woolen Colored Balls

Vocabulary words that can be used with this gift are as follows: positional words—*over, under, behind, in front of, beside, above, below, on, off, high, low, medium;* other vocabulary—*swing, fast, slowly, roll, jump, bounce;* and color words—*red, yellow, blue, orange, purple, green, primary, secondary, complementary.*

Gift 2—Wooden Sphere, Cube, and Cylinder

This gift mainly promotes understanding of and experimentation with the sphere, cylinder, and cube. Young children can stack these shapes and describe their parts. They can classify them. They can count the number of surfaces, edges, and corners. Have the children discover which ones roll and which ones do not roll. Spin them to discover what happens (the cube becomes a cylinder, the cylinder becomes a sphere).

Gift 3—Wooden Cube Divided into Eight Smaller Cubes

Vocabulary terms that can be used with this gift include the terms detailed in the following sections. Teachers can pass out copies of the large grid table found in Appendix B so children can see more clearly the shapes and forms related to the grid.

One-to-One Correspondence

The children place four blocks on the table. Then they match another four blocks one to one below them. The teacher asks, "Are there as many blocks on the top row as there are on the bottom row?"

Rational Counting by Ones

The children place all of the blocks on the left side. Each child moves each block one by one to the other side as they count. They can also count how many faces the cube has.

Rational Counting by Twos

The children place all the blocks on the left side. Each child moves two blocks to the other side as they count.

Dividing Blocks into Parts and Wholes

Have children place all eight blocks together. Have the children take four blocks apart on each side. Tell the children to place them back to make a whole. Have children take four blocks apart from the top. Tell the children to place them back to make a whole. Have the children take two blocks apart, so that there are four towers with two blocks each. Tell the children to place all four blocks together. Take two blocks apart from the top. Place them back to make a whole.

Seriation

Children can place blocks graduated in order from smallest to largest. They can use words such as *smallest to largest, narrowest to widest,* and *shortest to longest* by placing blocks together in twos and threes.

Graphing

Children can graph how many eyes, ears, noses, and mouths they have on their individual faces using the blocks.

Addition

The teacher can have the children play with the blocks and observe if the children place them in sets naturally. The teacher can tell the children that you can see three blocks in one set and five blocks in another set. The teacher can ask the children how many blocks they have altogether. Let children practice doubles (two and two, four and four, three and three). Children can then practice addition sums of eight (0 and 8, 1 and 7, 2 and 6, 3 and 5, 4 and 4, 8 and 0, 7 and 1, 6 and 2, 5 and 3).

Subtraction

There are seven types of subtraction problems that could be used, according to Carpenter, Carey, and Kouba (1990), and these can be applied to the blocks.

1. **Join, change, and unknown.** For example, "I have two blocks. How many more blocks will I need to make eight altogether?"
2. **Join, start, and unknown.** For example, "I have some blocks. Mary gave me two more blocks. Now I have eight blocks. How many blocks did I start with?"
3. **Separate, result unknown.** For example, "I have eight blocks. I gave Mary two blocks. How many blocks do I have left?"
4. **Separate, change, unknown.** For example, "I have eight blocks. I gave some to Mary . Now I have three blocks. How many did I give to Mary?"
5. **Part-part-whole, part unknown.** For example, "I have eight blocks. I separate four blocks. How many blocks are left?"
6. **Compare, difference unknown.** For example, "I have eight blocks. Mary has five blocks. How many more blocks do I have?"
7. **Compare, referent unknown.** For example, "I have eight blocks. I have three more blocks than Mary. How many blocks does Mary have?"

Multiplication

The children can play with the blocks in a naturalistic setting—a setting in which workable problems can be devised. For example, "Mary makes four stacks of blocks. She places two blocks in each stack. How many blocks are there in all?"

Division

Children can explore the blocks to understand the principles of grouping and sharing. *Grouping* is used to find out how many subgroups of a particular size a larger group contains. For example, "Mary has eight blocks. She wants to make buildings that are four blocks high. How many can she make?" *Sharing* is the process of dividing a larger group into a particular number of groups to find out how many items will be included in that number of subgroups. For example, "Two children are exploring the eight blocks. How many will each child get so that there are not any left over?"

Fractions

Froebel emphasized whole and parts in his work extensively. The students can see how many cubes fit into the larger cube. They then practice making ¼, ½, and ⅛ of the set of the blocks of eight.

Point

To show points in Gift 3, children can manipulate the cubes and discover the pointed parts where the straight lines come together to form a point. The teacher indicates to the children that this is a point.

Line

Children should feel the line on the cube and the teacher can say that these are vertical and horizontal lines.

Angle

The right angle is identified for the children. For children, the idea of the right angles would be just making a turn on a sidewalk. It could also be called a "square" corner.

Prism

Stack the eight blocks to make a prism or cube. What prism name does it have? Stack the eight blocks to form another prism. This is a rectangular prism.

Measurement

Children can use measurement words to describe how high the towers are. They can discuss whether they are the same, different, higher, shorter, or longer.

Gift 4—Wooden Cube Divided into Smaller Oblong Blocks

Teachers can pass out the large grid and allow the children to make discoveries about how many squares in the grid are covered up. After working with the large grid, the small grid can be distributed. The children can then make discoveries about how many squares are covered up with the rectangular prisms of the fourth gift. They can compare the rectangular prism shape of Gift 4 to the cube shape of Gift 3. The rectangular prism should be demonstrated as distinct from the cube. The faces of the rectangular prisms are rectangles not squares as is Gift 3. The vocabulary from Gift 3 can be used because they both have the same number of blocks and the same questions for one-to-one correspondence, rational counting by ones and twos, as well as dividing blocks into parts and wholes. Addition, subtraction (all seven types), multiplication, and division, fractions, points, lines, and right angles can be identified. They can experience using the rectangular prisms and seeing that it is easier to build with them than cubes; thus, this is the reason modular housing is composed of rectangular shapes.

Gift 5—Large Wooden Cube Divided into Smaller Cubes

Vocabulary words that can be used with this gift include *face, edge,* and *vertex.* These are all properties of prisms. The face is the flat part of the prism. The face of the cube is a square. A cube has six faces. The edges or line segments join together to make the faces.

This gift can be used with the large grid or the small grid as the activities are introduced.

One-to-One Correspondence

The children place four blocks on the table. Then they match four other blocks one to one below them. The teacher asks, "Are there as many blocks on the top row as there are on the bottom row?" This can be repeated with other prisms. The children can place four small triangular prisms below four halved triangular prisms. The teacher can ask, "Are there as many triangular blocks as there are cubes?"

Rational Counting by Ones

The children place all the blocks on the left side. Each child moves each block one by one to the other side as he or she counts by ones. They can count the cubes and the triangles and find out which has more.

Rational Counting by Twos

The children place all the blocks on the left side. Each child moves two blocks to the other side and counts by twos.

Rational Counting by Fives

The children place all the blocks on the left side. Each child moves five blocks to the other side and counts by fives.

Divide Blocks into Parts and Wholes

Have the children look at a cube. Place two large triangles together. Make a cube the same size as the first cube. Take them apart again. Have the children again look at a cube by placing four small triangular prisms together to make a cube. Take them apart and place them back to make a whole.

Seriation

Children can place blocks graduated in order from smallest to largest. They can use terms such as *smallest to largest, narrowest to widest, shortest to longest* by placing blocks together in twos and threes.

Graphing

Children can graph using the blocks. They can combine the blocks and make a graph birthdays. They can use words such as *less than, more than, the same as, the most, the least, some, all.*

Addition

The teacher can have the children play with the blocks and observe if the children place them in sets naturally. The teacher can tell the children that you can see three blocks in one set and five in another set. Ask "How many do you have altogether?" Let children practice doubles (two and two, four and four, three and three). Children can practice addition sums of 8 (0 and 8, 1 and 7, 2 and 6, 3 and 5, 4 and 4, 8 and 0, 7 and 1, 6 and 2, 5 and 3).

Subtraction

Use the seven types of subtraction problems described in the Gift 3 subtraction section.

Multiplication

The children can play with the blocks in a naturalistic setting. For example, "Mary Jo makes four stacks of blocks. She places two blocks in each stack. How many blocks in all?" This can be repeated with other combinations. In order to do multiplication, the student must understand what equal quantities are.

Division

Children can explore the blocks to understand the principles of grouping and sharing. *Grouping* is used to find out how many subgroups of a particular size a larger group contains. For example, "Mary has eight blocks. She wants to make buildings that are four blocks high. How many can she make?" *Sharing* is the process of dividing a larger group into a particular number of groups to find out how many items will be included in that number of subgroups. For example, "Two children are exploring the eight blocks. How many will each child get so that none is left over?"

Fractions

Froebel emphasized whole and parts in his work extensively. The students can see how many cubes fit into the larger cube. They then practice making $\frac{1}{4}$, $\frac{1}{2}$, and $\frac{1}{8}$ of the set of the blocks of eight.

Point

To show points in Gift 5, children can manipulate the cubes and discover the pointed parts where the straight lines come together to form a point. The teacher indicates to the children that this is a point.

Line

Children should feel the line on the cube and the teacher can say that these are vertical and horizontal lines.

Angle

The right angle is identified for the children. They should feel the right angle. The angle is created by intersecting rays or lines that meet to form a vertex. In order to understand the concept of *angle,* they should know that a circle is divided into 360 degrees and if it is superimposed over the angle where the sides intersect, it is the measurement of the angle. Some children in primary grades would be able to grasp this concept if they are able to superimpose a circle on the angle.

Prism

Stack the eight blocks to make a prism or cube. What prism name does it have? Stack the eight blocks to form another prism. This is a rectangular prism. Stack the blocks in other ways to form different size prisms.

Intersection

The concept of intersecting lines can be demonstrated by using the cubes to illustrate a pair of lines intersecting at a right angle. These lines are considered perpendicular, as opposed to parallel, which are lines that remain the same distance apart.

Gift 5 can also be used to show different kinds of polygons that can be made from cubes. For instance, a cube can be divided into two triangular equilateral prisms.

Gift 6—Large Wooden Cube Divided into Multiple Smaller Pieces

The teacher should let children make discoveries with the large and small grid and the prisms of Gift 6. Gift 6 extensions are a continuation of the activities in Gift 5.

Gift 7—Series of Colored Shapes

Gift 7 lends itself to wonderful exploratory work on the large and small grid where many discoveries with parquetry can be made.

One-to-One Correspondence

This can be done by matching the real shapes to shapes on a piece of paper.

Rational Counting

A game called "looking for four" can be used. Cats have four legs; squares, rectangles, and different forms of rectangles such as trapezoids, parallelograms, and rhombi have four sides.

Shapes

Triangles and their relationships can be shown. Equilateral (all sides equal), isosceles (two sides equal), and right triangle (one angle of 90 degrees) can be discussed.

Seriation

Seriation can take place by ordering the tile and combining tiles.

Fractions

Fractional parts of the various figures can be used. *Congruency* can be introduced by discussing smaller triangles shaped in an equilateral triangle as well as smaller shapes in a square. Children can make shapes as the teacher describes them. A *trapezoid* (quadrilateral) is composed of a square and two triangles. The children can rearrange the shapes in the trapezoid to make a parallelogram. A *parallelogram* is a quadrilateral that has two pairs of parallel sides. A *rhombus* is a quadrilateral that has two pairs of parallel sides. A *rectangle* is a four-sided figure with opposite sides equal and parallel, with each interior angle a right angle. An *octagon* is composed of four squares and four triangles.

Gift 8—Sticks and Rings

Children need to identify a circle, half circle, and arc and think about them in terms of fractions.

One-to-One Correspondence

The teacher places four children at the table. Each child is given one circle and two sticks, and the teacher asks, "Are there as many children as there are circles and sticks?" The teacher then passes out three more half circles and asks, "Are there as many half circles and sticks as there are children? Are there more children? How many more children?"

Rational Counting by Ones

Have children count each whole circle and each stick.

Rational Counting by Twos

Have children count the half circles and sticks by two.

Rational Counting by Fives

Place circles in groups of five. Count the circles by fives and repeat with half circles and arcs.

Divide circles and sticks into parts and wholes. Show the children a circle and then have them divide it into halves. Show them the longest stick and then have them find two smaller ones that make the same size when placed end to end, thus teaching halves. Place the two parts back into the circle. Show the children a circle and then have them divide it into fourths using quadrants. Place the four parts back into the circle.

Seriation

Children can place sticks and/or rings graduated in order from smallest to largest. They can use terms such as *smallest to largest, narrowest to widest, shortest to longest* by placing sticks and/or rings together in twos and threes.

Graphing

Children can graph how many eyes, ears, noses, and mouths they have on their individual faces using the rings.

Addition

The teacher can have the children play with the sticks and/or rings and observe if the children place them in sets naturally. The teacher can tell the children that you can see three rings together in one set and five sticks in another set. Ask, "How many do you have altogether?" Let children practice doubles (two and two, four and four, three and three). Children can practice addition sums of 8 (0 and 8, 1 and 7, 2 and 6, 3 and 5, 4 and 4, 8 and 0, 7 and 1, 6 and 2, 5 and 3).

Subtraction

Use the seven types of subtraction problems described in the Gift 3 subtraction section.

Multiplication

The children can play with the sticks in a naturalistic setting. For example, "Mary makes four stacks of sticks. She places two more sticks in each stack. How many sticks in all?" This can be repeated with other combinations.

Division

Children can explore the rings to understand the principles of grouping and sharing. *Grouping* is used to find out how many subgroups of a particular size a larger group contains. For example, "Mary has eight quadrants. She wants to make circles. How many can she make?" *Sharing* is the process of dividing a larger group into a particular number of groups to find out how many items will be included in that number of subgroups. For example, "Two children are exploring the eight circles. How many will each child get so that none are left over?"

Fractions

Froebel emphasized whole and parts in his work extensively. The children can see how many halves fit into a circle and discuss ½ of the circle. The children can see how many quadrants fit into the circle and discuss ¼ of the circle. They then practice the fractions ½ and ¼.

Point

To show points in Gift 8, children can manipulate the lines and discover the pointed parts where the straight lines come together to form a point.

Line

Children should feel the lines and make them both vertically and horizontally. Let them place the circles on the small grid and see how they fit within a square. Let them place them on the large grid and see what happens. Let them describe how the ½ and ¼ circle can make a complete circle.

Angles

The teacher can demonstrate that when a circle, which is 360 degrees, is superimposed over an angle, where the sides intersect the circle is the measurement of the angle.

Measurement

Measure how many small sticks it takes to make a long line on the large grid.

Gift 9—Points and Lines

The points are especially good on the small grids because they fit right in the square.

One-to-One Correspondence

The teacher places four children at the table. Each child is given one point. Ask, "Are there as many children as there are points?" The teacher passes out three points, then asks, "Are there as many half points as there are children? Are there more children? How many more children? How many fewer points?"

Rational Counting by Ones

Have children count each point of a different color.

Rational Counting by Twos

Have children count the points by twos.

Rational Counting by Fives

Have children count the points by fives.

The teacher can have children divide points into parts and wholes: Place all points of a certain color together. Take them apart. Place them back to make a whole or a line.

Seriation

Children can place points graduated in order from smallest to largest. They can use terms such as *smallest to largest* and *narrowest to widest* by placing blocks together in twos and threes.

Graphing

Children can graph quite easily with the points using any familiar topic such as hair color, number of brothers and sisters, favorite foods, favorite book, and kind of pets, using the graph paper. Vocabulary can be extended to more than, one more than, two more than, as well as one fewer than, two fewer than, and so forth.

Addition

The teacher can have the children play with the points and observe if the children place them in sets naturally. The teacher can tell the children that you can see three points in this set and five points in another set. Ask, "How many do you have altogether?" Let children practice doubles (two and two, four and four, three and three); research shows children learn doubles first. Children can practice adding sums of 8 (0 and 8, 1 and 7, 2 and 6, 3 and 5, 4 and 4, 8 and 0, 7 and 1, 6 and 2, 5 and 3).

Subtraction

Use the seven types of subtraction problems described in the Gift 3 subtraction section.

Multiplication

The children can play with the points in a naturalistic setting. For example, "Mary Jo makes four points. She places two points in each area. How many points in all?" This can be repeated with other combinations.

Division

Children can explore the points to understand the principles of grouping and sharing. *Grouping* is used to find out how many subgroups of a particular size a larger group contains. For example, "Mary has 16 points. She wants to make squares. How many can she make?" *Sharing* is the process of dividing a larger group into a particular number of groups to find out how many items will be included in that number of subgroups. For example, "Two children are exploring the 16 points. How many will each child get so that none are left over?"

Fractions

Froebel emphasized whole and parts in his work extensively. The children can see how many points fit into a square and discuss ½ of the square. The children can see how many quadrants fit into the square and discuss ¼ of the square. They then practice the fractions ½ and ¼.

Points

To show points in Gift 8, children can manipulate the points and discover the pointed parts where the straight lines come together to form a point.

Line

Children should feel the points and make lines with them both vertically and horizontally. Let them place the points on the small grid and see how they fit within a square. Have them place the points on the large grid and see what happens. Let them describe how the circle is inside of the square or vice versa.

Measurement

Measure how many points make two lines on the large square grid and how many squares make a line on the small grid.

Gift 10—Framework for Points and Lines

Gift 10 is a study of all previous gifts because lines and points are used to create three-dimensional figures that have flat surfaces. Froebel created an interest in the shapes and forms for construction. Geodesic domes and their construction can be discussed as well as lines, points, surfaces, and three-dimensional surfaces. In Gift 10, children use sticks and points (peas) to construct a geodesic dome, an advanced construction of Buckminster Fuller, which is a variant of the triangulation of the sphere. The items of Gift 10 form the bases of the post and beam used in traditional architecture. Other three-dimensional figures that can be constructed are: cube, noncubic rectangular prism, triangular prism, square pyramid, and triangular pyramid. Children should recognize the two-dimensional figures of the square, rectangle, various triangles, and circle. They should also recognize the three-dimensional shapes that they have constructed. Lines, vertices, and flat surfaces can be examined and summarized for children in the building process.

Grids Provide an Organizational Scheme for Studying Shape and Form

Vocabulary and Spatial Activities

Glossary of Terms

Polygon	Sides	Angles
Triangle	3	3
Quadrilateral	4	4
Pentagon	5	5
Hexagon	6	6
Octagon	8	8
Nonagon	9	9
Decagon	10	10

Triangles

A *triangle* is a three-sided polygon. Triangles have three line segments for sides and three angles. Triangles are classified by length of sides and sizes of their angles.

Equilateral triangles are triangles that have all sides equal in length, also known as *congruent*. These triangles also have all angles equal in measure.

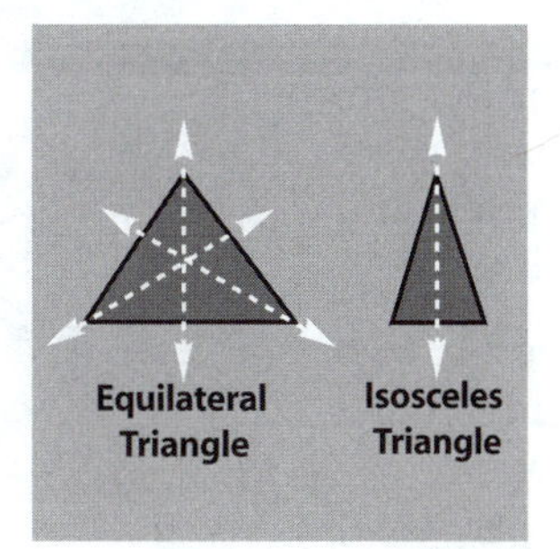

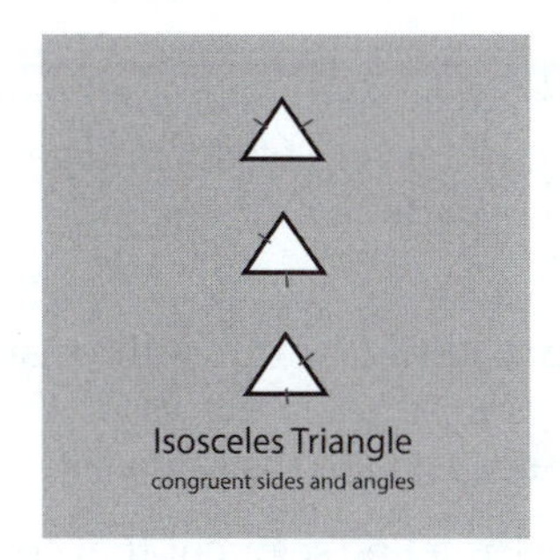

Isosceles triangles have two congruent (equal) sides and two congruent angles.

Scalene triangles have no congruent sides and no congruent angles.

Right triangles contain one right angle. The sum of the angles measures 180 degrees.

Acute triangles have three acute angles all less than 90 degrees, equaling 180 degrees.

Obtuse triangles have one angle greater than 90 degrees and two angles less than 90 degrees.

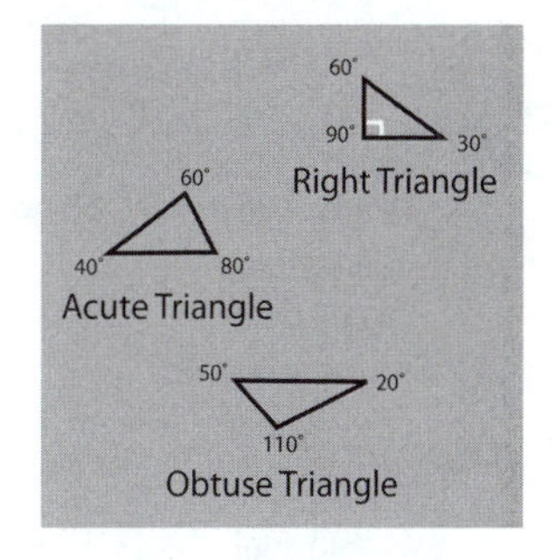

Circles

Semicircles are half circles and are named by three points on their circumference.

Arcs are part of a circle named by two or three points on the circumference of a circle.

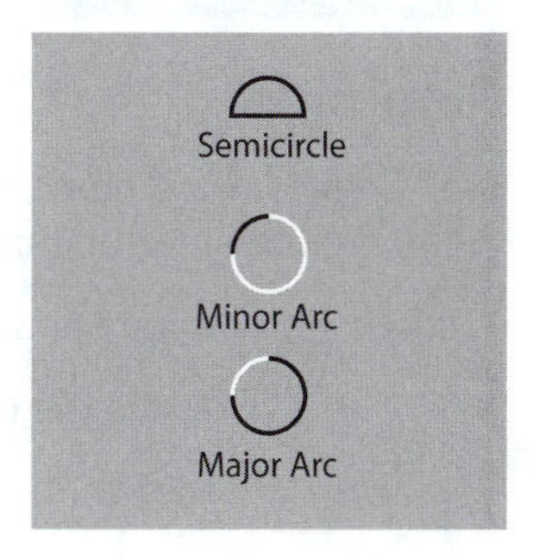

Quadrilaterals

A *quadrilateral* is a polygon with four sides.

Trapezoids are quadrilaterals that have one pair of opposite sides that are parallel.

Parallelograms are quadrilaterals that have two pairs of opposite sides that are parallel: examples are squares, rectangles, or rhombuses.

Rhombuses are parallelograms with two sets of parallel sides and four congruent sides.

Rectangles are parallelograms with two sets of parallel sides and four right angles.

Squares are parallelograms with four right angles and four equal sides.

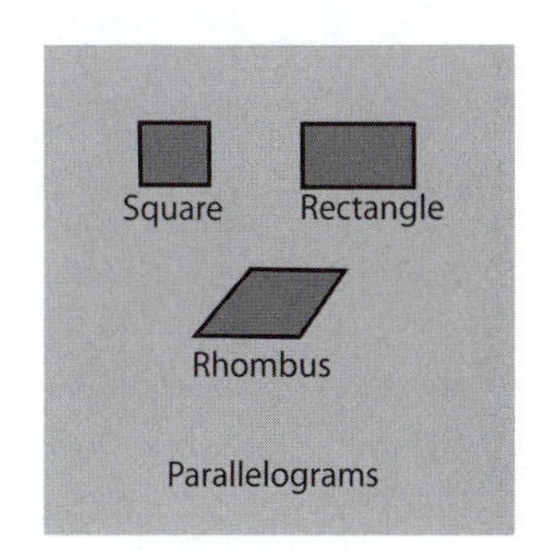

Prisms

Prisms are three-dimensional figures with length, width, and height with a polygon as a base. There are four parts of a prism: face, edge, vertex, and base.

Triangle Square

Triangular Quadrilateral

Prisms

A *face* is a side of a three-dimensional figure. Two faces of a prism are *bases;* they lie in parallel planes and are the same size and shape.

An *edge* is a line segment that connects two faces.

A *vertex* is the point formed by the intersection of three edges or three faces.

Prism Names

Prism names	Number of faces	Number of edges	Number of vertices
Triangular	5	9	6
Quadrilateral	6	12	8
Pentagonal	7	15	10
Hexagonal	8	18	12
Heptagonal	9	21	14
Octagonal	10	24	16

Pyramids

Pyramids are named by their bases; they have a polygon for a base and triangular sides that meet at a common point.

Bases have four points at the bottom.

Lateral faces are the triangular surfaces.

Faces are the base and lateral surfaces.

Edges are segments formed by the intersection of two faces.

Vertices are points formed by the intersection of three edges or three faces.

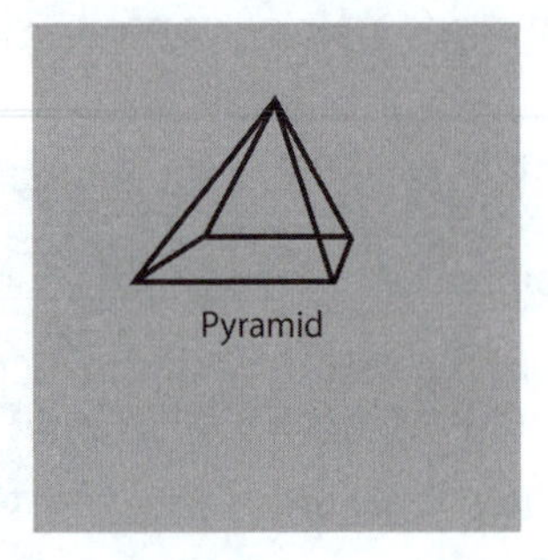

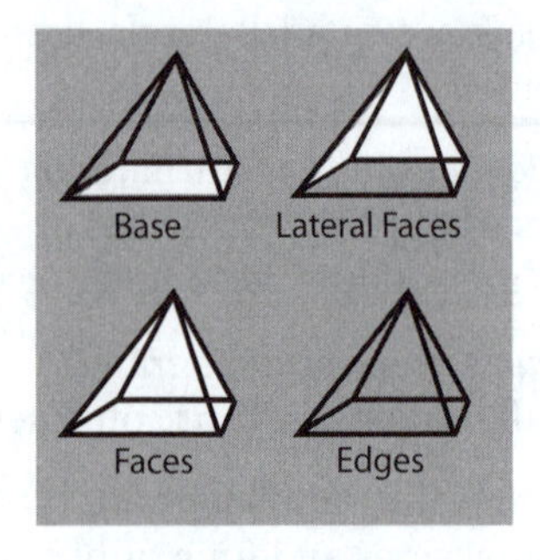

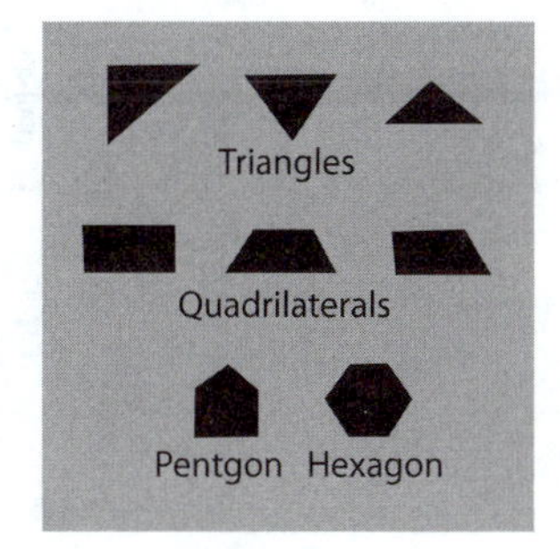

Pyramid Names

Pyramid name	Number of faces	Number of edges	Number of vertices
Triangular	4	6	4
Quadrilateral	5	8	5
Pentagonal	6	10	6
Hexagonal	7	12	7
Heptagonal	8	14	8
Octagonal	9	16	9

Congruent Figures

Congruent figures have the same shape and size.

Corresponding sides are congruent and fit exactly on top of one another.

Corresponding angles of two triangles are congruent if the corresponding angles and sides are congruent.

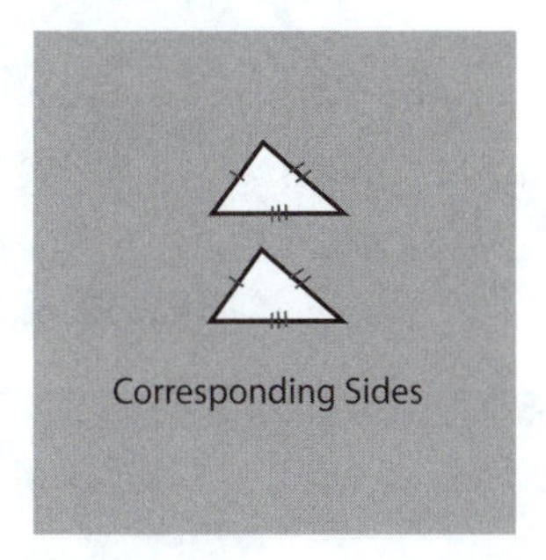

Similar Figures

Similar figures have the same shapes but not necessarily the same size.

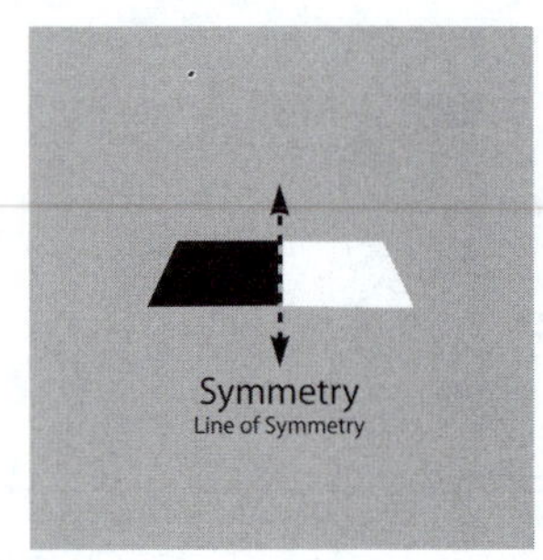

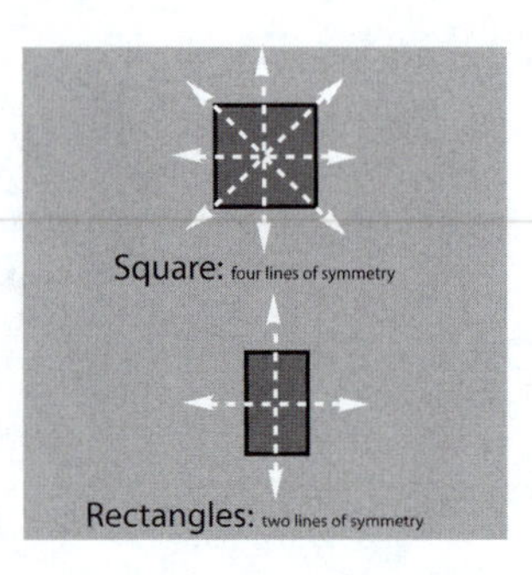

Symmetry

Two matching parts having the same measurements that are formed by placing a line down the center of a figure, creating two halves with the same size and shape, are said to be *symmetrical*. The line that divides the two halves is called the *line of symmetry;* some shapes have more than one line of symmetry.

Spatial Activities

The following are easy and inexpensive activities that emphasize spatial literacy.

Math

1. Tangrams can be used to offer children the chance to engage in puzzles and creative endeavors. There are seven tangram pieces that can be fitted together to make a square. Initial activities should include fitting two

pieces together to make a shape. As the children grow in their ability, they can use a greater number of pieces. They can also construct animals with the pieces.

2. Children can be asked to examine objects from their top, front, and side views.

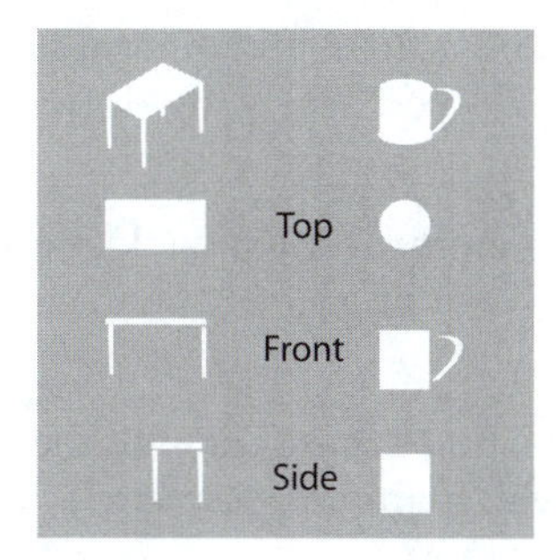

3. Children can be asked to perform *rotations*—turning a figure around on a point.
   a. Original
   b. Flip
   c. Rotate

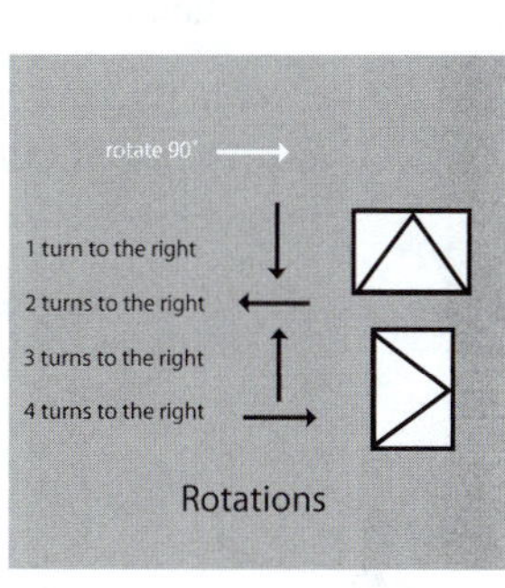

Rotations

4. Paper folding
   a. Make a cube from a three-dimensional pattern. Each of the patterns can be folded to make a cube.

Patterns to make a cube

   b. Make a cylinder from the pattern. Form the rectangle into a tube and use the circles for the bases.

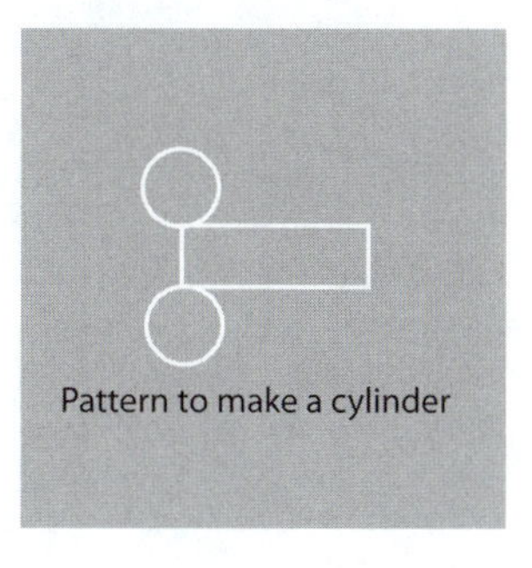
Pattern to make a cylinder

5. Draw a cube or a prism: 1) draw the base, 2) draw a second equal base, and 3) draw lines to connect the bases at their vertices.

Art

1. Display various art postcards, and determine which ones emphasize line. What kind of lines do you see? Why do you think the artist used these lines?
2. Lines can help us imagine things. Look at one of the pictures and imagine what the artist is saying. Share with the group what you think the artist is saying.
3. Using art postcards, find art works with the following shapes: rectangle, triangle, square, oval, diamond, semicircle, heart, spiral, crescent, pentagon, hexagon, or octagon.
4. Create figures in the following shapes: rectangle, triangle, square, oval, diamond, semicircle, heart, spiral, crescent, pentagon, hexagon, or octagon.

Games and Activities

N-Tropy

Re:creation Group Pic
Alberto House
Marino Way
Hogwood Lane Industrial Estate
Finchampstead, Berkshire RG40 4RF
United Kingdom

Phone (international): 44 (0) 118 973 6222
Fax (international): 44 (0) 118 973 6220
E-mail: info@recreationpic.com
Web site: http://www.recreationpic.com

This construction game demands balance, nerve, and calculated risk taking. First, students begin with an equal amount of playing sticks and take turns adding the sticks to create a structure on the three-dimensional frame playing board. The playing sticks must balance within the frame. If any of the sticks fall off during a student's turn, these sticks are added to that student's pile. The first player to get rid of all his or her sticks is the winner. This game results in a creative challenge that enhances students' own building abilities.

In the Garden Tessellations Puzzle

Tessellations
3913 E. Bronco Trail
Phoenix, AZ 85044

Phone: 800-655-5341
Fax: 480-763-6948
E-mail: Sales@tessellations.com
Web site: http://members.cox.net/tessellations/index.html

Garden-like items such as ladybugs, caterpillars, butterflies, and leaves fit together to form colorful patterned tessellations. Shapes include circles, stars, and pentagons, among others. This puzzle contains enough foam puzzle pieces for 10–15 students, as well as a set of instructions and a lesson guide covering the different types of mathematical symmetry, including tessellations, angles, and arcs. Each jar includes hundreds of colorful foam pieces, so each student gets a chance to create repeating patterns. Activity sheets challenge geometric problem-solving skills, illustrating why some shapes tessellate and others don't. This game is for ages K and up. *Note:* This game contains small parts and is not suitable for children under age 3.

Architectural Uberstix

Uberstix
P.O. Box 3351
Hailey, ID 83333

Phone: 800-524-4263
Fax: 608-362-8178
Web site: http://www.uberstix.com/

Using authentic blueprints, students can build representations of existing skyscrapers and bridges or create prototypes of their own designs. Students can apply for a building permit online that will show them the seismic and wind loads for their tower or skyscraper. Students can also go online to pinpoint the tower or skyscraper's position on a map and to see where other Uberarc builders have located their creations. Full-sized blueprints instruct how to build a 5-foot-tall skyscraper or tower. This teaches basics such as load-bearing walls, curves, and arches. *Note:* This game contains small parts and is not suitable for children under age 3.

Fractiles

Fractiles, Inc.
2525 Arapahoe Avenue, Suite E4-110
Boulder, CO 80302

Phone: 877-277-3201
Fax: 303-442-7776
E-mail: fractiles@fractiles.com
Web site: http://www.fractiles.com

Young students can learn about butterflies, snowflakes, optical illusions, and more—just by positioning the magnetic tiles on the activity board. Students can make a variety of colorful shapes and patterns with this unique art and puzzle toy. This product is intended for children ages 6 and up.

Magnetude

MindWare
2100 County Road C West
Roseville, MN 55113

Phone: 800-999-0398
Fax: 888-299-9273
Web site: http://www.mindware.com

Magnetude is a modular game with six identically shaped elements, connected by invisible internal magnets. Magnetude has been described as a small, modular "play art" object. Students can rearrange each piece to create new shapes and objects. Students exercise creativity while exploring the attracting and repelling forces of magnets.

The Great Origami Book and Kit

Sterling Publishing Co., Inc.
387 Park Avenue South
New York, NY 10016

Phone: 212-532-7160
E-mail: custservice@sterlingpublishing.com
Web site: http://www.sterlingpublishing.com

The art of folded paper links tactile and visual exploration. This big volume offers step-by-step instructions for 40 intricate shapes and comes with 90 sheets of 6 × 6-inch origami paper to get started. This book provides clear instructions on how to create eight basic shapes and then use those eight shapes to make more advanced origami creations.

Block Buddies

MindWare
2100 County Road C West
Roseville, MN 55113

Phone: 800-999-0398
Fax: 888-299-9273
Web site: http://www.mindware.com

With Block Buddies, students can use a variety of well-crafted wooden blocks to create their own design. This kit comes with 76 cards of colored block designs that students can create based on the images that they see on the cards. Some of the design images feature designs of various people, animals, and vehicles. The cards are separated into four levels of difficulty. *Note:* Block Buddies contains small parts and is not suitable for children under 3.

3-D Tangrams

MindWare
2100 County Road C West
Roseville, MN 55113

Phone: 800-999-0398
Fax: 888-299-9273
Web site: http://www.mindware.com

Four full tangram sets let students solve a visual challenge. These tangrams interlock and stand upright. Students can use three-dimensional tangrams to solve visual challenges. There is also a book with 100 puzzles and solutions included. This game is for one to four players and is recommended for children ages 4 and up.

Tangoes Jr.

MindWare
2100 County Road C West
Roseville, MN 55113

Phone: 800-999-0398
Fax: 888-299-9273
Web site: http://www.mindware.com

This product is made specifically for young learners, with a portable 12-inch-wide play case and seven magnetic tangram pieces that fit in a slide-out drawer. Sets include 11 cards with helpful hints. Choose from animals, objects, or people-themed Tangoes. With a large playing surface, seven magnetic puzzle pieces and recognizable puzzles, children can create many tangram images on a magnetic board. This product is recommended for children ages 3 through 6.

Pattern Play

MindWare
2100 County Road C West
Roseville, MN 55113

Phone: 800-999-0398
Fax: 888-299-9273
Web site: http://www.mindware.com

Pattern Play blocks are a great introduction to concepts such as sorting, matching, symmetry, congruence, and fractions. This kit consists of wooden block pieces that can be arranged on a wooden tray. Pattern Play introduces children to the concepts of building with unusual shapes and sizes to strengthen spatial skills. Pattern Play also includes a set of 40 pattern cards that give young students ideas to create new and interesting patterns. This game is recommended for children ages 3 and up. *Note:* This game contains small parts and is not suitable for children under age 3.

Superstructs

MindWare
2100 County Road C West
Roseville, MN 55113

Phone: 800-999-0398
Fax: 888-299-9273
Web site: http://www.mindware.com

Children can build structures using colorful sticks, multi-hole hubs, and tires. This product includes a step-by-step guide that illustrates how to create Ferris wheels, carousels, cranes, cars, trucks, and fun characters. Children can create anything from simple angles and straight lines to imaginative structures. This product is recommended for children ages 5 and up. *Note:* This product contains small parts and is not suitable for children under 3 years old.

Gears! Gears! Gears!

Learning Resources
Customer Service Department
380 North Fairway Drive
Vernon Hills, IL 60061

Phone: 800-333-8281
Fax: 888-892-8731
E-mail: info@learningresources.com
Web site: http://www.learningresources.com

Kids can explore simple mechanics and build patience and manual dexterity with pieces that snap together. This product contains colorful, spinning gears that can set young imaginations in motion. This product encourages kids to imagine and build characters, creatures, towers, buildings, vehicles, and more, allowing for many creative possibilities. This set comes with durable plastic gears, cranks, pillars, and connectors in a plastic bucket. This product is recommended for children ages 3 through 10.

I-Gami

Plastic Play, Inc.
1400 Bayly Street
Suite 6, Mall #2,
Pickering, Ontario L1W 3R3
Canada

Phone: 905-728-0063
E-mail: info@i-gami.com
Web site: http://www.i-gami.com

I-Gami is a plastic construction kit. The pieces in each kit are made of brightly colored bendable plastic that can be folded or snapped together with other pieces. Students can build huge creatures; vehicles; or complex geometric shapes such as spheres, hexagons, or truncated icosahedrons. The hollow constructions are lightweight and extremely durable. Each set contains 1,000 pieces, a sturdy plastic storage bucket, and directions for a variety of origami build-outs. Origami teaches children many spatial concepts.

Goobi Bars

Creative Zone Enterprises, LLC
P.O. Box 3535
San Dimas, CA 91773-7535

Phone: 888-784-6624
Fax: 888-584-6624
E-mail: info@Goobi.com
Web site: http://www.goobi.com

A Goobi Bar is an ergonomically designed plastic part with two magnets on each end with opposite polarity. The pieces are engineered to be easily held by both children and adults. These ultra-strong magnet-tipped posts snap into tripod joints to create many artistic and creative expressions. Goobi Bars can help teach children some basics of geometry, physics, architecture, and engineering. Playing with Goobi can enhance children's eye–hand coordination and improves their problem-solving skills. Kits can be purchased in both advanced or master packs. This product is recommended for children ages 5 and up.

Geofix Kits for Kindergarten to Grade 2

Didax, Inc.
395 Main Street
Rowley, MA 01969

Phone: 800-458-0024
Fax: 800-350-2345
E-mail: info@didax.com
Web site: http://www.didax.com

Geofix is an exciting tool for introducing three-dimensional shapes, math and science concepts, and design ideas. The Geofix construction system can be used from the early grades right through high school, with four interlocking shapes that snap together in an endless variety of three-dimensional models. Students can create multiple shapes in multiple sizes. Sets include a guide, 306 triangles, 120 squares, 50 pentagons, 24 hexagons, and a storage bin.

Empire State Building

Uberstix, LLC
P.O. Box 3351
Haley, ID 83333

Phone: 800-870-5908
Fax: 800-870-5908
E-mail: info@uberstix.com
Web site: https://www.uberarc.com

The UberArc 1200 Empire State Building allows students to hone their visual perception and engineering skills by building famous landmarks such as the Empire State Building. Students can use full-scale authentic blueprints to create a representation of the Empire State Building. Students can even apply for a building permit online and pinpoint their building's location on a map displayed to other UberArc builders. This kit is intended to teach students different basic building techniques to create load-bearing walls, curves, arches, and more. Pieces interlock so no tools are needed.

Intro to Structures, Bridges

K'NEX/The Rodon Group
2800 Sterling Drive
Hatfield, PA 19440

Telephone: 800-543-5639
E-mail: sales@rodongroup.com
Web site: http://www.knex.com

Students explore bridge types with this set specifically designed for classroom use. Build different models of arch, beam, truss, cable-stayed, cantilever, bascule, and suspension bridges. This set encourages teamwork and structural experimentation. This set is recommended for students in grades 3 through 6.

Blik Blok

MindWare
2100 County Road C West
Roseville, MN 55113

Phone: 800-999-0398
Fax: 888-299-9273
Web site: http://www.mindware.com

Students try to fit the blocks of this architect-created puzzle together to recreate the image on the front of the card, where a picture of an object appears along with directions of which blocks to use. On the other side of the card, there is an illustrated solution to the puzzle. This set includes 29 wood blocks and 100 puzzle cards with four levels of difficulty. The recommended ages for this product are age 8 and up.

Froebel Gifts Set

FroebelUSA (Red Hen LLC)
O-78 Leonard Street NW
Grand Rapids, MI 49534

Phone: 888-573-3436
Web site: http://www.froebelgifts.com

Recommended for teachers, architects, and artists who wish to understand and explore the creative possibilities of the original kindergarten gifts designed by Friedrich Froebel. The gifts are numbered 1 through 10. Conceptually, Gifts 1 to 6 can be thought to represent solids (three-dimensional), Gift 7 to represent surface (two-dimensional), Gift 8 to represent line, Gift 9 to represent point, and Gift 10 to represent point and line. The gifts represent a logical progression from the whole (unity) into parts (complexity) and a return to the whole. This idea of starting with the whole and moving out into the complexity of the parts is an important part of Froebel's philosophy. A child never completes or is finished with a gift, he or she just becomes ready for a different gift.

National Council of Teachers of Mathematics' Prekindergarten Through Grade 2 Curriculum Focal Points and Connections

Table E.1. Pre-K–Grade 2 curriculum focal points and connections compared with the expectations of the content standards in *Principles and Standards for School Mathematics*

Curriculum focal points and connections		Expectations of the content standards
Prekindergarten Curriculum Focal Points		***Number and Operations, Pre-K–Grade 2***
***Number and Operations:* Developing an understanding of whole numbers, including concepts of correspondence, counting, cardinality, and comparison**	**P, K**	Count with understanding and recognize "how many" in sets of objects
Children develop an understanding of the meanings of whole numbers and recognize the number of objects in small groups without counting and by counting—the first and most basic mathematical algorithm. They understand that number words refer to quantity. They use one-to-one correspondence to solve problems by matching sets and comparing number amounts and in counting objects to 10 and beyond. They understand that the last word that they state in counting tells "how many," they count to determine number amounts and compare quantities (using language such as *more than* and *less than*), and they order sets by the number of objects in them.	**2**	Use multiple models to develop initial understandings of place value and the base-ten number system
	K, 1	Develop understanding of the relative position and magnitude of whole numbers and of ordinal and cardinal numbers and their connections
	1, 2	Develop a sense of whole numbers and represent and use them in flexible ways, including relating, composing, and decomposing numbers
***Geometry:* Identifying shapes and describing spatial relationships**	**K, 1**	Connect number words and numerals to the quantities they represent, using various physical models and representations
Children develop spatial reasoning by working from two perspectives on space as they examine the shapes of objects and inspect their relative positions. They find shapes in their environments and describe them in their own words. They build pictures and designs by combining two- and three-dimensional shapes, and they solve such problems as deciding which piece will fit into a space in a puzzle. They discuss the relative positions of objects with vocabulary such as *above, below,* and *next to.*	**O**	Understand and represent commonly used fractions, such as ¼, ⅓, and ½ [In Grade 3 Curriculum Focal Points]
***Measurement:* Identifying measurable attributes and comparing objects by using these attributes**	**1**	Understand various meanings of addition and subtraction of whole numbers and the relationship between the two operations
Children identify objects as "the same" or "different," and then "more" or "less," on the basis of attributes that they can measure. They identify measurable attributes such as length and weight and solve problems by making direct comparisons of objects on the basis of those attributes.	**1**	Understand the effects of adding and subtracting whole numbers
	2	Understand situations that entail multiplication and division, such as equal groupings of objects and sharing equally
Connections to the Prekindergarten Focal Points		
Data Analysis: Children learn the foundations of data analysis by using objects' attributes that they have identified in relation to geometry and measurement (e.g., size, quantity, orientation, number of sides or vertices, color) for various purposes, such as describing, sorting, or comparing. For example, children sort geometric figures by shape, compare objects by weight *(heavier, lighter),* or describe sets of objects by the number of objects in each set.	**2**	Develop and use strategies for whole number computations, with a focus on addition and subtraction
	2	Develop fluency with basic number combinations for addition and subtraction

Reprinted with permission from *Curriculum Focal Points for Prekindergarten through Grade 8 Mathematics: A Quest for Coherence,* copyright 2006 by the National Council of Teachers of Mathematics.

Number and Operations: Children use meanings of numbers to create strategies for solving problems and responding to practical situations, such as getting just enough napkins for a group, or mathematical situations, such as determining that any shape is a triangle if it has exactly three straight sides and is closed.

Algebra: Children recognize and duplicate simple sequential patterns (e.g., square, circle, square, circle, square, circle).

Kindergarten Curriculum Focal Points

Number and Operations: **Representing, comparing, and ordering whole numbers and joining and separating sets**

Children use numbers, including written numerals, to represent quantities and to solve quantitative problems, such as counting objects in a set, creating a set with a given number of objects, comparing and ordering sets or numerals by using both cardinal and ordinal meanings, and modeling simple joining and separating situations with objects. They choose, combine, and apply effective strategies for answering quantitative questions, including quickly recognizing the number in a small set, counting and producing sets of given sizes, counting the number in combined sets, and counting backward.

Geometry: **Describing shapes and space**

Children interpret the physical world with geometric ideas (e.g., shape, orientation, spatial relations) and describe it with corresponding vocabulary. They identify, name, and describe a variety of shapes, such as squares, triangles, circles, rectangles, (regular) hexagons, and (isosceles) trapezoids presented in a variety of ways (e.g., with different sizes or orientations), as well as such three-dimensional shapes as spheres, cubes, and cylinders. They use basic shapes and spatial reasoning to model objects in their environment and to construct more complex shapes.

Measurement: **Ordering objects by measurable attributes**

Children use measurable attributes, such as length or weight, to solve problems by comparing and ordering objects. They compare the lengths of two objects both directly (by comparing them with each other) and indirectly (by comparing both with a third object), and they order several objects according to length.

2	Use a variety of methods and tools to compute, including objects, mental computation, estimation, paper and pencil, and calculators
	Algebra Pre-K–Grade 2
P, K	Sort, classify, and order objects by size, number, and other properties
P	Recognize, describe, and extend patterns such as sequences of sounds and shapes or simple numeric patterns and translate from one representation to another
P, K	Analyze how both repeating and growing patterns are generated
1	Illustrate general principles and properties of operations, such as commutativity, using specific numbers
K, 1 2	Use concrete, pictorial, and verbal representations to develop an understanding of invented and conventional symbolic notations
1, 2	Model situations that involve the addition and subtraction of whole numbers, using objects, pictures, and symbols
P, K	Describe qualitative change, such as a student's growing taller
1, 2	Describe quantitative change, such as a student's growing 2 inches in 1 year

Key: P, prekindergarten; K, kindergarten; 1, Grade 1; 2, Grade 2; O, outside pre-K–2; N, not identified at any level.

(continued)

Table E.1. *(continued)*

Curriculum focal points and connections

Connections to the Kindergarten Focal Points

Data Analysis: Children sort objects and use one or more attributes to solve problems. For example, they might sort solids that roll easily from those that do not. Or they might collect data and use counting to answer such questions as "What is our favorite snack?" They re-sort objects by using new attributes (e.g., after sorting solids according to which ones roll, they might re-sort the solids according to which ones stack easily).

Geometry: Children integrate their understandings of geometry, measurement, and number. For example, they understand, discuss, and create simple navigational directions (e.g., "Walk forward 10 steps, turn right, and walk forward 5 steps").

Algebra: Children identify, duplicate, and extend simple number patterns and sequential and growing patterns (e.g., patterns made with shapes) as preparation for creating rules that describe the relationships.

Grade 1 Curriculum Focal Points

***Number and Operations* and *Algebra:* Developing understandings of addition and subtraction and strategies for basic addition facts and related subtraction facts**

Children develop strategies for adding and subtracting whole numbers on the basis of their earlier work with small numbers. They use a variety of models, including discrete objects, length-based models (e.g., lengths of connecting cubes), and number lines, to model *part–whole, adding to, taking away from,* and *comparing* situations to develop an understanding of the meanings of addition and subtraction and strategies to solve such arithmetic problems. Children understand the connections between counting and the operations of addition and subtraction (e.g., adding two is the same as "counting on" two). They use properties of addition (commutativity and associativity) to add whole numbers, and they create and use increasingly sophisticated strategies based on these properties (e.g., "making tens") to solve addition and subtraction problems involving basic facts. By comparing a variety of solution strategies, children relate addition and subtraction as inverse operations.

***Number and Operations:* Developing an understanding of whole-number relationships, including groups in tens and ones**

Children compare and order whole numbers (at least to 100) to develop an understanding of and solve problems involving the relative sizes of these numbers. They think of whole numbers between 10 and 100 in terms of groups of tens and ones (especially recognizing the numbers 11 to 19 as one group of ten and particular numbers of ones). They understand the sequential order of the counting numbers and their relative magnitudes and represent numbers on a number line.

Expectations of the content standards

Geometry, Pre-K–Grade 2

P, K 1, 2	Recognize, name, build, draw, compare, and sort two- and three-dimensional shapes [Naming of three-dimensional shapes occurs in Grade 5 Curriculum Focal Points]
P, K 1	Describe attributes and parts of two- and three-dimensional shapes
1	Investigate and predict the results of putting together and taking apart two- and three-dimensional shapes
P, K	Describe, name, and interpret relative positions in space and apply ideas about relative position
P, K 2	Describe, name, and interpret direction and distance in navigating space and apply ideas about direction and distance
P, K N	Find and name locations with simple relationships such as "near to" and in coordinate systems such as maps. [This use of coordinate systems is not identified as a focal point or connection.]
O	Recognize and apply slides, flips, and turns [In Grade 4 Curriculum Focal Points]
1	Recognize and create shapes that have symmetry
P, K 1	Create mental images of geometric shapes using spatial memory and spatial visualization
1	Recognize and represent shapes from different perspectives
2	Relate ideas in geometry to ideas in number and measurement
P, K 1	Recognize geometric shapes and structures in the environment and specify their location

***Geometry:* Composing and decomposing geometric shapes**

Children compose and decompose plane and solid figures (e.g., by putting two congruent isosceles triangles together to make a rhombus), thus building an understanding of part–whole relationships as well as the properties of the original and composite shapes. As they combine figures, they recognize them from different perspectives and orientations, describe their geometric attributes and properties, and determine how they are alike and different, in the process developing a background for measurement and initial understandings of such properties as congruence and symmetry.

Connections to the Grade 1 Focal Points

Number and Operations* and *Algebra: Children use mathematical reasoning, including ideas such as commutativity and associativity and beginning ideas of tens and ones, to solve two-digit addition and subtraction problems with strategies that they understand and can explain. They solve both routine and nonroutine problems.

Measurement* and *Data Analysis: Children strengthen their sense of number by solving problems involving measurements and data. Measuring by laying multiple copies of a unit end to end and then counting the units by using groups of tens and ones supports children's understanding of number lines and number relationships. Representing measurements and discrete data in picture and bar graphs involves counting and comparisons that provide another meaningful connection to number relationships.

Algebra: Through identifying, describing, and applying number patterns and properties in developing strategies for basic facts, children learn about other properties of numbers and operations, such as odd and even (e.g., "Even numbers of objects can be paired, with none left over"), and 0 as the identity element for addition.

Grade 2 Curriculum Focal Points

***Number and Operations:* Developing an understanding of the base-ten numeration system and place-value concepts**

Children develop an understanding of the base-ten numeration system and place-value concepts (at least to 1000). Their understanding of base-ten numeration includes ideas of counting in units and multiples of hundreds, tens, and ones, as well as a grasp of number relationships, which they demonstrate in a variety of ways, including comparing and ordering numbers. They understand multidigit numbers in terms of place value, recognizing that place-value notation is a shorthand for the sums of multiples of powers of 10 (e.g., 853 as 8 hundreds + 5 tens + 3 ones).

Measurement, Pre-K–Grade 2

Level	Expectation
P, K 1, 2 N	Recognize the attributes of length, volume, weight, area, and time [Time is not identified as a focal point or connection.]
P, K	Compare and order objects according to these attributes
2	Understand how to measure using nonstandard and standard units
2	Select an appropriate unit and tool for the attribute being measured
2	Measure with multiple copies of units of the same size, such as paper clips laid end to end
2	Use repetition of a single unit to measure something larger than the unit, for instance, measuring the length of a room with a single meter stick
2	Use tools to measure
2	Develop common referents for measures to make comparisons and estimates

Data Analysis and Probability, Pre-K–Grade 2

Level	Expectation
K	Pose questions and gather data about themselves and their surroundings
P, K 1	Sort and classify objects according to their attributes and organize data about the objects
1	Represent data using concrete objects, pictures, and graphs
K, 1	Describe parts of the data and the set of data as a whole to determine what the data show
O	Discuss events related to students' experiences as likely or unlikely [In Grade 7 Curriculum Focal Points]

Key: P, prekindergarten; K, kindergarten; 1, Grade 1; 2, Grade 2; O, outside pre-K–2; N, not identified at any level.

(continued)

Table E.1. *(continued)*

Curriculum focal points and connections	
Number and Operations **and** ***Algebra:*** **Developing quick recall of addition facts and related subtraction facts and fluency with multidigit addition and subtraction** Children use their understanding of addition to develop quick recall of basic addition facts and related subtraction facts. They solve arithmetic problems by applying their understanding of models of addition and subtraction (such as combining or separating sets or using number lines), relationships and properties of number (such as place value), and use efficient, accurate, and generalizable methods to add and subtract multidigit whole numbers. They select and apply appropriate methods to estimate sums and differences or calculate them mentally, depending on the context and numbers involved. They develop fluency with efficient procedures, including standard algorithms, for adding and subtracting whole numbers, understand why the procedures work (on the basis of place value and properties of operations), and use them to solve problems. ***Measurement:*** **Developing an understanding of linear measurement and facility in measuring lengths** Children develop an understanding of the meaning and processes of measurement, including such underlying concepts as *partitioning* (the mental activity of slicing the length of an object into equal-sized units) and *transitivity* (e.g., if object A is longer than object B and object B is longer than object C, then object A is longer than object C). They understand linear measure as an iteration of units and use rulers and other measurement tools with that understanding. They understand the need for equal-length units, the use of standard units of measure (centimeter and inch), and the inverse relationship between the size of a unit and the number of units used in a particular measurement (i.e., children recognize that the smaller the unit, the more iterations they need to cover a given length).	

Connections to Grade 2 Focal Points

Number and Operations: Children use place value and properties of operations to create equivalent representations of given numbers (such as 35 represented by 35 ones, 3 tens and 5 ones, or 2 tens and 15 ones) and to write, compare, and order multidigit numbers. They use these ideas to compose and decompose multidigit numbers. Children add and subtract to solve a variety of problems, including applications involving measurement, geometry, and data, as well as nonroutine problems. In preparation for Grade 3, they solve problems involving multiplicative situations, developing initial understandings of multiplication as repeated addition.

Geometry and Measurement: Children estimate, measure, and compute lengths as they solve problems involving data, space, and movement through space. By composing and decomposing two-dimensional shapes (intentionally substituting arrangements of smaller shapes for larger shapes or substituting larger shapes for many smaller shapes), they use geometric knowledge and spatial reasoning to develop foundations for understanding area, fractions, and proportions.

Algebra: Children use number patterns to extend their knowledge of properties of numbers and operations. For example, when skip counting, they build foundations for understanding multiples and factors.

Literature, Readings, and Resources

Children's Block-Play Literature

General Readings on Buildings

Brown, D.J. (1991). *How things were built.* New York: Random House.

Liddiard, N. (1992). *The visual dictionary of buildings.* New York: Dorling Kindersley.

Munro, R. (1986). *Architects make zigzags: Looking at architecture from A to Z.* Hoboken, NJ: John Wiley.

Bridges

Adkins, J. (2002). *Bridges: From my side to yours.* Brookfield, CT: Roaring Brook.

Fandel, J. (2007). *Golden Gate Bridge.* Mankato, MN: Creative Ed.

Johmann, C.A., & Rieth, E.J. (1999). *Bridges: Amazing structures to design, build, and test.* Nashville, TN: Williamson.

Mann, K. (1996). *The Brooklyn Bridge.* New York: Mikaya Press.

Prince, A.J. (2005). *Twenty-one elephants.* New York: Houghton Mifflin.

Castles

Cole, J., & Degen, B. (2003). *Ms. Frizzle's adventures: Medieval castle.* New York: Scholastic Press.

Gravett, C. (2008). *Castle.* London: DK Eyewitness.

Macaulay, D. (1977). *Castle.* New York: Houghton Mifflin.

Houses

Dorros, A. (1992). *This is my house.* New York: Scholastic.

Galdone, P. (1972). *The three bears.* New York: Houghton Mifflin.

Gibbons, G. (1990). *How a house is built.* New York: Holiday House.

Horn, G.M. (2009). *Construction worker.* Pleasantville, NY: Gareth Stevens.

Liebman, D. (2003). *I want to be a builder.* Buffalo, NJ: Firefly.

Oxlade, C. (1994). *Houses and homes.* New York: Franklin Watts.

Steltzer, U. (1981). *Building an igloo.* New York: Henry Holt.

Wood, T. (1995). *See through history: Houses and homes.* New York: Viking.

Places of Worship

Macaulay, D. (1973). *Cathedral: The story of its construction.* Boston: Houghton Mifflin.

Macaulay, D. (2003). *Mosque.* Boston: Houghton Mifflin.

Ships

Batio, C. (2001). *Super cargo ships.* Osceola, WI: Motorbooks International.

Grahan, I. (1994). *How it goes: Boats.* London: Aladdin.

Holtzman, R. (2004). *Boats and ships.* North Kingston, RI: Moon Mountain Books.

Miller, W.H. (2001). *Picture history of American passenger ships.* Mineola, NY: Dover.

Stille, D.R. (2004). *Ships.* Minneapolis, MN: Compass Point Books.

Skyscrapers and Other Structures

Caney, S. (2006). *Ultimate building book.* Philadelphia: Running Press Kids.

Curlee, L. (2007). *Skyscraper.* New York: Athenaeum.

Gibbons, G. (1986). *Up goes the skyscraper.* New York: Macmillan.

Hopkinson, D., & Ransome, J. (2006). *Skyboys: How they built the Empire State Building.* New York: Schwartz.

Hunter, R.A. (1998). *Into the sky.* New York: Holiday House.

Johmann, C.A. (2001). *Skyscrapers.* Nashville, TN: Williamson Books.

Macaulay, D. (2000). *Building big.* New York: Houghton Mifflin.

Richardson, J. (1994). *Skyscrapers.* New York: Franklin Watts.

Stevenson, N. (1997). *Architecture.* New York: OK Publishing.

Sullivan, G. (2005). *Built to last.* New York: Scholastic.

Wilkinson, P. (1996). *Super structures.* New York: Dorling Kindersley.

Wood, R. (1995). *Legacies: Architecture.* New York: Thomson Learning.

Trains

Balkwell, R. (1999). *The best book of trains.* Boston: Kingfisher.

Gibbons, G. (1987). *Trains.* New York: Holiday House.

Children's Literature and Spatial Development

Frank Lloyd Wright and Buckminster Fuller

Fleming, D.B. (2004). *Simply Wright: a journey into the ideas of Frank Lloyd Wright's architecture.* Waunakee, WI: Castleconal Press.

Rubin, S.G. (1994). *First impression: Frank Lloyd Wright.* New York: Harry N. Abrams.

Snyder, R. (Ed.). (1980). *Buckminster Fuller: An autobiographical monologue/scenario.* New York: St. Martin's Press.

Geometric Concepts and Properties

Boyd, L. (1991). *Willie and the cardboard boxes.* New York: Viking.

Charosh, M. (1971). *Ellipse.* New York: Thomas Y. Crowell.

Clinton, S. (1986). *I can be an architect.* Chicago: Children's Press.

Edom, H. (1989). *How things are built.* Tulsa, OK: EDC Publishing.

Enrico, A. (1972). *Straight lines, parallel lines, perpendicular lines.* New York: Thomas Y. Crowell.

Froman, R. (1976). *Angles are as easy as pie.* New York: Thomas Y. Crowell.

Hix, K. (1978). *Geo-dynamics.* Calistoga, CA: Crystal Reflections.

Hutchins, P. (1971). *Changes, changes.* New York: Macmillan.

Jester, N. (1963). *The dot and the line.* New York: Random House.

Macaulay, D. (1977). *Castle.* Boston: Houghton Mifflin.

Macaulay, D. (1975). *Pyramid.* Boston: Houghton Mifflin.

Orii, E., & Masako, O. (1989). *Simple science experiments with circles.* Milwaukee, WI: Gareth Stevens.

Pienkowski, J. (1989). *Shapes.* New York: Simon & Schuster.

Pluckrose, J.J. (1986). *Shapes.* New York: Franklin Watts.

Sitomer, M., & Sitomer, H. (1971). *Circles.* New York: Thomas Y. Crowell.

Tompert, A. (1990). *Grandfather Tang's story.* New York: Crown.

Mapping and Spatial Skills in Geography

Chapman, G., & Robson, P. (1993). *Maps and mazes: A first guide to mapmaking.* Brookfield, CT: Millbrook.

Cicciarelli, J.T. (1996). *Maps.* Cypress, CA: Creative Teaching Press.

Fanelli, S. (1995). *My map book.* New York: HarperCollins.

Hartman, G. (1991). *As the crow flies: A first book of maps.* New York: Aladdin.

Knowlton, J. (1985). *Maps and globes.* New York: HarperCollins.

Nunn, T. (1996). *My global address.* Cypress, CA: Creative Teaching Press.

Petty, K., & Wood, J. (1993). *Around and about: Maps and journeys.* London: Aladdin.

Petty, K., & Wood, J. (1993). *Around and about: Our globe, our world.* London: Aladdin.

Sweeney, J. (1996). *Me on the map.* New York: Scholastic.

Taylor, B. (1994). *Maps and mapping.* London: Kingfisher.

Williams, R.L. (1996). *Can you read a map?* Cypress, CA: Creative Teaching Press.

Mapping Characters' Movements

Preschool and Kindergarten

Hoban, T. (1973). *Over, under and through and other spatial concepts.* New York: Macmillan.

Hutchins, P. (1968). *Rosie's walk.* New York: Aladdin Paperbacks

Rey, H.A. (1952). *Curious George rides a bike.* Boston: Houghton Mifflin.

Seuss, Dr. (1940). *Horton hatches an egg.* Boston: Houghton Mifflin.

First and Second Grade

Burton, V.L. (1971). *Katy and the big snow.* Boston: Houghton Mifflin.

Burton, V.L. (1939). *Mike Mulligan and his steam shovel.* New York: Penguin.

Fox, M. (1983). *Possum magic.* New York: Harcourt Brace Jovanovich.

McCloskey, R. (1976). *Make way for ducklings.* New York: Puffin.

McCloskey, R. (1978). *Blueberries for Sal.* New York: Scholastic.

McCloskey, R. (1978). *Lentil.* New York: Puffin.

McCloskey, R. (1980). *One morning in Maine.* New York: Puffin.

Third Grade

Holling, H.C. (1969). *Paddle-to-the sea.* Boston: Houghton Mifflin.

Holling, H.C. (1979). *Minn of the Mississippi.* New York: Houghton Mifflin.

Kellogg, S. (1984). *Paul Bunyan.* New York: Mulberry Books.

Kellogg, S. (1986). *Pecos Bill.* New York: Mulberry Books.

Lindbergh, R. (1990). *Johnny Appleseed.* Boston: Little, Brown.

Wilder, L.I. (1981). *Laura Ingalls Wilder Series: Little house in the big woods, Little house on the prairie, Farmer boy, On the banks of Plum Creek, By the shores of Silver Lake, The long winter, These happy golden years.* New York: Harper and Row.

Origami

Heukerott, P.B. (1988). Origami: Paper folding the algorithmic way. *Arithmetic Teacher, 35*(5), 4–8.

Juraschek, W. (1990). Getting in touch with shape. *Arithmetic Teacher, 37,* 14–16.

Kobayashi, K., & Sunayama, C. (1996). *Easy origami.* New York: Lark Books.

Neale, R., & Hull, T. (1994). *Origami, plain and simple.* New York: St. Martin's Press.

Temko, F. (2004). *Origami boxes.* Boston: Tuttle.

Shapes

Allington, R.L. (1979). *Shapes.* Milwaukee, WI: Raintree.

Carle, E. (1986). *The secret birthday message.* New York: Harper.

Crews, D. (1986). *Ten black dots.* New York: Greenwillow.

DePaola, T. (1975). *The cloud book.* New York: Holiday House.

Dodds, D.A. (1994). *The shape of things.* Cambridge, MA: Candlewick Press.

Ehlert, L. (1989). *Color zoo.* New York: J.B. Lippincott.

Emberley, E. (1961). *The wings on a flea: A book about shapes.* Boston: Little, Brown.

Freeman, M. (1969). *Finding out about shapes.* New York: McGraw Hill.

Hartman, G. (1992). *As the crow flies.* New York: Bradbury Press.

Hoban, T. (1970). *Shapes and things.* New York: Macmillan.

Hoban, T. (1974). *Circles, triangles and squares.* New York: Macmillan.

Hoban, T. (1983). *I read symbols.* New York: Greenwillow.

Hoban, T. (1983). *Round and round and round.* New York: Greenwillow.

Hoban, T. (1986). *Shapes, shapes, shapes.* New York: Greenwillow.

Hutchins, P. (1987). *Changes, changes.* New York: Macmillan.

Jonas, A. (1984). *Round trip.* New York: Mulberry.

Lerner, S. (1970). *Straight is a line.* Dons Mills, Ontario, Canada: Lerner.

Lerner, S. (1974). *Square is a shape.* Dons Mills, Ontario, Canada: Lerner.

MacDonald, S. (1994). *Sea shapes.* San Diego: Harcourt Brace.

McDermott, G. (1972). *Anansi the spider.* New York: Henry Holt.

McMillan, B. (1988). *Fire engine shapes.* New York: Lothrop, Lee & Shepard.

Shaw, C.G. (1947). *It looked like spilt milk.* New York: Harper Collins.

Tompert, A. (1990). *Grandfather Tang's story.* New York: Crown.

Yenawine, P. (1991). *Lines.* New York: Delacorte Press.

Yenawine, P. (1991). *Shapes.* New York: Delacorte Press.

Spatial Concepts

Hoban, T. (1972). *Push, pull, empty, full.* New York: Macmillan.

Hoban, T. (1973). *Over, under, and through and other spatial concepts.* New York: Macmillan.

Hoban, T. (1991). *All about where.* New York: Greenwillow.

MacDonald, S., & Oakes, B. (1989). *Puzzlers.* New York: Penguin.

McMillan, B. (1986). *Becca backward, Becca forward.* New York: Lothrop, Lee & Shepard.

Books and Articles for Further Reading

Froebel and Other Readings

Brosterman, N. (1997). *Inventing kindergarten.* New York: Harry N. Abrams.

Bultman, S. (2000). *The Froebelian Gifts.* Grand Rapids, MI: Kindergarten.

Corbett, B. (1989). *A century of kindergarten education in Ontario.* Mississauga, Ontario, Canada: The Froebel Foundation.

Downs, R. (1978). *Friedrich Froebel.* Boston: Twayen.

Foreman, G., & Hewitt, K. (1990). *The Learning Materials Workshop: Blocks.* Burlington, VT: Learning Materials Workshop.

Froebel, F. (1826). *On the education of man (Die muenschenerziehung).* Keilhau/Leipzig, Germany: Wienbrach.

Geary, D.C. (1994). *Children's mathematical development: Research and practice.* Washington, DC: American Psychological Association.

Hughes, J.L. (1910). *Froebel's educational laws: For all teachers.* New York: D. Appleton.

Weston, P. (1998). *Friedrich Froebel: His life, times, and significance.* London: Froebel College.

Reggio Emilia Readings

Abramson, S., Robinson, R., & Akenman, K. (1995). Project work with diverse students: Adapting curriculum based on the Reggio Emilia approach. *Childhood Education, 71*(4), 197–202.

Bisgaier, C.S., & Samaras, T. (2004). Using wood, glue, and words to enhance learning. *Young Children, 59*(4), 22–28.

Bredekamp, S. (1993). Reflections on Reggio Emilia. *Young Children, 49*(1), 13–17.

Cadwell, L.B. (1997). *Bringing Reggio Emilia home.* New York: Teachers College Press.

Edwards, C., Gandini, L., & Forman, G. (Eds.). (1998). *The hundred languages of children: The Reggio Emilia approach to early childhood education* (2nd ed.). Norwood, NJ: Ablex.

Firlik, R. (1996). Can we adapt the philosophies and practices of Reggio Emilia, Italy, for use in American schools? *Early Childhood Education Journal, 23*(4), 217–220.

Forman, G. (1996). A child constructs an understanding of a water wheel in five media. *Childhood Education, 72*(5), 269–273.

Gandini, L. (1993). Fundamentals of the Reggio Emilia approach to early childhood education. *Young Children, 49*(1), 4–8.

Giudici, C., & Rinaldi, C. (Eds.). (2001). *Making learning visible: Children as individual and group learners.* Reggio Emilia, Italy: Reggio Children.

Hendrick, J. (Ed.). (2004). *Next steps toward teaching the Reggio way: Accepting the challenge to change* (2nd ed.). Columbus, OH: Pearson.

Katz, L., & Cesarone, B. (1994). *Reflections on the Reggio Emilia approach.* Urbana, IL: ERIC Clearinghouse on Elementary Education.

Malaguzzi, L. (1993). For an education based on relationships. *Young Children, 49*(1), 9–12.

Schiller, M. (1995). Reggio Emilia: A focus on emergent curriculum and art. *Art Education, 48*(3), 45–50.

Sturloni, S., & Vecchi, V. (1999). *Everything has a shadow except ants.* Reggio Emilia, Italy: Reggio Children.

Recommended Resources for Block Play

Teaching Block Play

Bos, B. (1994). *Starting at square one.* Roseville, CA: Turn-The-Page Press.

Brosterman, N. (1997). *Inventing kindergarten.* New York: Harry N. Abrams.

Chalufour, I., & Worth, K. (2004). *Building structures with young children.* St. Paul, MN: Redleaf.

Consortium of National Arts Education Associations. (n.d.). *The national standards for arts education.* Retrieved from http://artsedge.kennedy-center.org/teach/standards

Croft, D.J., & Hess, R.D. (1985). *An activity handbook for teachers of young children.* Boston: Houghton Mifflin.

Day, B. (1996). *Early childhood education.* New York: Macmillan.

Foreman, G., & Hewitt, K. (1990). *The learning materials workshop: Blocks.* Burlington, VT: Learning Materials Workshop.

Frank, M. (1976). *I can make a rainbow.* Nashville, TN: Incentive.

Gura, P. (Ed.). (1992). *Exploring learning: Young children and blockplay.* London: Sage.

Hewitt, K. (n.d.). *Toying with architecture: The building toy in the area of play.* Katona, New York: Katonah Museum of Art.

Macaulay, D. (2000). *Building big.* New York: Houghton Mifflin.

Miller, S. (1997). *Problem solving safari: Blocks.* Torrance, CA: Totline.

National Council of Teachers of English and the International Reading Association. (2003). *Standards for English language arts.* Washington, DC: Authors.

Newburger, A. (2006). *Teaching numeracy, language, and literacy with blocks.* St. Paul, MN: Redleaf.

Provenzo, E., Eugene, F., & Brett, A. (1983). *The complete block book.* Syracuse University Press.

Robinson, H.F. (1983). *Exploring teaching in early childhood education.* Boston: Allyn & Bacon.

Walker, L. (1995). *Blockbuilding for children.* Woodstock, NY: Overlook Press.

Wellhousen, K., & Kieff, J. (2001). *A constructivist approach to block play.* Albany, NY: Delmar.

Weston, P. (1998). *Friedrich Froebel: His life, times, and significance.* London: Froebel College.

Software to Promote Challenging Learning Experiences in the Arts

Crayola Make a Masterpiece (IBM)

3D Castle Creator (Crayola)

Claris Works for Kids (Apple)

Create & Draw in Elmo's World (Mattel)

Disney's Magic Artist Studio (Disney Interactive)

Kid Pix Deluxe (Broderbund; recommended for creativity but the explosions may not be appropriate)

Orly's Draw-A-Story (Broderbund)

Sesame Street Create & Draw in Elmo's World (Mattel)

Sketchboard Studio (KB Gear Interactive)

Paintbrush (MS Windows)

Cartoon Maker (Disney)

Krazy Art Room (GuruForce, Inc.)

Tessellation Exploration (Tom Snyder)

Blue's Art Time Activities (Humongous Entertainment/Nickelodeon)

Make a Masterpiece (IBM/Crayola; the major competition to Kid Pix)

Computers and Spatial Development

National Council of Teachers of Mathematics
http://www.nctm.org

National Council of Teachers of Mathematics publishes reviews in its journal, *Teaching Children Mathematics*, and offers activities and lessons to teachers. Article downloads are free to members. Spatial development in young children is an area that is related to art.

International Society for Technology in Education
http://www.iste.org

International Society for Technology in Education publishes software reviews in its journal and provides services to schools to improve teaching, learning, and leadership in the use of technology.

Index

Page numbers followed by *f* indicate figures and those followed by *p* indicate photos.